HELL TO PAY

HELL TO PAY

The Unfolding Story of Hillary Rodham Clinton

BARBARA OLSON

Since 1947
REGNERY
PUBLISHING, INC.
An Eagle Publishing Company • Washington, DC

First paperback edition 2001

Library of Congress Cataloging-in-Publication Data

Olson, Barbara, 1955-
    Hell to pay : the unfolding story of Hillary Rodham Clinton / by Barbara Olson.
        p. cm.
Includes bibliographical references and index.
ISBN 0-89526-197-9 (acid-free paper)
1. Clinton, Hillary Rodham—Career in politics. 2. Clinton, Hillary Rodham—
Ethics. 3. Presidents' spouses—United States—Biography. 4. Presidents' spouses—
United States—Political activity. I. Title.

E887.C55 O47 1999
973.929'092—dc21
[B]   99-047548

Published in the United States by
Regnery Publishing, Inc.
An Eagle Publishing Company
One Massachusetts Avenue, NW
Washington, DC 20001
www.regnery.com

Distributed to the trade by
National Book Network
4720-A Boston Way
Lanham, MD 20706

Printed on acid-free paper
Manufactured in the United States of America

10 9 8 7 6 5 4 3 2

BOOK DESIGN BY MARJA WALKER
SET IN JANSON

Books are available in quantity for promotional or premium use. Write to Director of Special Sales, Regnery Publishing, Inc., One Massachusetts Avenue, NW, Washington, DC 20001, for information on discounts and terms or call (202) 216–0600.

CONTENTS

To my best friend and mentor,
my husband Ted,
and to the future for our grandchildren,
Hayley, Jillian, and Kirstin.

ONE
HILLARY'S BABY

"Life is a corrupting process from the time a child learns to play his mother off against his father in the politics of when to go to bed; he who fears corruption fears life."

— SAUL ALINSKY, *RULES FOR RADICALS*

D o you remember Hillary's preelection baby? In the summer before the 1996 election, when the Clintons' popularity had waned and it seemed as if the struggle for reelection might not succeed, Hillary Rodham Clinton let journalist Walter Isaacson know that she and the president had "talked about" adopting a baby. She let it slip that they were "talking about it more now." She added, "I must say we're hoping to have another child."[1]

That baby was never adopted, and the story dropped from sight. It seems the polling numbers weren't so bad after all, and the Clintons' Republican opponent, Bob Dole, was having trouble simply walking and talking at the same time.

But the baby story had its intended effect. It softened Hillary's image as a cold, steely ideologue in the aftermath of the health care debacle. Along with her book, *It Takes a Village*, the baby story allowed the American people to picture Hillary as a warm and caring person, a potential new mother, a caregiver.

Above all, it transformed her from a liability to an asset in Bill Clinton's bid for reelection to the presidency. To some, she is Saint Hillary. To others, a high priestess of feminism and a manipulator. Of course, Hillary is no Joan, Antigone, or Lady Macbeth, but she has played each role to the hilt.

I have come to know Hillary as she is—a woman who can sway millions, yet deceive herself; a woman who has persuaded herself and many others that she is "spiritual," but who has gone to the brink of criminality to amass wealth and power.

I came to know Hillary Rodham Clinton when I served as the chief investigative counsel for the House Government Reform and Oversight Committee, then chaired by the distinguished and gentlemanly William F. Clinger.

For months, five of us investigated the FBI and Travel Office scandals in a tiny windowless secure committee room on the first floor of the Rayburn House Office Building. This room was chosen after early drafts of our documents were mysteriously spirited from our garbage can to the press.

We changed our locks; not even the cleaning crews had access to our tiny room. I generally arrived at 6:30 AM and tried to leave for home before 8:00 PM. My colleague Barbara Comstock continued the vigil and wouldn't leave until around 4:00 AM. It was here that I pored over details of Hillary Rodham Clinton's role in several of the Clinton administration's unseemly political maneuvers. It was here that we wrote and rewrote the interrogatories for her to answer under oath and deposed her friends and loyal soldiers—from Harry Thomason, to Abner Mikva, to Bernie Nussbaum, to Bruce Lindsey.

The members of my seasoned investigative staff would each tell you they have never seen anyone better able to keep her stories, however improbable, straight. She was unflappable when presented with damning evidence and was adept at darting nimbly to a new interpretation that put that damning evidence in the best light.

I have never experienced a cooler or more hardened operator than Hillary Rodham Clinton. The investigators working for Independent Counsel Kenneth Starr found, as we did, that in one White House scandal after another, all roads led to Hillary. To investigate White House improprieties and scandals, the evidence necessarily led to *her* hidden hands guiding the Clinton operation.

We came to see that, essentially, Hillary is a woman animated by a lifelong ambition. That ambition is to make the world accept the ideas she embraced in the sanctuaries of liberation theology, radical feminism, and the hard left. We came to see her as a politician who invented her own strategies of protective coloration, who learned to mask her true feelings and intentions. She has become a master manipulator of the press, the public, her staff, and—likely—even the president.

Only in retrospect have we ever seen the mask slip. Only when we look back and remember the story line of last week, or last year, does the coyness of her soft words seem to be belied by the hardness of her deeds. The real Hillary is visible only when we wonder: What happened to the notion of that baby? Or when we ask ourselves what Hillary knew and when she knew about Monica Lewinsky—was it before or after she accused the *Washington Post* and every major news outlet of serving a "vast, right-wing conspiracy"?

More than twenty years before my investigation of her, Hillary Rodham sat in a similar room, perhaps with the same safes and creaky dials, to perform a similar investigation: Watergate. Few Americans realize the extent of the role that Hillary, as a Watergate investigator, played in destroying Richard Nixon. Few Americans realize the extent to which she burnished her political skills in the Watergate cauldron, practicing the bare-knuckle tactics of the highly politicized House Judiciary Committee on the Watergate Impeachment Committee.

Nor are many Americans fully aware of the extremes to which she has gone in order to protect and abet Bill Clinton's secret life. The supreme irony is that this 1960s liberal, as a partner to Bill Clinton, has become ever more darkly Nixonian in her outlook and methods—though without Nixon's self-knowledge, statesmanlike substance, and redemptive Quaker conscience.

Still, the "vast, right-wing conspiracy" was a touch of Nixonian rhetoric—albeit, from the left—for a woman with a Nixonian frame of mind. She has learned the skills of attack and counterattack from the best. White House Assistant to the President for Management and Administration David Watkins wrote that there would be "hell to pay" if the first lady's orders were not followed in dispensing of the career White House Travel Office employees. And he understated his case.

Over the years Hillary Clinton has assembled and skillfully used an arsenal of opposition researchers and private detectives that her one-time mentor, Dick Morris, now identifies as a "secret police" that has been used in "a systematic campaign to intimidate, frighten, threaten, discredit, and punish innocent Americans whose only misdeed is their desire to tell the truth."

Hillary is not merely an aider and abettor to this secret police operation. She has been its prime instigator and organizer. In the political life of the Clintons, it was she who pioneered the use of private detectives. It was she who brought in and cultivated the professional dirt-diggers and smear artists. It was she whose obsession with secrecy was so intense that when White House Counsel and former judge Abner Mikva finally bowed to the law and delivered subpoenaed documents, she and her White House scandal team lashed at him with such a vicious streak of humiliating profanity that he resigned. And then there is the public Hillary of *It Takes a Village*—gentle, mother-earth, and caring—sweet-talking the American people into socialism for their children.

Hillary Clinton is a determined, focused leader who rapidly rose to the top ranks of the radical left, and who now seeks to foment revolutionary changes from the uniform of a pink suit. She used Arkansas as a laboratory for her ideas. As first lady, she tried to wield direct power on the national level and failed. Now she is inventing a career beyond her husband's, to make her own place in history—to find a path to ultimate power. But serving as the junior senator from New York will not provide a stage big enough for such ambitions. Like Eleanor Roosevelt before her, Hillary Clinton seeks nothing less than an office that will give her a platform from which to exercise real power and real world leadership.

TWO
DREAMS OF POWER

"It is not enough to persuade them of your competence, talents, and courage—they must have faith in your ability and courage. They must believe in your capacity not just to provide the opportunity for action, power, change, adventure, a piece of the drama of life, but to give them a very definite promise, almost an assurance of victory."

— SAUL ALINSKY, *RULES FOR RADICALS*

In 1975, the year that Hillary would marry Bill Clinton, she entertained the notion of becoming a United States Marine.

She was a Yale law graduate living in Fayetteville, Arkansas, but still well known and well regarded among the liberal luminaries of the East. A year before, as a congressional staffer working on Watergate, Hillary had helped force a Republican president to resign. Her efforts as a dilettante advocacy lawyer on behalf of the Children's Defense Fund and her self-important, sophomoric writings arguing for a radical expansion of children's rights had established her as a rising star in the liberal policy firmament.

Now she was teaching at the University of Arkansas law school with her future husband. Everyone knew the next act: She would marry Bill, and he would run for statewide office.

Yet one day this lady law professor sailed down to a Marine Corps recruitment office and offered herself up as an officer in the U.S. Marine Corps. She was rejected, because of her age and her myopia, she says. But she obviously had much more working against her. And why would she want to leave the man she loved, her career, and her friends to join the military? A patriotic desire to serve her country? To prove her worth?

This episode has long been a standing joke among her friends, seen as a moment of fanciful lunacy, perhaps her way of issuing a direct challenge to the very heart of American masculinity: Does the Marine Corps have the guts to take in someone like me? She may even have believed she would have lasted past noon of her first day of Marine Corps boot camp. Or perhaps she sought to give her politically ambitious young husband a layer of defense against future draft-dodging charges. There is, however, another interpretation.

PURSUING POWER

Perhaps Hillary was looking far off, into the distance, not at her husband's needs and possibilities, but at her own. Perhaps she knew that if she ever ran for office, she would have an invaluable advantage as a female candidate if she had a record of military service that so many of her male contemporaries lacked.

Like so many politicians, the need for elected office had come early to her. She had become vice president of her junior class in high school.[1] She was elected to student government twice in college. The second time as president of her class at Wellesley, a position that allowed her to make a grandiose, cant-laden commencement speech that transformed her into a radical celebrity.

Now the Ford years had come, and the storms that had ravaged America's campuses were quieting. Vietnam was winding down, and there was little possibility of a war that would take her, as a Marine reservist, too far away from Bill and her new civilian life.

Hillary had already put together quite a resume as a campus leader, a law professor, and an embryonic legal scholar. Imagine how a Marine Corps ring would have rounded out that image? She would have macho credentials that would prove she could run with the boys to balance her blooming feminist and leftist stature.

Hillary has never been a piker in the dream department. As a teenager, she yearned to become the first woman astronaut. Like the marines, NASA rejected her, and it is no coincidence that her husband has made a point of pouring millions of dollars into programs to train women astronauts. As an adult, she now yearns to become the first woman to be elected president of the United States of America. Why else would she be running for the U.S. Senate? Certainly not for money.

HarperCollins editor Judith Regan offered Hillary $5 million for her memoirs.[2] She could easily pull down $50,000 per speech in lecture fees and honoraria that are forbidden to senators. She could make a senator's salary in three days as a civilian.

Such a life, however, would lack the accoutrements of power. Jean Houston, the spiritualist and certified FOH, speculated for the *Washington Post* that being Hillary was like being Mozart with his hands cut off.[3] Hillary undoubtedly believes it.

She began her time as first lady as the second part of the two-for-one deal, a near equal of the president, and a part of a White House triumvirate in which she was as powerful as the vice president.

The collapse of her health care plan put her on the defensive. And then it got worse. The press discovered her fingerprints, figuratively and sometimes literally, on scandal after scandal—from the firing, smearing, and attempted framing of the White House Travel Office staff, to the ransacking of White House Deputy Counsel Vince Foster's office after his suicide, to billing records that materialized in the White House residence like a gift from the starship *Enterprise*. She began to look like an albatross, and lost clout, becoming the weakest member of the triumvirate.

After a lengthy period of petulance and sulking, suddenly all of that was behind her. The president had his own scandal, one entirely of his own making, and one in which she was the most visible and pathetic victim. The world poured out its heart to her, and admired her posture of stoic dignity while her husband and everyone else in Washington seemed to be throwing their sense of self-respect out the window. The year of Monica restored her popularity.

"Like the moon," ex-advisor Dick Morris wrote in his memoirs, "Hillary only shines or—one suspects—receives affection, when her husband is most luminous. She seems most brilliant when Saturday-night Bill has strayed, gotten caught, and needs his wife to rescue him."[4]

CROSSING HER RUBICON

This time the klieg lights had really come up on an appalling and pathetic Saturday-night Bill. And Hillary shined more brightly than she ever had in her life.

During the 1998 elections, the president's appearance before Democratic crowds in New York evoked polite applause. But when she was introduced, the faithful erupted in cheers. As she basked in the radiating warmth of adoring crowds, it seemed as if the time had finally come to strike out on her own.

Hillary found receptive audiences—and presidential-level press coverage—when she visited laid-off textile workers in New York and the enclaves of rich movie stars and celebrities on Long Island.

Something like this had happened once before, on a more modest scale. After Hillary had helped her husband pass his educational agenda as governor of Arkansas, there had been a boomlet of support for a candidacy of her own as governor. She could succeed and extend the Clinton era in much the same way as Lurleen Wallace had extended that of her husband, George, in Alabama.

For a brief time, both Clintons entertained the notion and studied the polls. Hillary told her friend and law partner Webb Hubbell how her candidacy "might energize a new generation of females in the state."[5] But the dreams, frustratingly, had to be deferred. The polls and strategists, the only real gods in the Clintons' place of worship, argued convincingly for Bill to run for another term as governor.

Now here it was again, a tantalizing opportunity, a thrilling chance, a new possibility in which it would be her political needs and her time in the sun that would dominate their political marriage.

On the very day the nation heard Monica Lewinsky give her first interview on ABC's *20/20*, Hillary visited the Adrien Block Intermediate School in Flushing, Queens, New York. The visit of a first lady to a public school would normally merit scant media attention. On this visit, when she walked into the auditorium, Hillary must have been momentarily blinded by the lights of twenty-five television cameras from the networks, from cable, and from stations as far away as Berlin and Tokyo.

Ever since the eighth grade, Hillary had relished, and privately stoked, public speculation from her friends and allies that she would run for public office. Now her good friend and advisor, Susan Thomases, whetted Hillary's appetite to run for the Senate in New York. Other friends and admirers had been handing out titillating rumors to favored media allies like bon-bons. She was no longer denying them. She crossed her Rubicon, or at least the Hudson, on a spring day when Staten Island Democratic leader Robert Gigante leaned over and asked her point blank if she had any news.

"Yes," she said.

"Does that mean you're running?"

"Yes," she said.[6]

She started working a list of two hundred prominent activists and liberal leaders throughout New York State put together by former White House Deputy Chief of Staff Harold Ickes, the bare-knuckled strategist and longtime street fighter of New York politics. Political consultant Mandy Grunwald;

avaricious fund-raiser Terry McAuliffe; pollster Mark Penn; media consultants like David Doak and Hank Morris; and liberal stalwarts like William Lynch, the former deputy mayor in the Dinkins administration, all began to orbit the Hillary camp. A New York political team had visibly coalesced as Hillary began the public spectacle of scouting for a home in Westchester and let it be known that the Clintons planned to vacation in New York.

At this same time, the president began to voice doubts about Al Gore's electability to friends and reporters. If he was to have a legacy, it would likely have to come from someone else. And once elected to the Senate, wouldn't Hillary be on the fast track for a presidential run?

When Dan Rather asked her on a *60 Minutes II* interview about running for the presidency, Hillary uttered a coy giggle and said, "Oh my gosh, that's not possible, I don't believe."

"You've thought about it, though, haven't you?"

"No, I haven't," she insisted.

"You've never considered it?"

"People have said that to me, but it is something that I don't take seriously at all; it's not even in the universe of my thinking."

Of course, that statement, like so much that Hillary and her husband say, was a lie. The truth is that a run for the presidency has long been in the universe of her thinking. It was probably in her mind that day she flirted with the Marine Corps. Nor is this just her own profound fantasy. Many people around Hillary—including her longtime advisor, Betsey Wright, who had been the "bimbo-eruption" firefighter during the 1992 campaign—had long urged her to set her sights on the presidency.

THE PATH TO POWER—NEW YORK?

By May 1999 friends of Hillary were letting it be known that they saw great promise in the first lady's candidacy for the United States Senate from New York. Robert F. Kennedy had done it, and within the first few years of his first term he had created a national platform that had positioned him, at the time of his death, at the threshold of the White House. "If Gore loses next year, then it's Hillary in 2004," one Hillary campaign insider told the press.[7]

If the Senate was all she wanted, if her ambition was truly to be one of one hundred U.S. Senators, there was an easier path open to her. In 1998 Illinois Republican Peter Fitzgerald beat Carol Moseley Braun, an incumbent weakened by her dubious handling of campaign money and flirtation with the bloody, dictatorial regime in Nigeria. Yet Fitzgerald managed to win with only 51 percent of the vote.

Hillary could target that Illinois Senate seat from her home state, and stay in the public eye by taking an appointive position such as president of the World Bank—a position that she has left waiting as an option. Then, well before the 2004 election, she could move back to the state of her birth and upbringing. She could announce her candidacy at the Hillary Clinton Park in Chicago. The crowds in Chicago would be no less enthusiastic than those in New York. Scores of former high school classmates and friends could form an advance guard of volunteers.

A race in Illinois would be fitting.

It would be closer to a sure thing.

Fitzgerald is the perfect opponent for Hillary: A white, male conservative easily portrayed as out-of-touch, as a Republican extremist. She could carry this off just as she and her husband had done before to the former—and frankly "progressive"—House Speaker Newt Gingrich and, most unlikely of all, the mild-mannered, by-the-book Independent Counsel Kenneth Starr. Fitzgerald could be overwhelmed in Hillary's pincer movement, an old-fashioned gentleman caught between her moderate and persuasive demeanor, and her killer instincts.

If she runs in New York instead, Hillary will likely face New York Mayor Rudolph Giuliani. This former U.S. attorney treats political opponents in the same way he treated criminal defendants on Wall Street: by handcuffing them, shackling them together, and running them past the press in abject humiliation.

Mayor Giuliani is a candidate with monumental achievements to brag about. Under his watch, crime has dropped in New York's seventy-six precincts by 50 to 90 percent in three years. Homicides are down 70 percent. Giuliani has literally saved thousands of lives, and thousands of women are not rape victims today because of his policies. He has made New York City safe again and brought prosperity to the Big Apple. The city economy is booming. Fueled at the high end by an unprecedented stock boom, and at the low end by a continuous influx of talented and eager immigrant labor, New York is bursting with financial and human capital.

In a hypothetical early matchup poll, Hillary had led Mayor Giuliani 49 percent to 38 percent. But things changed rapidly when the reality of her potential candidacy began to set in. Pat Caddell, the political consultant who helped elect Jimmy Carter, publicly compared Hillary's campaign to "Ted Kennedy's deflated 1980 challenge of Carter." He added, "Her poll numbers are high in part because of her first victim status as a wronged woman, but that won't last."[8] By March 1999, Giuliani could point to a Marist Institute for Public Opinion poll that showed Mrs. Clinton's initial boomlet of support evaporating to 50 percent against 46 percent for Mr. Giuliani, a statistical dead heat. "Take a look at today's Marist and see if she's crowned a winner," Mr. Giuliani said.[9] As the summer grew hot, Hillary's numbers moved up and down, but regularly put her anywhere between two and ten points behind Giuliani.

Some Democrats began to sense disaster—not electoral disaster, necessarily, but a fund-raising disaster that could cripple Democratic chances in other races, including the presidential race. Hillary is the party's prime fund-raiser. A direct mail letter Hillary signed for the Democratic Senatorial Campaign Committee in 1998 raised three times more than expected, a total of $3 million. As a candidate needing $20 million to run in New York, Hillary is draining dollars away from Democratic candidates.

Writing in the *New Republic*—a magazine ardently in Vice President Al Gore's corner—journalist Michelle Cottle predicted that Hillary could become another "Ted Kennedy-like demon with which to frighten Republican donors into departing with their cash."

"She could divert resources from other candidates, politicize their races in ways that don't play well beyond the Upper West Side, and become a rallying point for conservatives still itching to exploit anti-Clinton sentiment," Cottle wrote. "She could, in other words, do precisely what her husband has done time and again—sacrifice the good of her party and her cause to satisfy her own ambitions."

Ex-New York governor Mario Cuomo agreed with that

analysis saying that the wooden vice president would need Hillary on the stump to "lend the campaign a flash and pizzazz." Unsaid by Cuomo, but clear to all, was that a Hillary candidacy would allow the capital of world media once again to recycle the scandals of the Clinton years and her role in them. Mountains of dirty laundry would be recycled to hang into the sunshine.

Tough questions that can be ducked by a first lady cannot be ducked by a Senate candidate. Referring to her spectacular ability to turn a $1,000 investment in cattle futures into a small fortune, conservative columnist George F. Will asked, "If you are that gifted with money, will you promise to seek a seat on the Finance Committee?"[10]

She will also have to explain to New York City's Jewish voters why she has a lifetime record of support for the Palestine Liberation Organization (PLO). The same Hillary who will be donning yarmulkes and making her appeal in the synagogues of New York—and who now says, in defiance of Clinton administration policy, that Jerusalem rather than Tel Aviv should be the capital of Israel—is the same woman who was chairing the New World Foundation when a $15,000 grant was awarded to a group called Grassroots International. Grassroots International had direct ties to the PLO.[11]

Hillary claims she didn't vote on those funds. But this is the same Hillary warmly cited by New Age thinker Michael Lerner for joining her husband "to call for a Palestinian state that would agree to live in peace with Israel."[12] While recent polls show considerable softening toward a Palestinian state among American Jews, this is hardly the issue she needs to win in New York. "You favor carving a Palestinian state into Israel's back," George Will challenged her. "Schools run by the Palestinian

Authority, which would run such a state, teach (among other anti-Semitic propaganda) that the Holocaust is a Zionist lie. How is Israel helped by a contiguous state run by Holocaust deniers?"[13]

DECEPTIVE APPEARANCE

Then there is the carpetbagger charge. Robert F. Kennedy did not have a cakewalk to the Senate. In fact, with much more experience in New York than Hillary, he barely managed to win in 1964—the year that Lyndon Johnson and many other Democrats won in an immense landslide.

The power of celebrity may pale in the face of attacks like this one from Republican Congressman Rick Lazio: "Hillary Clinton, first of all, has never lived a day of her life [in New York] outside the Plaza Hotel...." Representative Lazio went on to add: "You just heard in the report before that her political people are looking for her to visit some families. Well, she wouldn't need that if she had her own family in New York. This is a woman who has never sent her children to school in New York, has never paid Mario Cuomo's taxes, needs an exploratory committee to find Binghamton and Rochester and Utica and Long Island. This is the wrong person for New York. This is someone who roots for the Chicago Cubs over the New York Mets. How can we have that?"

As if in response, a New York Yankees baseball cap materialized on Hillary's head like the Whitewater billing records had once materialized in her White House residence. Suddenly we heard that she was a longstanding Yankees fan. Out of nowhere the Yankees of October 1998 became White House guests in July 1999. Just as she felt she needed to wrap herself in motherhood for the 1996 election, she was determined to wrap herself in a New York Yankees pennant for the year 2000 senatorial election.

But I know that if it's a struggle over who is the bigger Yankees fan, Hillary is sure to lose to a man like Giuliani, who actually kept a Yankee Stadium bleacher chair in his office when he worked in the Department of Justice.

Nor can she count on strong coattails from her husband. Bobby Kennedy could rely on the reflected glory of a martyred brother. Consumed by some form of respectable legacy, Bill Clinton on the other hand has seen his popularity sink to its lowest point, weighed down by scandal after scandal.

"Please, please, please run, Hillary," says Republican political consultant Mike Murphy on MSNBC. "Why? Because she is a loser and she will draw Democrat money from all over the country into New York, where she will lose."[14]

"Come," veteran New York commentator Jimmy Breslin purred on CNN, "but please don't cry when you lose."[15] She entered the Senate race on the strength of a boomlet of popularity, only to face insurmountable odds in the form of an entrenched and relentless opponent, her own record on the PLO, and her shared record of scandal with her husband.

This is the appearance of things to come. It may be a deceptive appearance. Nothing written here is unknown to Hillary. She is weighing other factors, making other calculations. Remember, this was the couple who was once swept out of power in 1980, only to rebuild patiently the Clinton image and retake the governor's mansion. This is the couple who was down-and-out in the New York presidential primary, only to retake it in a maudlin national appeal on *60 Minutes*.

This is the couple who suffered the loss of their health care bill, a suicide by an intimate friend in the White House, a baker's dozen scandals, only to be returned to the presidency in 1996 in a cakewalk. If Hillary is running, she has a plan.

One plan is to immunize herself on the PLO charge. Most saw through Hillary's pandering to the New York Jewish community in August of 1999 when news of her long-lost Jewish stepgrandfather suddenly surfaced, just when the PLO charges against her were heating up.

If Benjamin Netanyahu will be working the stumps in New York, so will an even greater authority on the security of Israel—Prime Minister Ehud Barak—and so will James Carville—the political commando who helped to take Netanyahu out and put Barak in. Barak is personally grateful to the Clintons for publicly supporting him, and for lending him their political operatives. He is willing to return the favor. Barak has let it be known that his government will roll out a red carpet for the visiting first lady, and will go out of its way to demonstrate that she offers no threat to Israel.[16] There is a reason why Hillary visits all the right "I" countries so dear to New York voters: Israel, Italy, and Ireland. She knows who butters the political bread.

ON THE OTHER HAND...

And what about Mayor Giuliani?

No New York mayor since 1868 has made it to higher office. Not Jimmy Walker, not John Lindsay, not Ed Koch. A woman born in Illinois is not much more geographically distant from Buffalo than someone who lives in Manhattan. In many ways, she is culturally much closer.

In some quarters, there is concern that Rudy Giuliani will not successfully rouse the conservative faithful. Some GOP voters are still bitter over his eleventh hour endorsement of

Democrat Mario Cuomo just before Cuomo lost the governorship in 1994 to Republican George Pataki.

As a final testament to Hillary's chances, consider former
United States Senator Alfonse D'Amato who, after a bruising
year investigating the Clintons, was on the comeback trail in
New York until he ran smack into Hillary. She raised more
than a million dollars for his victorious opponent and publicly
ridiculed him as "Senator Tomato." She destroyed D'Amato
and the most powerful Republican machine in the state.

THE ANSWER

So why would Hillary put herself through such a dangerous
and difficult race?

Because she can win. And something else.

When asked in 1994 about the prospect of his wife running for president, Bill Clinton said, "Oh, she'd be great at it.
But I don't think she'd ever run—not in a hundred years!"
The reason, he said, was "she was not interested in being in
elected office and she always said that publicly."[17]

Perhaps it all depends on her definition of what "not
interested" is.

THREE
"SEE HOW LIBERAL I'M BECOMING!"

"It is useless self-indulgence for an activist to put his past behind him. Instead, he should realize the priceless value of his middle-class experience. His middle-class identity, his familiarity with the values and problems, are invaluable for organization of his 'own people.'"

— SAUL ALINSKY, *RULES FOR RADICALS*

illary Rodham—as she was known until she changed her name after a half-dozen years of marriage—seems to have been born ambitious.

The same focused young woman keeps appearing throughout the pages of *Eyrie*, the Maine South High School yearbook, and *Southwards*, the school paper. Here she is in 1963, a sophomore and class council representative. There she is as a junior, on the Cultural Values committee. Think about that!

Some teenagers are diffident, shy. They half-look at the camera, embarrassed to be in school publicity shots. The photos of Hillary show poise, confidence, and a level stare.

GOLDWATER GIRL

She is the daughter of Hugh and Dorothy Rodham, middle-class and comfortable who have been established in Park Ridge, Illinois, since Hillary was four. Park Ridge is a suburb of Chicago, white and conservative, mid-America in the middle of America. It is near the site of the first McDonald's. Hillary Rodham is not hard to read. She's a daddy's girl. A Goldwater girl.

She popped up as chairman of the Republican organization in the mock election debate, and in a photo playfully holding up her dukes against her Democratic opponents. She wore a Goldwater sash and gave a five-minute speech on behalf of the Republican presidential nominee and Republican Senate candidate Chuck Percy. She led a student council effort to clean up obscene graffiti that marred a South High wall. She made the honor society. She made her television debut as a backup member of the school's team on *It's Academic*.

By her senior year, Hillary was in full stride: She was class council vice president, served on the Pep Club, won a science award, excelled at speech and debate, received the Daughters of the American Revolution Award for citizenship, and was a National Merit finalist.

There are signs that she was respected, but not terribly well liked. *Southwards* revealingly predicted that she would become nun "Sister Frigidaire." Another *Southwards* item, with a crude drawing of Hillary, is headlined: "Lawyer Hillary Reviews Career."

And early ambivalence about her ability—or willingness—to make it on her own was suggested when asked about her ambitions after high school. Hillary Rodham said, "To marry a senator and settle down in Georgetown"—a curious response for someone who had nourished such intense early ambition.

Furthermore, somewhere, something wasn't quite right. The daddy's girl would soon become a feminist activist and critic of the nuclear family.

In November 1973 Hillary Rodham wrote an article for the *Harvard Educational Review* that advocated a radical expansion of the rights of children. In it, Hillary Rodham revealed an important aspect of her political agenda: Support for the liberation of children from "the empire of the father."

This word choice gives a glimpse into her inner life. "I grew up in a family that looks like it was straight out of the 1950s television sitcom, *Father Knows Best*," Hillary would later write.[1]

But, in retrospect, it may also have been as icy, tense, controlled, and artificial as a sound stage.

BABY BOOMER SUBURBIA

Hugh Rodham was a salty, tobacco-chewing, self-made man, whose primary way of showing affection was through sarcasm and whose instant response to any achievement by his overachieving daughter was to dismiss it and raise the bar even higher. Hillary had to jump high to be daddy's favorite.

Years after his death, she is jumping still.

Discipline and acceptance of the hard realities of life were a Rodham family tradition. Hugh Rodham's father, an English immigrant, had gone to work in a lace factory at age eleven.

Hugh, sandwiched between two brothers, grew up in Scranton, Pennsylvania, in a competitive environment that spurred him on to win an athletic scholarship to Penn State, where he made the football team. After graduating in 1935, he returned home to sell lace curtains. Hugh soon abandoned Scranton for Chicago, where he became a textile salesman.

Perhaps the most formative experience of Hugh's early life was as a chief petty officer in the Navy during World War II, when he drilled recruits at a Great Lakes naval base. It was perhaps there that the Rodham style was perfected, one in which life became a constant drill. This was a style he would take with him into civilian life, one in which only intense, cheerless, and concentrated effort could ward away the specter of the poorhouse.

Hugh came to own and run his own plant, where he made screen-printed draperies and fabrics. He did the buying, the printing, the sewing, and the selling. Big hotel chains and airlines became his best customers. He acquired a good home in a prosperous suburb. He bought a Cadillac and became a Taft Republican.

On occasion, Hugh put his two sons, Hughie and Tony, to work, making it clear at dinner that an extra potato that evening was their reward. He drove his family relentlessly, and often asked his children, "Do you want us to end up in the poorhouse?"

If Hugh's early life was pure Horatio Alger, Hillary's mother, Dorothy Howell, had a childhood that was positively Dickensian.

Dorothy must have put forward a confident appearance when she first met Hugh as a young secretary at the Columbia Lace Company. There was likely little outward sign of the devastating childhood she had endured.

She had been born to teenaged parents in Chicago. Her parents split up and sent eight-year-old Dorothy and her three-year-old sister alone on a cross-country train to live with their paternal grandparents, also English immigrants, in Los Angeles.

The image of two little girls, forlorn and forsaken, sank deep into young Hillary's mind and is often pointed to in her political speeches.

"When my mother first told me how she cared for her sister during the three-day journey, I was incredulous," Hillary wrote. "After I became a mother myself, I was furious that any child, even in the safer 1920s, would be treated like that."[2]

California in the 1920s may have seemed like paradise, but Hillary's grandmother was a harsh taskmaster and her grandfather was distant. Young Dorothy relished the occasional kindness of strangers and relatives, a teacher who bought her milk, a great-aunt, a kind family who took her in as a boarder.

The Rodhams were married in 1942. Their first child, Hillary, was born in 1947, followed by Hughie and Tony.

Park Ridge offered the Rodhams a world of safety, neighborliness, and good schools. A typical baby boomer suburban life. Children moved in constant action up and down the block, in and out of houses, from softball to tag.

August vacations were spent at Hillary's grandfather's cottage on Lake Winola, near Scranton, where the kids trekked local mountains, and fished and swam in the Susquehanna River. At Park Ridge, Hillary fell into place, becoming both playmate and self-conscious leader.

The Hillary legend began early. The story has been repeated often by writers from Gail Sheehy to David Maraniss how Hillary, shortly after moving to Park Ridge, was hit by Suzy, a local bully. Hillary recounts that she ran home in tears and terror, only to be told by her mother, "There's no room in this house for cowards."

The story continues that Hillary walked up to Suzy standing amid a group of boys and gave her a good pop, thus earning young Hillary the acceptance and respect of the other kids. Thereafter, we are told, Hillary played with the boys, fought with the boys, and held her own with the boys. One can expect to see this scenario dramatized on tape for a Democratic National Convention some time in the future: It is the beginning of her legend.

Hillary soon became a high achiever, "winning so many awards," according to her mother, "it was embarrassing."[3] She was a Brownie, then a Girl Scout whose sash sported as many pins and medals as the breast of a four-star general.

Dorothy was determined to be the kind of mother that she had never known. She was nurturing, an emotional counterweight to Hillary's stern father. She was resourceful and imaginative, one time making a miniature world for Hillary's dolls by filling a cardboard box with sand, and using a mirror to make a lake, and twigs for the forest.

"She organized our daily lives and fed us with her devotion, imagination, and great spirit," Hillary wrote of her mother. "She attended every school and sports event and cheered for us whether we scored or struck out. She taught Sunday school, helped out at our public school, and was there when we came home for lunch. She entertained our friends, took us to the library, and made sure we did our chores."[4]

On the other hand, Hillary portrays her father as hard, cold, and demanding. She proudly showed her father report cards with a column of A's. His reaction was always, "You must go to a pretty easy school."

After Hughie won a football game 36 to 0, completing ten out of eleven passes, Hugh said, "You should have completed the other one."

Hugh was the kind of father whose withholding of affection may have inspired overachievement, but it also seems to have created a reservoir of resentment for a young woman who would later write a whole book about the value of nurturing.

Hillary fantasized early on with becoming an astronaut. Hillary and Hughie spent many hours in the basement on pretend flights to the moon. "She would always drive and I would always have to sit in the back," Hughie would later say of their imaginary journeys.[5]

At age fourteen, Hillary wrote a letter to NASA inquiring about how a young lady could aspire to become an astronaut. She recalls that she was "infuriated" by a reply that told her that only boys could become astronauts.

If the heavens were closed to her, the next world was not. She followed the example of her father, a devout Methodist who taught his children to kneel by their beds and pray every night. "We attended a big church with an active congregation, the First United Methodist Church in Park Ridge," Hillary wrote. "The church was a center for preaching and practicing the social gospel, so important to our Methodist traditions. Our spiritual life as a family was spirited and constant. We talked with God, walked with God, ate, studied and argued with God."[6]

At an early age, Hillary absorbed the lessons of the Methodist church, and was shaped by the power of its social gospel. The United Methodists now claim more members than the Episcopalians, Presbyterians, Congregationalists, and American Baptists combined, dominating the National Council of Churches.

Like all Christians, Methodists believe in salvation through grace. But John Wesley, Oxford scholar, failed missionary to Georgia and peripatetic revivalist in the British Isles, distinguished Methodism from other Protestant denominations by injecting it with the doctrine of the "second blessing"—the dynamic interaction of human will and divine grace that could lead toward spiritual perfection.

In the late nineteenth and twentieth centuries, Methodist theology, awakened by the powerful assertions of social science, began to stir a new awakening to the issues of class and race. The compelling power of this new social gospel had resonated with the Methodist commitment to the quest for human perfectibility. "Be doers of the word and not hearers only," is a phrase often heard in the Methodist church.[7]

Also, of all the denominations, Methodism perhaps had gone the farthest in advocating the "Social Creed" and its quasi-socialist concept of progress. Of all the denominations, Methodism had been the most militant opponent of the saloon and advocate of temperance and prohibition. It was this strain of Methodism, the deep eddies of the Christian left, that gave Hillary Rodham her moral and political bearings and perhaps her highly attuned sense of self-righteousness. "I wrestle nearly every day with the biblical admonition to forgive and love my enemies," she wrote in *It Takes a Village*.[8]

Her Methodism would emerge in her spirited attacks on corporations, on tobacco, on pharmaceutical and insurance companies. It became the root of her worldview, one in which it is never enough to attack an opponent's actions. One must also expose his motives, and use that perspective to destroy both the action and its proponents. For the natural companion of a doctrine of perfectibility is a conviction in the existence of evil—and immorality—of one's enemies. Hillary's America is a starkly Manichean universe, one in which she perceives the enemies of progress as numerous, powerful, and clever—in fact, as the "vast right-wing conspiracy."

Hillary began her life in the church cleaning up, reading scripture lessons, and participating in Christmas and Easter pageants. Then she met the Reverend Don Jones, and it was that meeting that began the external change in the Goldwater girl.

THE UNIVERSITY OF LIFE

Hillary was a fourteen-year-old ninth grader when the Reverend Donald G. Jones arrived as the new youth minister. He was an intense, energetic thirty-year-old, newly minted from divinity school in Manhattan. The students, not Jones, called the class "The University of Life." It was an apt name, for the Reverend Jones possessed an expansive mission to open his students to his view of the wider world and transform them.

Don Jones was determined to break open the comfortable cocoon of Park Ridge and expose his protégés to the disturbing realities of the contemporary world. He brought in an atheist to debate the existence of God. He upset the congregation with a discussion of teenage pregnancy. He conveyed his deep commitment to the theology of Paul Tillich, who redefined Christianity in terms of the German idealistic tradition and existentialism. Jones believed, as Tillich wrote, that the major flaw of contemporary Christianity was its deep roots in middle-class culture. Its revival, Tillich argued, could come only from a critique of society that took its inspiration from Marxist lines of thought.

In this new spin on Christianity, sin and grace, death and redemption were no longer the key features of theology. The major problem facing American youth, the Reverend Jones informed his students, was a crisis of meaning and alienation. Hillary carried this forward to her "politics of meaning."

The Reverend Jones jolted his students with a bracing mixture of counterculture and high culture, the poems of e.e. cummings, J.D. Salinger's *The Catcher in the Rye*, and a discussion on Picasso's *Guernica*. He drew explicit parallels between the utopia of Karl Marx and the heavenly kingdom. He took the group into inner-city Chicago, where Hillary for the first time came to know poor people, "trailer people," black people, Hispanic people—families who, he taught, would not have been welcome in Park Ridge, even if they could have afforded it.

The University of Life took Hillary and her friends to nearby farms, where the students set up a program to baby-sit migrant children while the parents toiled. For the first time, Hillary performed social work for the poor, this time for Hispanic migrant laborers and their families.

"I don't think those kids had ever seen poverty before," Reverend Jones recalled to Arkansas journalist Meredith Oakley. "Religion, going to church, tended to function there for most people to reinforce their rather traditional conservative values, and so when I came in and took that white, middle-class youth group into the inner city of Chicago, that was quite radical."[9]

According to Hillary, no experience with the University of Life had a greater effect on her than an outing, on one spring night in 1962, when the Reverend Jones took the students on a church bus to Orchestra Hall on Michigan Avenue to hear a lecture by Dr. Martin Luther King, Jr.

Dr. King spoke on "Sleeping Through the Revolution," challenging the audience to awaken to the challenge of ensuring the civil rights of all. King met with the students one by one backstage. Hillary shook his hand and later recalled the experience as "eye-opening."[10]

Later, Hillary met Barry Goldwater after reading *The Conscience of a Conservative*. But the lessons from the lantern-jawed Arizonan were losing ground to Reverend Jones and the University of Life.

Two years after coming to Park Ridge, the Reverend Jones went on to teach in New Jersey, eventually becoming a professor of theology at Drew University. Many of his congregants were glad to see him go, regarding him as a radical leftist preacher of the "social gospel." But he had left a process of change within the girl who had once been crestfallen when Barry Goldwater had lost in his race for the presidency. She no longer trusted the "conscience of a conservative," but found herself thinking more and more in terms of mass social action, of a Christian socialism where the restraints of Christianity gradually gave way to the demands of politics and power.

High school and the University of Life gave Hillary leadership training and a growing sense of mission, but she was still not picking up awards for congeniality. She describes one incident at a chilly soccer game when, after remarking on how cold it was, a competitor said, "I wish people like you would freeze to death." When Hillary asked how the girl could feel that way when the girl didn't even know her, the young soccer player responded, "I don't have to know you to hate you." Hillary recounted this story years later as one of her first experiences with discrimination. But the other girl was white. Hillary apparently just couldn't understand that maybe there was something about her that the other girl just didn't like.

HIPPIEDOM AND THE STRUGGLE AGAINST EVIL

Hillary graduated in the top 5 percent of her class (somewhere around fifteenth place), and was voted "most likely to succeed." She was also a National Merit scholar and had firmly established herself with her high school faculty as a student leader.

"She was set on going to an all-girls' school," Dorothy Rodham said.[11] Hillary considered Radcliffe and Smith, but decided on Wellesley once she saw a photo of its charming campus, surrounding a lake. She was smitten. It seemed a natural destination, where the motto is "not to be served, but to serve."

Hillary has a reputation for being smart, but was not the natural student that her future husband was, who could breeze through a lesson and get it down cold. She had to apply herself. And she did so at Wellesley, where she became a Durant scholar, one of the highest academic honors then bestowed on a Wellesley student.

As a high school student, Hillary had always been indifferent to cosmetics. "When she was fifteen or sixteen and the other kids started to use makeup and fix their hair, she wasn't interested," Dorothy recalled. "That used to annoy me a little bit. I used to think, 'Why can't she put on a little makeup?'" Still, it wasn't until she went to Wellesley that she adopted a hippie leftist look.[12]

Hillary was "finding" herself. Still, some men were attracted to her. Geoff Shields, a Harvard junior who met Hillary when she was a freshman, and who dated her for two years, said that Hillary "tended to listen more than talk. But as time went by, she solidified her beliefs." Many of their dates, he said, were spent sitting with friends over a beer or a soft drink, "talking in an animated way about politics and government and social issues," among them civil rights, civil liberties, and the war in Southeast Asia.[13]

As far as connecting with the currents of liberalism, Wellesley in the late 1960s was the "university of life" writ large. Wellesley students, noted Eleanor "Eldie" Acheson, granddaughter of Truman's secretary of state and later placed by Hillary in Janet Reno's Department of Justice, tended to "become right-thinking"[14]—meaning left-thinking, of course, because in the world of Hillary Clinton "left" is right and "right" is a conspiracy.

During her freshman year, Hillary wrote a letter to Reverend Jones exulting in the election of liberal Republican John Lindsay as mayor of New York. Still a Republican, she admitted that she was "leaning left." She added, "See how liberal I'm becoming!"[15]

Hillary also called herself "an ethical Christian," remaining physically aloof from much of the counterculture. Friends do not recall her smoking marijuana or drinking to excess. Unlike many of her colleagues, she did not jump feet first into the bacchanal of the late 1960s. But her social activism continued to grow.

Hillary took time from her studies to work trying to teach poor black children in Roxbury to read. She was active in student war protests and increasingly vocal in private over her opposition to the war. In each instance, Hillary was forced to think—as she did at Park Ridge—of operating outside the bounds of her immediate surroundings. Blacks made up less than two percent of Hillary's Wellesley class. Few Wellesley girls had family serving in Vietnam. Hillary knew that she was sheltered. And the feeling that evil ran amok outside was at

times overwhelming. On the day that Martin Luther King, Jr.,
was murdered, Hillary burst into her suite, startling her
roommate, threw her book bag across the room, and yelled, "I
can't stand it anymore. I can't take it." She soon broke into
sobs.[16]

Hillary participated in antiwar marches in Boston. The
assassination of Robert F. Kennedy moved her to withdraw
from the campus Young Republicans and volunteer for antiwar candidate Eugene McCarthy in New Hampshire. When
he dropped out of the Democratic presidential primary,
Hillary struggled over whether to support Hubert Humphrey.

It was not an easy decision. She had gone home to
Chicago in time to witness the bloody clash between Mayor
Daley's police and antiwar protestors. There had been a brief,
last struggle in her mind between the liberal Republicanism of
the Ripon Society and the Democrats her father had taught
her to despise. She went to the Republican National
Convention with a group of liberal Republicans who wanted
to draft Nelson Rockefeller. When Nixon was nominated,
that left her with the choice of supporting Vice President
Hubert Humphrey or sitting it out.

Perhaps she should have joined her leftist colleagues in
despising Humphrey as a tool of President Johnson, as an
apologist for the war she opposed and detested, and against
whom she had organized a student strike. But she was not
ready to go that far. "She finally came around," says Eldie
Acheson. "She even distributed literature [for Humphrey] in
New Hampshire."[17]

The break with her past was now complete; the liberation
from the grip of her father's convictions. From here on out,
the Republicans were the enemy, and the enemy was allied

with evil—the evils of war, racism, sexism, and poverty. In this struggle against evil, Hillary accepted the necessity of "party discipline," campaigning for Democrats regardless of her personal assessment of a particular candidate.

By her senior year, the time had come to do more than advocate. The time had come for Hillary to run for office. She became one of three candidates running for president of the student government. None received the endorsement of the *Wellesley News*. "They each expressed a desire for greater student jurisdiction in social matters and a more responsible role in academic decision making," read a news editorial, "but all three were equally vague as to exactly how they would implement the change in the power structure to achieve the second objective."[18]

A *Boston Globe* profile recounted her reactions after she won. In her exuberance, she took aside one of her professors. "I can't believe what has just happened," she said. "I was just elected president of the government. Can you believe it? Can you believe that happened?"

In that same 1993 *Globe* profile, her friend and to this day loyal supporter Acheson recalled that as student body president, Hillary was "a sophisticated coalition builder who provided extremely strong and very sensible leadership. Some people were shrill, accusatory, and adversarial to the administration of the college, but she artfully and very respectfully led student government to where it was an important factor at the school."

Others did not see her tenure in such glowing terms. At times, Hillary displayed the toughness she would become known for later.

Marshall I. Goldman, a professor who taught Russian economics, pleaded with students not to disrupt classes with a two-day strike to conduct teach-ins on the Vietnam War and race relations. "Let's give up weekends, something that we enjoy. Don't give up classes—that's not a sacrifice."

"I'll give up my date Saturday, Mr. Goldman, but I don't think that's the point," Hillary fired back. "Individual consciences are fine, but individual consciences have to be made manifest."[19] She meant that giving up a date on Saturday night would do nothing to register the anger of the movement on the establishment. If throwing a little sand in the gears was necessary, she was ready to do it.

Hillary pushed for, and won, the school's recruitment of more black students. Joining the egalitarian trend that was so fashionable at the time, she fought for, and won, pass-fail classes. She sought and achieved changes to the rule that students had to wear skirts to the dining hall. And, resonating with another popular movement of the sixties, she supported opening Wellesley's dorms to visits by men.

Hillary took away from her experience a reputation as a leader, a woman who could win over the administration to the changes that were sweeping across universities, across the nation. She was a person of her culture and the times, and she demonstrated keen instincts for being at the front of the popular causes of the day.

"She was so ambitious," a classmate recalled in a 1993 *New Yorker* profile.

"She already knew the value of networking, of starting a rolodex, even back then. She cultivated relationships with teachers and administrators even more than with students. While she was noticed across the board and she had her circle of friends, I would not say she was popular. She was a little too intimidating for that."[20]

Hillary's last act at Wellesley was to create a defining radical moment for her in 1969. She gave a commencement address that has been mythologized by her adherents as "The Speech," the touchstone that friends, journalists, biographers, and future Republican opposition research analysts have returned to again and again.

THE SPEECH

It was the spring of 1969. Richard Nixon was president, and it was becoming increasingly clear that his promise of "peace with honor" was not intended to be a surrender. Tons of bombs were raining on Hanoi. Draft riots and resistance to the war intensified, and the campuses of America were in turmoil.

The commencement speaker at Hillary's graduation was Senator Edward Brooke, the first African American to sit in the United States Senate since Reconstruction. He was a liberal Republican from Massachusetts and an accomplished lawyer who had once smashed organized crime rings as a prosecutor.

As a Young Republican, Hillary had once supported Senator Brooke. She had even campaigned for him in her sophomore year. But now he was tainted, beyond repair, given his partisan association with Nixon (though Brooke would later help sink the nomination of G. Harrold Carswell, Nixon's appointee to the U.S. Supreme Court).

There was widespread interest among Hillary's friends, especially Eldie Acheson, in staging a counter-commencement. After much back-and-forth, University President Ruth Adams reluctantly agreed to allow a designated speaker to have a few words at the commencement. According to Joyce Milton's *The*

First Partner, Adams extracted a promise from Hillary that she would submit a prepared text of her remarks and stick to it.

For three days, Hillary and her friends put together a speech. To this day, Hillary's staff do not expect the speeches they produce to be delivered as written. On the stump, Hillary extemporizes, pulls together her theme with reactions to what has just been said.

Her first big speech was a forerunner of that style. It was pure reaction, a rebuke that reads polite on the page, but was hard, even rude, when delivered.

Senator Brooke, when he spoke, expressed empathy with the students and their anguish over racial and social injustice as the root cause of human misery and the chief obstacle to the proper development of our nation. He praised Hillary's generation as an expression of an America that "has identified more precisely than ever before the nature and magnitude of its acute social problems." He even sounded themes that should have played well with Hillary—that society has a responsibility to alleviate poverty, hunger, unemployment, inferior education, and inadequate health care. Brooke's Republicanism was not the "individual responsibility" ethos of Barry Goldwater, but the liberal Republicanism that had resonated in Hillary's social conscience.

But then he went on to speak the unspeakable on an American college campus in 1969. "Whatever the romantics may say about violence in our national life," Brooke said, "the use of force is repugnant to the spirit of American politics." He denounced the radical Students for a Democratic Society and suggested that the fringes of the protest movement might be giving comfort to America's enemies.

This was more infuriating to Wellesley's fashionable left-
ists than hearing Vice President Spiro Agnew directly lash
into the students without apology or restraint. That this combination of criticism and "empathy" enraged young Hillary
shows how radicalized she had become. It wasn't enough to be
a black liberal Republican with a liberal social agenda because
liberal Republicans weren't willing to go all the way and
expunge by force the evil that Hillary saw manifest in the
Vietnam War, resistance to every demand by the civil rights
movement, and in failure to eradicate poverty.

"Senator Brooke gave an address that was pretty close to
being just absolutely disconnected with the four years of our
experience at Wellesley," says Acheson. "Hillary decided it
could not go unremarked upon, and before her speech, gave
an extemporaneous critique of Brooke's remarks."[21]

In 1992, in a *Newsweek* interview with Eleanor Clift,
Hillary characterized Brooke as giving "a very traditional,
conventional speech in which he basically took a kind of
Republican apologist line about what was happening, what
President Nixon was doing."

Hillary Rodham Clinton continued: "It was exactly the
kind of message my classmates felt they didn't want as their
last remembrance of Wellesley. When I spoke, I responded to
his not really having addressed the concerns of the people
about to go into this world."[22]

Noted feminist *bête noire* Camille Paglia has given a sexual
interpretation of what happened on that spring day. She won-
dered if Hillary was "lashing out in a visceral response to the
invasion of her all-woman's school by a glamorous, lordly male
who, from my one passing encounter with him as he sauntered
elegantly down the Capitol steps in 1972, had a distinctly

roving eye."[23] Whatever the cause, something about Brooke pushed Hillary's button as she stepped before the podium.

Introduced by College President Ruth Adams as "cheerful, good-humored, good company, and a good friend to us all," Hillary quickly extinguished all hopes that charity, generosity, respect, and good manners might reign that day. Surprise, then shock, rippled through the audience as Hillary ripped into a United States senator, a civil rights icon, a black man before a liberal audience.

"Part of the problem with empathy with professed goals is that empathy doesn't do anything," she said, with the pompous, angry, impatient, and self-righteous tone that was so typical of campus "leaders" of that era. "We've had lots of empathy; we've had lots of sympathy, but we feel that for too long our leaders have used politics as the art of the possible. And the challenge now is to practice politics as the art of the making what appears impossible, possible."

After bitterly rejecting Senator Brooke's effort to express support for her colleagues' ideals, she characterized him as a craven apologist for Nixon. She then went on to attack the dispassionate terminology that she perceived was being employed to evaluate her country's many ills.

"What does it mean to hear that 13.3 percent of the people in this country are below the poverty line? That's a percentage. We're not interested in social reconstruction; it's human construction. How can we talk about percentages and trends?"

Hillary said of her classmates: "Our attitudes are easily understood having grown up, having come to consciousness in the first five years of this decade—years dominated by men and dreams, men in the civil rights movement, the Peace Corps, the space program—so we arrived at Wellesley and we found, all of us have found, that there was a gap between expectation and realities. But it wasn't a discouraging gap and it didn't turn us into cynical, bitter old women at age eighteen. It just inspired us to do something about that gap."

Hillary reminded everyone of the many concessions that she and her classmates wrested from the school administration. The rest of the speech was part sixties psychobabble, with its undertones of German existential philosophy, and part youthful, egocentric angst.

"We are, all of us, exploring a world that none of us understands and attempting to create within that uncertainty," she said. "But there are some things we feel, feelings that our prevailing, acquisitive, and competitive corporate life, including tragically the universities, is not the way of life for us."

After this impenetrable declaration, she went even further into the depths of murky sixties thinking: "We're searching for more immediate, ecstatic and penetrating modes of living." A line for which one craves Camille Paglia's exegesis.

Much of the rest of the speech discussed "authentic reality" versus "inauthentic reality." Performed by a spirited woman to an audience of young women of similar leanings, it undoubtedly made a strong impression of youthful idealism. But is entirely incomprehensible today.

Even in today's liberal culture, such a convoluted stew would be seen not as a courageous declaration of identity, but as a hopeless meandering of feminist platitudes and catchy sound bites that would cause listeners, students, and faculty alike to look away out of embarrassment for the speaker. As a style it could be called the first person, subjective.

Another student who gave a commencement address at Brown University that year exemplified the same self-indulgent style and non-linear thought processes. That student, Ira Magaziner, was brought twenty-four years later to the White House by first lady Hillary to create and manage her health care proposal.

Echoing Hillary's ascent into rhetorical fantasy, the theme of Magaziner's address was "realities exist but they're not real to me." Magaziner, soon to head to Oxford as a Rhodes scholar, said, "I can't believe us spending millions of dollars to send soldiers to West Germany to engage in a war game. I can't believe financing the burning of our crops while millions starve. I can't believe analysts seriously discussing how decisions are made by whether Johnson or Nixon feel that their place in history is going to be preserved if they make certain decisions while people die." You can tell why Hillary and Ira became such close compatriots.

Magaziner and Hillary Rodham can be forgiven for these youthful flights because they were repeating a peculiar self-centered idealism, seemingly rooted not so much in morality as in aesthetics: A view that somehow the world and society had a responsibility to produce results that made the student, or teacher, or community activist feel better personally.

The elites of American education, the best and the brightest, sought to create protégés by giving young leaders an unprecedented freedom to discover their own truths. And they did: They found truths no one before or since has quite recognized. This generation of leaders, chosen, taught, and celebrated by elite academics embraced an inexpressible ideal, whose core characteristic was a feeling of unending entitlement.

The world had to do more than improve. It was expected to reorder itself, to become a great pinwheel to spin around tender egos and emotional needs.

Whatever the reaction of listeners in Hillary's Wellesley graduation audience like Paul Nitze, the diplomat, and Eldie's distinguished grandfather Dean Acheson (he actually later asked Hillary for a copy of her speech), the reaction of Hillary's peers was immediate and unanimous. They gave her a seven-minute standing ovation. Hillary was soon profiled with other young Americans in a *Life* magazine piece, titled "The Class of '69." Looking bespectacled and bemused, an excerpt of her speech ran under her photo: "Protest is an attempt to forge an identity."

Later, she confessed that she had celebrated at the end of commencement day by breaking a campus rule. She swam in the school's Lake Waban. She stripped to her bathing suit, and carefully folded her clothes and glasses on the shore, only to have them confiscated by a security officer. "Blind as a bat, I had to feel my way back to my room," she said.[24]

Hillary took off that summer with other students to do odd jobs around the country, winding up in Alaska. She took a job at a fish cannery, where she informed the owner that she did not believe that his fish appeared fit for consumption. She may have expected him to close down his cannery and change his methods. Instead, he fired her.[25]

SAUL ALINSKY, HILLARY'S RADICAL PROPHET

When William Jefferson Clinton took the oath of office, Wellesley suddenly adopted a new-found policy of putting the thesis of any graduates who became first lady under lock and key. It is hard to imagine that this unique provision was adopted without the strong support, if not the instigation, of the highly secretive first lady.

The contents of Hillary's thesis, and why she would want

it hidden from public view, have long been the subject of intense interest. Most likely, she does not want the American people to know the extent to which she internalized and assimilated the beliefs and methods of Saul Alinsky.

It was Alinsky, legendary organizer and left-wing folk hero, who was responsible for bringing Martin Luther King, Jr., to Chicago. Hillary first met him under the auspices of the Reverend Jones and the University of Life. Born in Chicago in 1909, Alinsky did graduate work at the University of Chicago in criminology. He studied prison life at Joliet State Prison and took a particular interest in the Capone gang.

He emerged as a radical leader when he joined forces with the impoverished families of the "Back of the Yards" area in Chicago, near the old stockyards, site of Upton Sinclair's *The Jungle*. Skillfully building up local support and enlisting the backing of the Catholic Church, he campaigned for increased social services and enhanced government support for housing programs.

"I acted in such a way that within a few weeks, the meat-packers publicly pronounced me a subversive menace," Alinsky later wrote. "The *Chicago Tribune*'s adoption of me as a public enemy of law and order, a radical's radical, gave me a perennial and constantly renewable baptismal certificate in the city of Chicago."[26]

Alinsky assembled a staff of followers that drew from the lessons learned in the 1930s. In time, they spread their organizing mission to the black ghetto of Rochester, New York, and the Mexican-American barrios of California. Alinsky became a confederate of both Martin Luther King and California farm-worker organizer Cesar Chavez. He took it as a matter of pride that he was arrested frequently and touted that he was under FBI surveillance.

In 1947 Alinsky wrote *Reveille for Radicals,* a best-seller in which he argued against the labor model of trying to reform capitalism, arguing instead for a more direct takeover of power. The sequel, *Rules for Radicals,* published in 1971, had a galvanizing effect on the young radicals wending their way through the elite universities of the East Coast. The generation of social protest had found its Socrates in this portly, balding man with the wizened face.

One of Alinsky's adherents was Dick Morris, future Clinton political consultant, who incorporated Alinsky's methods in running draft clinics and busing thousands of students to the peace marches in Washington. Another was Hillary Rodham, future first lady and "co-president" of the United States.

To understand Hillary and much of her subsequent life, it is important to learn the philosophy and tactics of the mentor who has had more apparent influence on her than any other.

For Alinsky, the goal of the political organizer is to help his followers accumulate power. He harbors the strong belief that the role of the organizer is to be a neutral agent, a kind of ideological agnostic seeking no particular outcome and advancing no philosophy other than the winning of power.

The trick, Alinsky suggests, is taking on whatever protective coloration one needs to win the trust of one's charges. To this degree, he offers nothing but stinging criticism for any organizer whose language or demeanor turns off would-be followers. He admonishes the children of the SDS (Students for a Democratic Society) generation to change their off-putting dress and language, to not be ashamed of their middle-class roots. "Our rebels have contemptuously rejected the values and ways of life of the middle class," he writes in *Rules for Radicals*. Alinsky teaches:

> They have stigmatized it as materialistic, decadent, bourgeois, degenerate, imperialistic, war-mongering, brutalized, and corrupt. They are right; but we must begin from where we are if we are to build power for change, and the power and the people are in the big middle-class majority. Therefore, it is useless self-indulgence for an activist to put his past behind him. Instead, he should realize the priceless value of his middle-class experience. His middle-class identity, his familiarity with the values and problems, are invaluable for organization of his own people.
>
> He will know that a square is no longer to be dismissed as such, instead, his own approach must be "square" enough to get the action started.[27]

He was aware that America gave the radical much more opportunity to accomplish his aims than in other countries.

> True, there is government harassment, but there still is that relative freedom to fight. I can attack my government, try to organize or change it. That's more than I can do in Moscow, Peking, or Havana.... Parts of the far left have gone so far in the political circle that they are now all but indistinguishable from the extreme right.[28]

Alinsky excelled at the outrageous. He once suggested buying one hundred tickets to the Rochester symphony, and giving them to the first one hundred blacks who responded to an offer of a free dinner of baked beans. The establishment, Alinsky wrote, would not in its wildest fears "expect an attack on their prize cultural jewel, their famed symphony orchestra. Regular stink bombs are illegal and cause for immediate arrest, but there would be absolutely nothing here that the Police Department or the ushers or any other servants of the establishment could do about it." Alinsky delighted in the idea that "the law would be completely paralyzed."[29]

The idea of a bean-generated gas attack, silly as it sounded, was the kind of weapon Alinsky was adept at crafting—acts designed to reduce an enemy to powerlessness through ridicule. "People would recount what had happened in the symphony hall and the reaction of the listener would be to crack up in laughter. It would make the Rochester Symphony and the establishment look utterly ridiculous.... Imagine the tension at the opening of any concert! Imagine the feeling of the conductor as he raised his baton!"[30]

Among Alinsky's key tactics are these:

- *Power is not only what you have but what the enemy thinks you have.*
- *Never go outside the experience of your people.* Alinsky would not have urged migrant laborers to adopt the techniques of, say, striking Parisian students.
- *Whenever possible go outside of the experience of the enemy.* Here he approvingly cites General Sherman's defiance of the traditional military doctrine of his time, disconnecting his army from supply lines and living off the land.
- *Make the enemy live up to their own rule book. "You can kill them with this, for they can no more live up to their own rules than the Christian church can live up to Christianity."* Alinsky excelled at forcing his opponents to violate their own standards, and then force them to capitulate out of shame.
- *Ridicule is man's most potent weapon.*

There was another rule that has been so thoroughly absorbed and implemented by Hillary, the Clinton operation, and their team of private investigators, dirt diggers, and apologists, that it now defines her and her husband.

Alinsky was an advocate of "mass jujitsu." In many of his forms of attack, he advocated letting the enemy move first, and then use his own momentum against him.

But Alinsky also had a rule for pure attack. "Pick the target, freeze it, personalize it, and polarize it."

Senator Brooke was the first victim of Hillary's skill at freezing, personalizing, and polarizing. There have been many others.

In the fall of 1968, Hillary informed her thesis advisor, political scientist Alan Schechter, that she would write a paper questioning how much control poor people should have over programs designed for their benefit. She interviewed Alinsky, and concluded that Johnson-era programs did not go far enough. The problems of poverty made it necessary for a fundamental shift in the structure of power.

Hillary would later look back warmly at her philosophical mentor in a 1993 *Washington Post* interview. Nowhere does she recognize the classical liberal critique that the relentless pursuit of power is antithetical to democracy.

LAW SCHOOL LIBERALISM

Hillary briefly entertained an offer of an internship with Saul Alinsky, but opted instead for law school. Put off by the sexism and snobbery of a Harvard law professor, she chose Yale.

Harvard offered a traditional legal education. Yale Law School was a better fit for Hillary, as much an endless social science seminar and finishing school for radicals at the time than anything else.

At Yale, Hillary's rolodex of lifetime political contacts grew fat. It was here that she established a friendship with future Labor Secretary Robert Reich; future U.S. Trade Representative Mickey Kantor; future Deputy Secretary of State Strobe Talbott; and future Justice Department nominee Lani Guinier.

And, of course, the ultimate connection, her future husband, the future president of the United States.

For all the protest at Wellesley, the level of activism was tame at the women's university in comparison to the strident protests at Yale in the 1970s. The university functioned then, as it functions today, in the style of a classic medieval academic city. A citadel of higher learning, Yale draws up its gates at night to protect itself from New Haven's rampant crime—the ever-present threat of robbery, rape, and murder.

Much of the city—black, poor, and threatened by muggers and drug dealers—is a natural and convenient venue for the ideas and experimentations of the social scientists who work on the safe side of the drawbridge.

The New Haven/Yale dichotomy has long been the defining feature of the community. In 1970 the parallel between a mostly white, academic castle in a neighborhood that is mostly black and poor charged the atmosphere with danger, excitement, and possibility. In this mix, students sought to make law school as relevant as possible to the larger social issues; indeed, to make it a tool of social change.

"With its accumulated resources," student Robert Borosage wrote in a 1970 issue of the *Yale Review of Law and Social Action*, "the law school could have attempted to define and protect the public interest in the legal process, or at minimum, those interests which were poorly represented."

At many law schools, student defiance went only so far before meeting steel. At Yale, it met only mush.

The school had long since accepted pass-fail grading, responded to disruptive and dangerous outbursts by students with mournful apologies, and reacted to threats by flinging open dormitory doors to visiting radicals.

It also, of course, offered access to some of the most distinguished names in legal scholarship. On the left was Burke Marshall, perhaps the leading civil rights advocate of the time. To the right—and there was almost no one to the right—was future Supreme Court nominee Judge Robert Bork, Sr., clearly an anomaly.

Much later in an address to law students, former Yale law professor Judge Bork said, "America is being governed by Yale law graduates with 1960s attitudes.... Law schools... have become politicized.... The legal system has started to judge by ideology, not law." The judge spoke of his former students Bill and Hillary Clinton: "I used to say they were both my students. Now I say they were just in the room."

Such "straight" professors as Judge Bork were tolerated as a necessary evil, a sop to ideological balance that was otherwise ignored.

"The professors' assumptions, undefined and unrevealed, were to be accepted by each of the students," wrote student radical Robert Borosage. "This led to rather amusing results, property taught as if the market system still worked, and antitrust as if the notion of state capitalism had never occurred to anyone.

"[L]ike intellectuals in Stalin's Russia, students played one role in public and another in private," Borosage wrote. "They went through the motions of acquiring a legal education, but contributed little of themselves in the process."[31]

More typical of the Yale style of legal education was Charles Reich, whose book, *The Greening of America*, became a 1960s leftist bible (later lampooned by columnist George F. Will as the worst book ever written). Still to the left, but well within the legal establishment, were the staid champions of legal realism, theorists who advocated the expedient use of law as a means for advancing social progress. Legal realism had already come to dominate the activist jurisprudence of the Warren Court. Its most forceful and perhaps most eloquent adherent was Justice William O. Douglas.

Here at the apex of *avant guarde* American legal philosophy in the seventies, the relativism of the liberal elders had created consequences they could neither contain nor control.

THE CRITS

Duncan Kennedy was Yale Law's leading radical legal theoretician, founder of Critical Legal Studies, or Crits as we knew them. Crits applied to the law the same deconstructionist methodology that French philosophers, such as Jacques Derrida, had once applied to literature. Law, no less than literature, was best viewed as a "social construct" that expressed the needs of the prevailing power structure. It would need to be deconstructed to understand its roots in the power structure, and then reconstructed to build a new and better society. American law was necessarily an expression of bourgeois values and an instrument of oppression wielded by a corrupt authority.

Crits were explicitly Marxist in their dialectical methods, and interested in revolutionary change, not in reform. Judge Bork says the Crit movement's "mindless form of leftist politics" and "crude anti-intellectualism would not have been tol-

erated on any decent law school faculty" prior to the radical
sixties generation. "That it thrives now," he says, "speaks volumes about the political and intellectual atmosphere in many
of today's most prestigious law schools."[32]

For many classical liberals—and conservatives like Yale
graduate and Supreme Court Justice Clarence Thomas—law
is rooted not in "the power structure," but in the words of our
Constitution. But for the followers of Critical Legal Studies,
the law is an empty vessel, a semantic weapon backed by the
threat of state coercion that can be used on behalf of the powerful or the powerless. As Judge Alex Kozensky explains, the
Crits believe the law is rooted as much in the text as in "what
they had for breakfast" on any particular day.

Duncan Kennedy—whose ultimate goal was to radicalize
as many students as possible—became a tenured professor at
Harvard, where his philosophy took root and ultimately influenced much of the Clinton judiciary.

HILLARY AND THE BLACK PANTHERS

With her sandals, stringy hair, Coke-bottle glasses, and a black
arm band worn in remembrance of the dead at Kent State,
Hillary was gaining prominence in the Yale protest movement.
She was seen leading demonstrations on the great and small
issues of the day, many of them targets of opportunity, from
the Vietnam War to the lack of tampons in the women's rest
rooms. One of Hillary's professors at Yale was Thomas
Emerson, known as "Tommy the Commie." It was through
Professor Emerson that Hillary had been introduced to
defense attorney Charles Garry, who guided her involvement
in the support and defense of the Black Panther Party.

Members of the Black Panther Party, including the infamous Bobby Seale were being tried in New Haven for murdering one of their own. The victim, Alex Rackley, had been suspected by the Panthers as a police informant. What was certain was that he had been brutally tortured, beaten, scalded, mutilated, and killed. The evidence against the Black Panthers was overwhelming—including an audio tape of part of the "trial" to which Rackley was subjected. Two Panthers confessed to shooting Rackley as part of a plea bargain. But Bobby Seale fought extradition from California and became another target of opportunity, much more appealing than issues on feminine hygiene, and a rallying point for student radicals who idolized the Panthers as the leaders of a necessary black insurrection against the repressive white establishment.

That the Black Panthers could actually be guilty was an idea that had never occurred, or mattered, to their defenders, who were not at all fazed by a Black Panther Party that justified the rape of white women by black men as a political act of protest against white oppression, or that glorified the killing of police officers—or, in their words, "pigs."

Yale was a natural forum, perhaps battleground, for the privileged white students who wanted to show their solidarity with the Black Panthers and the forces of revolution against the presumed racism of American law.

A protest, centered around a May Day strike, was set to occur on the Yale campus. Possibly intimidated by the still-fresh images of Kent State, and consistent with Yale's supine reaction to virtually every radical student initiative of the era, Yale President Kingman Brewster issued a statement sympathizing with the students and the plight of the Black Panthers. Then he opened the college dorms to demonstrators, whether they were students or not, and allowed Black Panther lawyer Charles Garry to make his residence on campus.[33]

Hillary formed a close association with Garry, and manifested no misgivings by the violent rhetoric of his clients, who called for police assassinations and said, "If Bobby dies, Yale fries."[34] As part of her coursework with Professor Emerson, Hillary attended the Black Panther trials and put her considerable leadership and organizational skills to work in organizing shifts of fellow students to monitor the trial and report alleged civil rights abuses.

LEFT COAST RENDEZVOUS

Robert Borosage, the student writer, was another radical leader who had become a colleague and close acquaintance of Hillary's. Borosage later went on to lead a left-wing think tank called the Institute for Policy Studies, which supported Cuban expansion into Grenada and Angola, and Daniel Ortega and his Soviet-backed Sandinistas in Nicaragua.

Hillary's friendship with radicals like Garry and Borosage led Hillary to all the fashionable "chic," as writer Tom Wolfe put it, reaches of the left including Robert Treuhaft and Jessica Mitford.

Treuhaft was a former lawyer for the Communist Party. His wife, the late Jessica Mitford, was famous in muckraking circles for savaging the American funeral home industry in *The American Way of Death*. They were both committed Communists. Stalinists, in fact.

David Brock, in *The Seduction of Hillary Rodham*, quotes historian Stephen Schwartz as saying that this was not a pair of cuddly modern-day Fabians:

> This was a group of hard Communists who had been running the
> Communist Party of Northern California.... It was a political

organization whose loyalty to the Soviet Union was explicit, whose discipline was Stalinist, and whose intellectual attitudes were mainly Stalinist....

Treuhaft is not like the Black Panthers. Treuhaft is a man who dedicated his entire legal career to advancing the agenda of the Soviet Communist Party and the KGB.[35]

Treuhaft had formally left the Communist party in 1958, but only because it had lost so many members that it was no longer a viable organization. Mitford, an unreconstructed acolyte of Joseph Stalin, would later condemn the Hungarian Freedom Fighters who threw Molotov cocktails at Soviet tanks as "grasping neo-Fascist types."[36]

In 1972 Treuhaft offered Hillary a summer internship working on behalf of indigent criminal defendants in Berkeley. Hillary accepted and worked for Treuhaft for a summer. She later paved the way for Mitford to lobby Governor Bill Clinton on the death penalty.[37]

Hillary has never repudiated her connection with the Communist movement in America or explained her relationship with two of its leading adherents. Of course, no one has pursued these questions with Hillary. She has shown that she will not answer hard questions about her past, and she has learned that she does not need to—remarkable in an age when political figures are allowed such little privacy.

THE RADICAL WRITE

At Wellesley, Hillary began to follow radical publications. At Yale, she served the movement as an editor. She also became a writer herself, defining and extending the terms of a Crit idea, the burgeoning field of "children's rights."

At first, radical politics had started as an outgrowth of her Methodism. Now it became increasingly driven by a realization that her goals could be achieved only by the application of power.

"My sense of Hillary is that she realizes absolutely the truth of the human condition, which is that you cannot depend on the basic nature of man to be good and you cannot depend entirely on moral suasion to make it good," the Reverend Jones told reporter Michael Kelly in his courageous 1993 "Saint Hillary" piece in the *New York Times Magazine*. "You have to use power. And there is nothing wrong with wielding power in the pursuit of policies that will add to the human good. I think Hillary knows this. She is very much the sort of Christian who understands that the use of power to achieve social good is legitimate."[38]

For Hillary, the convergence of power and Christian ends had come together in *Motive*, a magazine for college-age Methodists.

"I still have every issue they sent me," Mrs. Clinton would later say as first lady.[39] She told a writer for *Newsweek* that she still treasured a 1966 *Motive* article by theologian and SDS leader Carl Oglesby called "Change or Containment."

Oglesby is variously described as a Marxist or Maoist theoretician, in the piece so admired by Hillary, Oglesby defended Ho Chi Minh and Castro, and Maoist tactics of violence. "I do not find it hard to understand that certain cultural settings create violence as surely as the master's whip creates outcries of pain and rage. I can no more condemn the Andean tribesmen who assassinate tax collectors than I can condemn the rioters in Watts or Harlem or the Deacons for Defense and Justice. Their violence is reactive and provoked, and it remains culturally beyond guilt at the very same moment that its victims' cultural innocence is most appallingly present in our imaginations."[40]

"It was the first thing I had ever read that challenged the Vietnam War," Hillary said, adding that *Motive* had given her the impetus to move from being a Goldwater Republican to a McGovern Democrat.

At Yale, she found the chance to participate in radical scholarship more directly. A good, though not brilliant, law student, she could have played the angles and tried to make the *Yale Law School Journal*, the obvious route to prestige and a solid job offer to a partner-track position with a big law firm. Perhaps she doubted her ability to make the *Journal* on merit. Or perhaps for other reasons, she chose instead to serve as one of the editors of the *Yale Review of Law and Social Action*, where she worked side-by-side with future Clinton insiders Mickey Kantor and Robert Reich.

Founded during Hillary's first year at Yale Law School by a group of third-year students, the *Review* was more than just a radical version of the traditional law journal. It was to be a purveyor of radical scholarship and ideas. Hillary served as one of the *Review*'s initial nine editors, critiquing articles and offering her advice.

The maiden issue of the *Review* in 1970 declared, "For too long, legal issues have been defined and discussed in terms of academic doctrine rather than strategies for social change."

There were articles by or about William Kunstler, Charles Garry, and Charles Reich of *Greening* fame. Although not a legal scholar, radical gadfly Jerry Rubin appeared in the *Review* to exhort parents "to get high with our seven-year-olds" and students to "kill our parents."

"Only gradually," two *Review* editors note on a profile of Rubin's appearance at Penn State, "does the dialectic of the new myth appear. Youth's language is its strength. For a moment, Rubin plays McLuhan. The youth culture, particularly their language, is continually being commercialized by the Establishment. 'We have revolutions in toilet paper, sex through Ultrabrite, trips to the Bahamas, Dodge rebellions. But the key word is fuck; they (Rubin smiles) can't co-opt fuck.'" By the 1990s, it became apparent that Rubin was as wrong about that as he was about everything else.

Rubin was told by a student in the audience that his father was a judge. "To this, Mr. Rubin queried, 'Why don't you kill him?' Of course, we all thought he was joking but then, he explained how it really would be dramatic and dwelled on the subject of assassination to the point where none of us in the room doubted his seriousness."

A more typical *Review* article discussed rent strikes, under the heading "The Law as a Tactic," the Crit concept of law as a means "both to protect the strikers and educate them."

The combined second and third law issues of the *Review* in the fall/winter of 1970, on which Hillary served as associate editor, centered on Bobby Seale and the Black Panther trials. It included many cartoons depicting the police as hominid pigs, their snouts wet while they mutter, "niggers, niggers, niggers, niggers." Another cartoon, under the caption "What Is a Pig?" shows a wounded pig-man, bruised, bandaged, and on crutches from a severe beating. The answer to the question in the cartoon is "A low natured beast that has no regard for law, justice, or the rights of people; a creature that bites the hand that feeds it; a foul depraved traducer, usually found masquerading as the victim of an unprovoked attack."

Another cartoon, under the caption "Seize the Time!" shows a pig-man surrounded by flies, decapitated and cut in half.

Other articles were less gruesome in presentation, if not intent. James F. Blumstein, fourth-year law student, and James Phelan, second-year law student, for instance, wrote "Jamestown 70," a radical manifesto that proposed "migration to a single state for the purpose of gaining political control and then establishing a living laboratory for experimentation." They write:

> Revolution is impossible when armed revolt by the citizenry-at-large would inevitably be put down by the military might at the disposal of those in control. We see the best way out in reeducating this nation to its heritage; reopening the frontier, where alienated or deviant members of society can go to live by their new ideas; providing a living laboratory for social experimentation through Radical Federalism; and restoring effective political communication in a multimedia society.
>
> What we advocate is the migration of large numbers of people to a single state for the express purpose of effecting the peaceful political takeover of that state through the elective process. The goal of this takeover would be to establish a truly experimental society in which new solutions to today's problems could be tried, an experimental state which would serve as a new frontier and encourage imaginative local innovation.

The goal was to forge a society based on "a New Consciousness."

"Experimentation with drugs, sex, individual lifestyles or radical rhetoric and action within the larger society is an insufficient alternative. Total experimentation is necessary."

The marches on Washington, Woodstock—they had all

been lost, were nothing but drops in the great, oblivious sea of apple pie consumerism. It was time for those with a heightened consciousness to migrate to a safer place, much as African Americans migrated from the sharecropper farms of the South to create their own new realities in Chicago and New York.

"An American-style Kampuchea," is the memorable description Daniel Wattenberg used to describe "Jamestown 70" for the *American Spectator* magazine.[41]

For all its utopianism and fantasy-like qualities, radical federalism was a kind of a Frederick Jackson Turner thesis for the psychedelic frontier. It may even have led to the settlement of so many hippies in Vermont and Northern Idaho—or San Francisco.

Hillary complained that early drafts of "Jamestown 70" were "mental masturbation." She worked with its authors to make it more specific, more "down to earth."

Wattenberg reported that "Hillary provided a detailed sympathetic critique of the article, according to a source at the journal. Her main problem with the piece was that it was long on rhetoric, short on action."[42] For Hillary, the mental exercise of imagining a "New Consciousness" was fatuous unless there were forceful steps that could be taken to enact it.

While some 1960s radicals on the wilder fringes might have been merely self-indulgent fantasists, or spoiled college kids seeking to avoid the responsibilities of their parents, Hillary was a budding Leninist. Menshevik, Bolshevik, Trotskyite—they were all debating societies. What really mattered to Lenin—and what Saul Alinsky taught Hillary to value—was *power*.

DEFENDER OF VIOLENCE

At the end of the Johnson administration, Eugene Rostow, one of the main policy architects of the Vietnam War, returned from the State Department to the Yale Law School faculty.

After Rostow's office was ransacked by antiwar vandals, "a number of us identified with the antiwar movement, including Hillary, were considering going to Rostow and saying even though we disagree with you on the war, this is unforgivable. Hillary took a different approach, one of our few disagreements," a Hillary colleague told David Brock. "She said, 'You know, I wouldn't put down those people so easily. You've got to understand the rage they feel. You know, because they are disenfranchised; they are not empowered.' She was sort of taking the position that well, our real enemies are society and the establishment."[43]

Throughout her life, Hillary has been marked by a desire to dedicate her life to achieve a transcendent ideal. That ideal has changed over the years. It was represented first by Barry Goldwater, then by liberal Republicans like John Lindsay. Then it became George McGovern, the Black Panthers, the Crits, and even Stalinists like Jessica Mitford and Robert Treuhaft.

Like others of her time, she had begun her journey on Eisenhower's interstate highway system only to find herself deep in the Ho Chi Minh trail; from the comforts of prosperous 1950s American suburbia to a Marxist critique of everything that had shaped her, Hillary had liberated herself from Hugh Rodham and his grim empire. While her family had struggled to get ahead, their money, the expensive education they provided Hillary, allowed her to be a free agent, exploring, assessing, finding her own path in a way her parents could not have dreamed for themselves. Now Hillary believed she had the answers she sought. Now was the time for action.

She found a partner, a fellow power seeker who would take her to the unlikely destination of Arkansas.

FOUR
OF ONE MIND

"What was my alternative? To draw myself up into righteous moral indignation, saying, I would rather lose than corrupt my principles, and then go home with my ethical hymen intact?"

— SAUL ALINSKY, *RULES FOR RADICALS*

When told that he had become president, Harry Truman said that he felt as if all the stars and moon had fallen on him. Ronald Reagan, in his memoirs, recalled walking into the White House with Nancy, seeing the furniture from their home moved into the grand rooms of the mansion, and suddenly being overwhelmed by the realization that the presidency was truly his to command.

In their respective memoirs, the Clintons will one day each tell of similar emotions on their first day as president and first lady. Untold, likely, will be the real tone and tenor of that day, or the reason for their very public fight that day as reported by *Time* magazine. Standing on the steps of Blair House on Inauguration Day, 1993, Bill Clinton yelled at his wife through the cold morning air. "Fucking bitch!" he screamed, causing Secret Service agents and well-wishers to cower. "Stupid motherfucker," was the reply from our first lady.[1]

This was a rare lapse in a carefully contrived image. For the most part, the public sees the marriage the Clintons wish us to see. There is the loving couple on the beach, studiously unaware of nearby photographers, gently dancing in each other's arms to a lovers' waltz only they can hear. There was the tender moment during the State of the Union address when the president looked up from the podium, made direct eye contact with his wife, and mouthed the words, "I love you" for the entire viewing audience to see. One could only marvel at the chutzpah that it took for Bill Clinton to try such a stunt in the midst of the Monica Lewinsky scandal. It was a moment that seemed like a scene out of a 1950s grade "B" movie.

Given all that is known about the Clintons today, it is likely this moment *was*, in fact, scripted by someone with a Hollywood or television soap opera touch. Their good friends, television sit-com producers Harry and Linda Bloodworth-Thomason, were indeed called back to the White House during the impeachment crisis to manufacture the best possible pro-Clinton gloss to the spectacle. It has taken every trick in the book—from Hollywood advice to trashing former presidents from Washington and Jefferson to Eisenhower and Reagan—to keep the myth of the Clinton's marriage alive. Hillary even went so far as to blame her family's troubles on "a vast right-wing conspiracy" to laying it off on child abuse from an argumentative grandmother.

The president she now claims is a victim of a weakness for which he is not responsible. The victim of personal tragedy: "There was terrible conflict between his mother and grandmother," Hillary told an interviewer in the premier issue of *Talk* magazine in August 1999. "A psychologist once told me that for a boy, being in the middle of a conflict between two women is the worst possible situation. There is always the desire to please each one."

So the president, according to the most recent Clinton theory, cannot help himself. Torn between a doting mother and a devoted grandmother, he must now try to please every woman he encounters. This, we are expected to believe, justifies exposing himself to Paula Jones, groping Kathleen Willey, and forcibly raping Juanita Broaddrick. These and scores of similar incidents Hillary expects us to believe are merely sins of weakness, if they are sins at all, to be laid at the feet of his deceased mother and grandmother. The sins of malice by comparison are those of Kenneth Starr's, Henry Hyde's and every journalist who has ever tried to tell the truth about the Clintons.

Hillary's comments were a dramatic affirmation that the true nature of the Clintons' relationship is that they are of one *mind*, if not one flesh. They are united by an insatiable drive for power and prominence, by a calculating belief that their grip on power is more important than any abuse of it, and justifies the comprehensive employment of Saul Alinsky's principles to manipulate the public mind to maintain that position of power.

Decades before her "vast, right-wing conspiracy" *Today* show defense of her husband during the "Year of Monica,"

Hillary was well aware that her husband was incorrigibly promiscuous. For reasons which are now much more apparent, Hillary chose to pretend that she believed his denials. As she has from the very beginning of their relationship, Hillary has again and again acted to protect Bill Clinton from the consequences of his actions.

Before they were even married, during his first political campaign, Hillary went through Bill Clinton's desk on a search-and-destroy mission to tear up phone numbers she knew he collected during the day's campaigning. Most self-respecting women would have left. Hillary chose to stay. She behaves as both a desperate lover, and like a frantic campaign manager protecting a flawed candidate. Over time, protecting Bill has been more about the perpetual campaign and less about the marriage. Hillary, it seems, long ago accepted Bill Clinton as someone who could advance her goals, as a necessary complement to her more intellectual cold-blooded pursuit of power.

After all, it is Bill, not Hillary, who can seem to search one's soul with his blue eyes. It is Bill Clinton who can give "the meaningfuls" as no other. It is Bill more than Hillary, who can engage people around a coffee counter or across the nation on television. She accepts him as he is, because he is willing to return the favor. He is the willing vehicle for her ideas and her quest for power. And he could be the launch pad for a presidential candidacy of her own.

Still, it is important to remember that their romance did not begin as a power play or a purely political partnership.

POWERS OF PERSUASION

Candidate Clinton told *Newsweek* of his first encounters with Hillary Rodham at Yale Law School: "And I saw her across the hall. And I'd been trying to work up the guts to talk to her. And she threw a book down at the end of the library—it's a long skinny room—and she walked the length of that room and she said, 'Look, if you're going to keep staring at me and I'm going to keep staring back, we should at least introduce ourselves. My name's Hillary Rodham. What's yours?' At that moment," he now claims, "I could not remember my name."[2]

They had been introduced before at the cafeteria by mutual friend Robert Reich, who had known Clinton at Oxford, and Rodham from a meeting of student leaders on academic reform at Dartmouth College.

Hillary had her eyes cast on Bill for some time. She had first heard his jocular boasting about the size of Arkansas watermelons. She took in the sight of the tall young man, his easy manner and aggressive charm, and liked what she saw.

For his part, Bill claims to have been impressed by such a direct, forward young woman, so different from the demure and passive girls he had pursued in Arkansas. Once Bill said he lingered around the line for class registration to talk to her, only to have his cover blown by a registrar.

"Bill, what are you doing here? You already registered."[3] He may have been a little embarrassed. Hillary had to have been more than a little flattered. They had already talked to each other for an hour. Bill patiently went through registration with her, and then took her to the campus art museum, where he gave her his first display of his powers of persuasion by talking a custodian into opening the closed museum so he could give his newfound girlfriend a private tour.

What did he see in Hillary?

He saw an accomplished and determined woman, a campus leader, a dedicated activist. She arrived at Yale already famous for her appearances on *College Bowl*, the television quiz show, and for her speech denouncing Senator Brooke.

"The story of what she had done at Wellesley preceded her. We were awed by her courage," a law school friend told David Maraniss.[4] Hillary was "deliberately unattractive," a male classmate later told *Vanity Fair*. "I believe it came down to her self-consciousness about her own looks."[5]

Michael Medved, the future conservative movie critic and a Yale Law classmate, remembered Hillary as definitely not "date bait." And perhaps, in a way, that was her attraction to the Arkansas playboy.

Bill, ever the connoisseur of women, was worldly and political enough to see beyond the southern-born underpinnings of his Arkansas upbringing. He recognized that Hillary's long unkempt hair, her sandals and frayed jeans, and her owlish frames represented her sense of how she fit into Yale and her statement of how she wanted to be perceived there. As a girl, her mother Dorothy recalled, Hillary had thought "makeup was superficial and silly. She didn't have time for it."[6] She wasn't going to compete on her looks or her charm. Her appearance was her statement, a declaration of her need to appear serious.

It was also obvious that Hillary was not a low maintenance woman. But Bill wasn't frightened off. He enjoyed the intellectual sparring and even the arguing. He seemed to relish having a woman who was assertive and willing to challenge him. He seemed to see a challenge to his usual taste in women, and perhaps a challenge to him to overcome Hillary's somewhat icy and formidable facade.

What did Hillary see in Bill?

In most circles, a Rhodes scholar is a standout. But at a

prestigious law school like Yale, such prior distinctions are canceled by a mutual sense of belonging to a select group. In fact, many of Bill's classmates mistook him for a country bumpkin, seeing in him a young man whose nostalgia for his home state was cloying. A boy who spent far too much time waxing poetic about Arkansas. Tales of its pie fairs, watermelon festivals, and quaint country outings like the Toad Suck Daze Fair, the festival in Conway where the governor always entered a frog in the race. And some of Bill's colleagues resented the presumptuousness of his open ambitions for elected office.

It was assumed that once out of Yale, they would all become something—some would be elected to the Senate or governorships, some would become federal judges, some would become partners in powerhouse law firms. It just wasn't seen as proper form to talk about it. To Hillary, Bill must have seemed refreshingly honest and guileless about his dreams and desires. Bill Clinton admitted openly to everything he wanted. "Bill's desire to be in public life was much more specific than my desire to do good," she once said.[7]

A friend recalled, "The fact that Bill knew he was going to run for political office was very attractive to Hillary."[8] Bill had a background that must have seemed quaintly exotic to a young woman from a midwestern suburb. Her life in Park Ridge had been quintessential suburban America, the place where the generation that had survived the Great Depression and the Second World War sought to realize the fruits of victory and prosperity in a stable and orderly environment.

The true home of William Jefferson Clinton was as different as any place could be in America. And, contrary to the carefully nurtured image, for most of his young life, that place was the brazenly tacky Hot Springs, not Hope. Long after World War II, Hot Springs still existed as an anachronism from the Prohibition era, an inland French Quarter where every bar had the seedy glamour of the speakeasy, where gambling machines and card games operated in full view of the law, and where city fathers did not dare denounce the local houses of prostitution, lest they offend the madams who paid them handsomely, and who often knew way too much to risk offending.

It was almost as if Bill Clinton had been raised on a riverboat by a riverboat gambler. The mother he idealized as a sardonic observer of the human condition was seen by many as a barfly with a heart of gold. Local hearsay held that Bill was the bastard son of a car salesman, not Virginia's husband, Bill Blythe of Texas, a traveling salesman who was killed in a car wreck. This story is probably not true. Despite the timing of Bill's caesarian birth less than eight months after Blythe returned from active duty in Italy, young Billy Blythe seemed very much his father's son. Bill's strong jawline, which he likes to project in a bold profile for photographers, is an obvious inheritance from his mother. Otherwise, Bill Blythe could be Bill Clinton's brother. He had the same friendly lines about the eyes, a similarly open and handsome face punctuated by that same rakish, slightly bulbous nose. Like his son, Blythe was an inveterate salesman, a man with an easy gift for conversation who made his living ingratiating himself with others.

There are other similarities as well. The number of times Blythe was married, or whether he was legally a bigamist at the time of his marriage to Virginia, is unclear. What no one disputes is that he was a full-time lady's man, a familiar figure from a time in America when a salesman's car would be parked one night at a widow's home, the next night at the home of a lonely waitress he had met at a diner.

In his early years, Bill was raised by his maternal grandmother while Virginia attended nursing school. Later, he and his half-brother were raised by Roger Clinton, a Good Time Charlie who weaved in and out of their lives. Roger steadily grew more abusive, both verbally and with his fists, one time stomping Virginia on the floor and hitting her over the head with a shoe.[9]

During the presidential campaign, Clinton did not have a PT-109 story to tell like his idol John F. Kennedy. In its place he related the defining moment of his young manhood: The day he marched into the middle of a fight and ordered his stepfather never to touch his mother again. The fighting did not end, although the marriage did. A short time later, Virginia relented and took back her husband, though his presence in the house this time was on borrowed grace.

Given such a place and such a past, another child might have been molded into a Puritan. William Jefferson Clinton absorbed all that was around him and became a true product of Hot Springs—but with prodigious talents to go with his wide-open early influences. He was raised to appreciate that one could live comfortably with contradictions, that part of the art of living was to rise above, duck around, and skate through the ambiguities and embarassing interuptions of life.

Virginia had told her boys that they had to brainwash themselves, to put unpleasant memories out of their mind. "Construct an airtight box," Virginia told them. "I keep inside it what I want to think about. Inside is white, outside is black.... This box is strong as steel."[10] This was the same box

President Clinton told the American people that he placed all
the scandal allegations.

Bill Clinton's easy way with people was augmented by a
cavalier, often reckless, attitude towards the truth, an
approach that seems to have freed him from the restraints of
a conscience or even an awareness of his own duplicitousness.

Yet, for all his sunny disposition, Clinton possessed a firey
temper similar to Hillary's and a saturnine moodiness in private. "Mood swings come upon Clinton frequently," Dick
Morris writes in his memoirs, *Behind the Oval Office*. "Far
from the affable, kinetic figure he shows in public, he is most
often morose in private...."[11]

Morris had an intense twenty-year relationship with the
Clintons. Though Morris is now estranged, his writings, filled
with striking metaphors, carry a tone of authenticity burnished perhaps by his own embarassing sex scandals and con-
comitant public humiliation.

Morris writes of Hillary and Bill: "Warm-blooded animals
carry within them the ability to adjust their body tempera-
tures, but cold-blooded creatures need outside warmth from
the sun to keep them warm inside."

Hillary is warm-blooded. She is driven, but she does not
need outside sources of warmth to be comfortable in her own
skin. Left to herself, she contentedly reads biographies, takes
walks, or, according to *Washington Post* journalists, communes
with Eleanor Roosevelt. Bill, on the other hand, needs living
people to warm him up and craves constant reassurance and
approval, just to feel alive.

Left to himself, Bill Clinton can be a sullen figure lost in long
bouts of self pity; a man who displays a volcanic temper toward
his staff and who can barely stand to be himself, by himself.

"Bill Clinton can be elusive. He'll just disappear on you. One minute you think he's right there on your wavelength, and the next minute you're turning your head to look for him. He gets distracted, disenchanted, bored, or annoyed and stops the meetings or phone calls.... "[12]

As a love interest, it is unlikely that Hillary had an inkling at first of Clinton's many dark sides. After all, at the beginning of their relationship she was another source of outside radiance and warmth—someone whom he needed to seduce, literally and figuratively.

A commitment to political change was still the defining feature of her life—love or no love. Had Clinton been an acolyte of Judge Bork or a Nixon Republican (a handful did exist on the Yale campus), there is very little likelihood that personal attraction could have trumped ideology. As it turned out, Bill Clinton's outlook was very close to her own, at least it appeared that way to her, and despite his political ambitions, he was willing to argue that the whole American system was corrupt and beholden to corruption, and endorse the far left philosopher Herbert Marcuse's view that America's version of freedom and democracy was a fraud.

If Hillary liked the fact that he would join her on the radical ramparts, she also admired his intellect. She was a good student, but it required hard work. Clinton, by many accounts, could waste much of his time reading philosophy and murder mysteries, do a quick study of someone else's notes, and ace the exam.

"Magically, before examinations, he borrowed some good notes, mine among them, disappeared for three weeks, and performed quite well," one colleague remembered.[13]

They were both deep in extracurricular activities, though both Bill and Hillary disdained interest in buffing their

resumes with the usual apprenticeships on the law review. The
law review would have required hard work—not a little of it
tedious and decidedly unglamorous, and not very political.
Hillary was immersed in her work with children. Bill spent his
spare time working for a local Senate political campaign.

Like Hillary, Bill also had a deep grounding in religion,
though in many ways it was a different religion. To say that he
was a southern Baptist and she a Methodist is to gloss over the
vast cultural rift between her church and the people and places
Bill knew. Bill attended the Park Place Baptist Church in Hot
Springs, where the Christianity he learned was closer to that of
the tent than that of Hillary's studies of seminarians such as Paul
Tillich. Later, when he returned home, Clinton would venture
to Pentecostal revival meetings at Redfield, Arkansas, where he
would join a quartet of pastors to sing "Amazing Grace," and
join in their passionate expressions of belief. At Oxford, Bill may
have walked the same cobblestone streets and quads as John
Wesley and his "methodical" Bible study group. But he was
more at home campaigning in Arkansas among singing, dancing, shouting Pentecostals, his own saxophone in hand.[14]

Of course, with Bill, the personal is always political. He
found Pentecostal pastors useful as his ambassadors to the
religious right. While Hillary went to Methodist services in
Little Rock, Bill joined the largest Baptist congregation in the
state, the only one on statewide television every Sunday
morning, where he volunteered as a member of the choir.
Though Bill had no time for choir practice, he rarely missed
the chance for the citizens of Arkansas to see him behind the
preacher, hymnal in hand (much like the Bible he studiously
displayed while walking into church during his presidency),
singing to the glory of God.

Race was another factor that made him attractive to Hillary. At Wellesley, Hillary had gone out of her way to befriend African Americans, making a point of taking a black friend with her to church. Bill had a more comfortable relationship with blacks, less of an ideological need to cross racial barriers and more of an interest in them as potential future constituents. When Bill walked over to a group of black students, isolated at one end of a table at the Yale cafeteria, he did so out of an apparent interest in communicating, winning them over, and making them like him—people to be enlisted as future supporters. "I was one of ten African Americans in a class of one hundred twenty-five students," William T. Coleman III, son of a prominent figure in the Ford administration, recalled. "From the first day of law school, the African-American students gravitated toward each other and almost immediately began to form close bonds. By the second week of class, there was a black table in the cafeteria. This self-segregation was readily acknowledged and accepted by the majority student body, with one notable exception. A tall, robust, friendly fellow with a southern accent and a cherubic face unceremoniously violated the unspoken taboo by plopping himself down at the black table. His presence at the table at first caused discomfort. Many of the black students stared at him with expressions that suggested the question, 'Man, don't you know whose table this is?' The tall fellow with the southern accent was oblivious to the stares and engaged us in easy conversation."[15]

THE WINNING FORMULA

Bill Clinton's next roommate was to lead to something more permanent. The Clinton-Rodham romance deepened, and they soon moved in together in a student apartment for $75 a month. At this stage in their relationship, friends remember,

their arguments were mostly friendly ones, dinnertime conversation over the issues of the day. The moment of truth
came in 1972, when Hillary was to have graduated. The
choice she made tells of the deepening of their relationship,
and her hopes for a union with Bill. For the first time in her
meteoric educational career, Hillary chose to slow down, to
remain at Yale taking an extra year to graduate until Bill
Clinton finished in 1973.

In the years to come, they worked together as co-depen-
dents, as campaigners, as co-governor and co-president. The
first project in which they put their minds together was as student lawyers arguing before a mock trial, the coveted Prize
Trial. To all appearances, the trial appeared real, with local citizens and students brought in to serve on the jury and play-act
the role of witnesses.

Bill and Hillary were brought in to argue for the prosecution in a case in which a policeman had been accused of murdering "longhairs." Bill and Hillary crammed for a month,
spending every spare moment prepping and challenging each
other to do their best.

One spring day, they began their argument before Abe
Fortas, former justice of the U.S. Supreme Court.

"Clinton was soft and engaging, eager to charm the judge
and jury and make the witnesses feel comfortable, pouting
when a ruling went the other way," recounts Clinton biographer David Maraniss. "Rodham was clear and all business."
One observer remembered "that Rodham was never concerned about stepping on toes whereas Clinton would mas-
sage your toes."[16]

Despite their best efforts, they lost the trial. But it was
here that they hit on a winning formula that would serve them

well in all the political trials to come. Bill does a great "good
cop," the one who speaks more from sadness than from anger,
who seeks to co-opt, not to condemn. Hillary, harder to attack
behind the shield of a woman's vulnerability, is the tough
prosecutor, the one to level a charge or counter an attack with
one of her own.

Their next partnership was in the McGovern campaign,
in the summer and fall of 1972. Bill worked as coordinator of
the McGovern campaign in Texas, a campaign based in a
dusty office on Sixth Street in Austin, but one that perhaps
should have been based in the Alamo.

Hillary was sent to San Antonio, where she led a
Democratic voter registration drive. Even in a losing campaign, there are new influential friends to be made, new addi-
tions to the rolodex. One of them was a woman who would
eventually become the master of the Clinton rolodex, future
Little Rock chief of staff Betsey Wright. Wright is known to
most Americans as the person who would later coin the term
"bimbo eruption" and was portrayed as the rough queen of
opposition research in *Primary Colors*.

There also were visits to each others' parents. On a trip to
Park Ridge, Illinois, Bill Clinton made his customary good
first impression. "I was cutting the grass," Tony Rodham says,
recalling one day when he was eighteen years old. "He
climbed out of the car, came right over and started helping me
cut the grass. We had a nice little chat, and, of course, I had
something else I wanted to do so Bill immediately volunteered
to help finish the job with the grass. I think Dad came out of
the house and put a stop to it."[17]

Hillary's family liked the engaging young man, but Hugh
had his doubts. "My father was more concerned that he was a

Democrat than [from Arkansas]," Hillary said. "Great arguments, great arguments."[18]

THE CHOICE

About that time Bill, like Hillary, was given an opportunity to work on the House Judiciary Committee impeachment investigation of Richard Nixon. Had he done so, he would have set the groundwork for what would have been the political irony of the century. Instead, Bill decided to accept a job teaching law at the University of Arkansas at Fayetteville as a stepping stone to elected office. It was Hillary who was recruited to serve as counsel on the House Judiciary Committee, working long hours on an investigation that would lead to a committee vote that would result in the resignation of President Nixon. Yet well before the fatal moment came, a full month before, she flew down to Fayetteville to interview for a professorship of her own. The interview went well, and she was accepted.

While still in Washington, Hillary spoke often of her Arkansas boyfriend, her mood often turning on whether he had called. There were signs that she worried about whether he was spending time with other women. Hillary often declared to her colleagues that her boyfriend in Arkansas was going to become president someday.

No sooner had Richard Nixon walked down the red carpet, and given his broad wave and victory sign before boarding the plane that would carry him into exile, than Hillary asked her roommate, Sara Ehrman, to drive her to Arkansas in a 1968 Buick. During the trip, Ehrman tried to talk her out of it. Two years shy of thirty, Hillary had had opportunities galore: Offers from law firms, top positions in

the Democratic Party, leadership positions in major associations—it was there for the taking.

If she stayed back East.

If she remained in Washington or moved to New York.

If she forgot about this guy from Arkansas.

"You have the world at your feet," Ehrman said. "Why are
you throwing your life away for this guy?" When the two
stopped in Charlottesville, Virginia at Monticello, Ehrman
reminded her they were still close to the Washington Beltway,
time enough to go back. Hillary would hear none of it.[19]

Enormous adjustments were necessary when she arrived in
Arkansas. "I grew up in the Land of Lincoln, and spent enormous amounts of time as a child studying Illinois and
American history, reading biographies of Lincoln, making field
trips to Springfield and other places that had some association
with Lincoln," Hillary reminisced.[20] "So he [Lincoln] had a
very big place in my historical imagination. I mean, it was just
an open-and-shut case that Abraham Lincoln was by far the
greatest President, because he had saved the Union and came
from Illinois. I remember clearly one time traveling with my
family on a trip to Florida, when I was nine, I think," Hillary
said. "We got to Vincennes, Indiana, which is very southern
Indiana, and checked into a little motel that had a little tiny
TV. For the first time I saw a TV series called *The Gray Ghost*,
which was about a Confederate soldier. And I was just astonished that anybody would have a television series in which the
hero was a Confederate solider. And then as we traveled farther
south, I remember being in Alabama and stopping at gas stations where they sold Confederate flags and things like that."

Bill Clinton was the first person she had ever met from
Arkansas. One time he picked her up at the airport and pro-

ceeded to make a hard sell for living in the South. What should have been a one-hour drive to Hot Springs took eight hours as he gave her a tour of state parks, scenic overlooks, favorite barbecue spots, and his favorite fried-pie place.

"My head was reeling because I didn't know what I was going to see or what I was expecting," Hillary later said.[21] "I had a lot of apprehension, partly because I didn't know anybody and did not know how I'd be received.

"The people were warm and welcoming to me. I felt very much at home," she told *Newsweek*. "And it was a shock to me because I had never lived in the South or in a small place before. It gave me a perspective on life and helped me understand what it was like for most people.... I think I've had a more interesting time of it than I would have if I had chickened out and not followed my heart."[22]

Yet, her awareness of being a Yankee outsider grew as she looked around her prospective future home, a hybrid state between the Ozarks and the muddy flats of the Mississippi River.

The time had also come for Hillary to be judged by Bill's family. One can imagine Virginia's inner reactions when she saw Hillary. "Virginia loathed Hillary then," Clinton friend Mary Fray recalled. "Anything she could find to pick on about Hillary she would. Hillary did not fit her mold for Bill."[23] Even Bill knew that Hillary's "look" could be a public problem, and assigned a friend the task of finding ways to mute the hippie Hillary with a few traditional southern touchups.

But Clinton's mother could never warm to this harsh, Yankee outsider. Perhaps Virginia was the kind of mother who would always be jealous of any woman who attached herself to her beloved older son. More likely, she may have imagined Bill marrying the kind of woman who would make a great playmate, someone who would be fun to be with, someone who could cut up and carouse, someone, perhaps, like Bill's longtime occasional girlfriend Dolly Kyle Browning, an attractive blonde, who would later urge Clinton to seek treatment for his "sex addiction." But if Virginia wanted a good-looking southern girl to show off as a daughter-in-law, Bill could not have disappointed her more.

To Hillary, Virginia must have appeared like a clown, with her penciled-in Joan Crawford eyebrows, and her Tammy Faye Bakker thick powder and heavy coat of lipstick. There was a long testy period of sounding each other out.

According to friend Carolyn Staley, Bill sat his mother down, and told her in no uncertain terms that he would never "marry a beauty queen." It was to be Hillary or nobody.[24] And they would live in Fayetteville, the home of the University of Arkansas.

THE NARROW CENTER

"If Arkansas is an hourglass, then Fayetteville is the narrow center," former Razorback offensive tackle Webb Hubbell recalled in his memoirs:

> All these young people grow up all over the state in towns like Mountain Home and Bald Knob and De Valls Bluff and El Dorado (here pronounced El Do-ray-do), and then at a certain point the kids all leave those hamlets and go off to the University of Arkansas at Fayetteville.
>
> There, the continuity of the statewide bond is forged. For four years these people from all corners eat together, drink (a lot) together, sleep with one another, cheer for the Razorbacks together, and in so doing they form alliances, marital and other-

wise, that will affect the future of the state for years. Because, after college, having all passed through that unifying filter, they disperse once again back into the wider (but still not very wide) geography, taking with them an expanded field of acquaintances, loyalties, and bonds.

As a result, everything in our state—including its business and politics, which you can't separate from everyday life—is intensely personal. That's why it's like Main Street. Everybody's on a first name basis. And that means that political talk is personal talk, and business deals are personal deals, and personalities are more than issues. Furthermore, they don't want this system to change.[25]

Bill Clinton had made a shrewd job choice. As his students graduated, they fanned out across the state with stories about their gregarious, energetic young professor who had been a Rhodes scholar and who was sure to make a name in Arkansas politics.

One thing was clear once Hillary and Bill settled in Fayetteville, they could not continue to live together. Having a liberal firebrand of a girlfriend was a detriment enough. Living in sin with her in Arkansas during the 1970s would have been political suicide.

It was during this time, as a law professor, that Hillary made a lifelong friend in political scientist Diane Blair, whose husband, Jim, became the general counsel for Tyson Foods, the giant poultry producer. Later, as governor, Clinton presided over the wedding of Diane and Jim. Jim Blair was so much older and more distinguished looking, that when they traveled out of state he was mistaken for the governor, and Clinton as a junior member of his entourage.

"Jim and I became friends with Bill and Hillary before Bill held any office, before Jim was at Tysons, indeed, before they were the Clintons and we were the Blairs," Diane Blair recounts in *The Clintons of Arkansas*.[26] They had first met Bill at the 1972 Democratic National Convention. For a long time, Bill had sung Hillary's praises to Diane, promising her that they would be fast friends.

"I asked him why he didn't marry this wonderful woman and bring her back to Arkansas with him. He would love to, he said, but Hillary was so uncommonly gifted and had so many attractive options of her own that he felt selfish about bringing her to what would be his state and his political future."[27]

Diane was impressed with Clinton's sensitivity. It piqued her interest in Hillary all the more. She was not disappointed. In Hillary, the new law school professor, she found a soulmate.

"As two of the few female faculty members, we were acutely aware of the suspicion with which many old-timers still regarded women in academe," she recalled. Hillary was one of the few women practicing law in northwest Arkansas, and was inevitably tagged a "lady lawyer" by a local judge.[28]

They became regular lunchmates, tennis partners, and sounding boards about life in Fayetteville.

Hillary, always with an excess of energy, devoted much of her time to establishing a legal clinic to train local law students in the legal needs of indigent people. She also secured funds from the Legal Services Corporation to operate a legal aid bureau in Northwest Arkansas.

Hillary had done her part. The time had come for Bill Clinton to make his intentions clear. Once, while driving around Fayetteville, the young couple had noticed a small brick-and-stonework house for sale. Then Hillary left for a trip to Illinois and the East Coast to explore her options.

When she returned, Bill drove her to the little house, offering a key and a ring.

They were married two months later, in October 1975, in a modest ceremony. It would have been common for an Arkansas woman to have spent a great deal of time preparing for her wedding. Hillary bought her dress at the last minute, an off-the-rack item from Dillards department store.

They didn't plan a honeymoon. Later, Hillary's mother found a good package deal including Hillary's brothers. So the young couple honeymooned in Acapulco with Hugh, Dorothy, Hughie, and Tony in tow.[29]

THE SECRET POLICE

What explains the eventual evolution of the Clintons' marriage into a dynamic political partnership, the constant undercurrents of anger and recrimination, the shouting and the throwing of lamps and books? How did they become so angry at each other that they would destroy the memory of Inauguration Day for one another, the day their lifelong dreams were fulfilled, with a public display worthy of James Carville's acid term, "trailer trash"?

There is another side to their early relationship. Hillary was well acquainted with Arkansas long before she moved to Fayetteville. She had lived in Arkansas for part of 1974, when Bill Clinton had decided to run against incumbent Republican Congressman John Paul Hammerschmidt. The Clintons and their boosters rarely talk about that race, and for good reason. It was during this time that Hillary learned all too well what kind of husband Bill Clinton would make.

Two legacies were created during this period. First, in the Clinton marriage, the personal fused with the political. The risks that Bill Clinton took with his relationship with Hillary were inseparable from the risks he took with his own career.

The second legacy is the need for what Clinton consultant and friend Dick Morris called "the secret police." Hillary learned about private investigators in her work on behalf of the Black Panthers and the Communist apologists Robert Treuhaft and Jessica Mitford. Now Hillary was constantly checking up on Bill, not just to learn the extent of his betrayals, but to assess the danger he posed to their joint political career.

Hillary began her surveillance of Bill during this period in simple ways, eavesdropping and checking his desk. While Hillary knew Bill was cheating, she didn't know that Mary Lee Fray—the woman charged with making Hillary more attractive—was also the shepherd who kept the doors revolving so that Hillary never bumped into what she called "Bill's special friends." Clinton campaign coordinators Neal McDonald remembered that Bill "had a girlfriend in every county."

While Hillary assumed that her intellect would keep Bill at her side, Mary Lee Fray lamented that Hillary "had a weight problem and she wouldn't diet.... She didn't have a body for a dress. So I told her to at least buy some nice underclothes."[30]

If it came to a choice between changing her lingerie or snooping on Bill, Hillary preferred to search for scraps of paper with phone numbers on them and tear them up, mutilating the paper as though it were a Black Panther informant betraying Bobby Seale to "the pigs."

'HOW'D YOU GET AWAY WITH IT?'

Bill Clinton was only twenty-eight years old in the summer of 1974. He looked little like the man in the Oval Office with the

$500 California haircut. He was pasty, gangly in the limbs, and pudgy around the stomach and hips. In old photos, he looks every bit like the momma's boy that he was.

"I had never before met a candidate my own age with side-burns and hair as long as mine," said Dick Morris, who met Clinton three years later. "I'd also never before met a south-erner who talked fast."[31]

Still, there was something about Bill Clinton. Something far beyond an educational resume that made people take notice of him. He had the charisma and the presence that made plausible a run for office before he was thirty.

Taking on Representative John Paul Hammerschmidt was a bold move. Republicans were few in Arkansas. But Hammerschmidt was well-entrenched, a popular GOP con-gressman who relied on a strong base in Fort Smith, which, at the western-most boundary of the state, was as close as you could get, politically and geographically, to Oklahoma. Hammerschmidt, a veteran, carefully tended to the concerns of the large community of retired military personnel in the area.

Moreover, with the power of big money, television, and the franking privilege, it had become harder than ever to dis-lodge an incumbent. It is a mark of Clinton's political judg-ment that he foresaw that the usual rules of politics could be rewritten in 1974. Despite the statesmanlike handling of Watergate by many leading Republicans, the public was determined to vent its anger by turning a large number of them out of office. Clinton correctly predicted the political tsunami that would sweep in a whole generation of Democratic politicians, the so-called "Watergate babies."

He was determined to become one of them. And he knew

just how to do it. The trick, he explained to a committee of local labor leaders, was to use every available opportunity to tie Hammerschmidt to Nixon. Any vote, any position, any statement Hammerschmidt made could be turned into a weapon if it mirrored the Nixon position. The unions were so impressed by Bill's deft understanding of the challenge ahead that they switched their endorsement from a primary challenger to the young law professor.

The Clinton campaign opened for business in an old bungalow on College Avenue. Paul Fray, and his wife Mary, in whose wedding Bill had served as best man, ran the campaign.

In many ways, this race was classic Bill Clinton. It reflected his frenetic pace and his utterly disorganized style.

As a professor, Bill Clinton was notorious for losing blue books and exams (including one of a student who later presided over his sexual harassment trial and who found he had lied under oath to her face, Judge Susan Webber Wright).

Clinton drove the backroads of Northwest Arkansas in his green AMC Gremlin, often missing events or appointments because he'd feel the need to stop at a local roadhouse to praise the local pie and flatter a local precinct woman or mayor.

Bill was diligent about collecting business cards and names, stuffing them in his pockets. Once back at campaign headquarters, he'd pile them up on his desk and forget about them.[32]

Old photos from the campaign show a headquarters full of bright young people. They were hardly, however, a microcosm of the district Bill sought to represent. The men wore long hair, full sideburns, baggy shirts, and worn-out jeans. There were times when the scent of marijuana rolled out of

Clinton phone banks, and the campaign symbol might as well have been a hand-rolled cigarette.

If his staff was indiscreet, Bill Clinton himself was an encyclopedia of improprieties. One was a pesky little habit of encouraging women to feel like they had a shot at a permanent relationship with him—a charm he was still practicing a quarter-of-a-century later on a young White House intern named Lewinsky.

Hillary must have already been aware of her boyfriend's far-reaching sexual appetites. She had encouraged her father, rock-solid Republican that he was, to move to Arkansas and drive around in his Cadillac putting up "Clinton for Congress" signs. Hugh Rodham brought Hughie with him. (Eventually the whole family moved to Arkansas. Hughie and Tony attended the University of Arkansas. Hugh and Dorothy retired to Little Rock to be near their granddaughter, Chelsea.)

Apparently, Hugh agreed to help this young man, if that is what his daughter wanted. While Hillary worked night and day for the House Judiciary Committee in Washington, D.C., she was hoping that having her father and brother nearby might help to restrain Bill's Rabelaisian appetite for sex.

It was, however, a hopeless enterprise. Nothing has forced Bill Clinton to walk the straight and narrow. Not threats of divorce from his wife. Not the threat of destroying a promising political career. Not the need to appear on *60 Minutes* in the midst of a presidential campaign and not the risk of a humiliating scandal by having sex wih a young intern in the Oval Office. Certainly having his main girlfriend's dad and little brother on the campaign would not deter him.

Vigorous pursuit of the opposite sex is natural and even

healthy, especially in youth. At some point, however, youthful indiscretion and sexual promiscuity turns unhealthy, into obsession, and can become an unacceptable character flaw. In 1992 the campaign made much of the famous photo of Bill Clinton, then sixteen and part of a Boy's Nation delegation to the White House, in which he firmly shook the hand of President John F. Kennedy.

The president and teenager make eye contact in that photo. They seem locked on to one another. It was the perfect campaign photo for Bill Clinton. At century's end, after all that is known about these two men, it is also a moment of irony, one that is deep and poignant.

Bill Clinton had, like John F. Kennedy, become an aggressive, out-of-control womanizer, someone who aspired to be both married and enjoy his charm and sexual magnetism by indulging in quickies in a backseat, a basement, or a room off the Oval Office. Bill Clinton went beyond wildest rumors of JFK—to being credibly accused of going beyond quickies to sexual harassment and forcible rape.

"His identification with JFK was particularly evident to me," Dick Morris wrote, "in 1995 when Clinton returned from a President's Day interview with the media where he was asked, 'If you could ask your idol, John Kennedy, one question and only one question, what would it be?'

"'I'd want to ask him, you know, how did you do it?' Clinton jokingly confided. 'How'd you get away with it?'"[33]

Investigative reporter James B. Stewart unearthed a story from Bill's attendance at family counseling sessions for his half-brother Roger, then a cocaine addict. He told the therapist that he was born sixteen and he would always be sixteen. Bill said that Hillary was born forty, and that she'd always be forty.[34] One might think, at a minimum, that this was an awful thing to say about his wife. But it also underlined that his mother Virginia might have known her son better than he knew himself—and maybe he would have been calmer, happier, tamer if he had married a Gennifer Flowers or a self-confessed sex addict like Dolly Kyle Browning.

Bill Clinton had many girlfriends stashed around the district. Some of them were willing to be casual part-timers. At least one, a woman in Fayetteville, worked at campaign headquarters and thought of herself as Bill Clinton's girlfriend, possibly his future wife. Bill did nothing to dissuade her or any of the others.

And the only thing that kept him from being even more reckless was when Hillary called from Washington saying she was going to sleep with someone else—a fairly pathetic tactic, but one that had Bill in tears begging her not to ruin their relationship. And she didn't. Instead, she came to Arkansas to join the campaign.

Bill's "hippie girlfriend" brought a semblance of order to the campaign. Names of potential supporters and contributors were catalogued. Bill was forced to allow himself to be "advanced," to at least try to adhere to a disciplined schedule of appearances.

Hillary's steely commitment and her bossy and bickering attitude alienated many staffers, and angered Bill's old friends, Paul and Mary Fray.

For the campaign staffers, the stress of managing the Bill and Hillary relationship—which was already metamorphosizing into a political partnership and a more political issue—combined with the constant challenge of getting the candidate from point A to point B, began to tell.

Still, given the strength of the Democratic vote in the hamlets of the district, and the building wave of public anger over Watergate, Fray knew that Bill Clinton did, indeed, have a shot. But given the state of the Clinton campaign, they would need a boost to win, and that boost would come from money that would buy votes.

"There's no doubt that the system is corrupt," one Clinton supporter later told the press. "I don't think it's a function of Democratic politics or of any party politics. It's really a function of no-party politics."[35]

"Walking around" money was a southern tradition. It was taken for granted that the Democratic party had the right to work with labor unions and church groups to disburse large sums of cash to bribe people to vote. Bill himself had handled piles of such money for the McGovern campaign in Texas.

Now it was his turn.

Paul Fray matter-of-factly explained to the candidate that dairy interests in the state were willing to put up the cash to buy absentee ballots. All Bill had to do was say "yes."

Left to himself, there is little doubt what he would have done. But Hillary had not yet become the operator she was later to become. From an adjoining room, she found out about it and allegedly killed the deal.

Allegedly on election night, Fray made one last desperate effort to buy the election. Hillary refused, and Mary Fray joined her. Perhaps wiser than her husband, Mary Fray knew that if caught, Bill would hang Paul Fray out to dry. This triggered what aides called "the hen and the rooster fight."[36] The fight ignited again, when it was evident that the margin of Bill Clinton's imminent defeat was fewer than 10,000 votes—votes that Fray thought he could buy. Presaging the battles that would later rock the White House, writer David Brock describes a raucous scene: "Telephones and books sailed across the room, smashing windows. Fray blamed Hillary, Hillary blamed Fray, and Mary Lee blamed Bill.... Hillary got an earful about Bill from Mary Lee. 'I threw all the trash on Bill,' Mary Lee said. 'The deceit started with hiding the girl-friends. This is the first time Hillary found out about a lot of things.'"[37]

Many irretrievable things happened that night.

One was the utter destruction of the friendship between Bill Clinton and Paul and Mary Fray.

Also destroyed were Hillary's hopes that she could return to Washington as a congressman's wife and resume her career as a legal activist. If she wanted to marry Bill, she was doomed to life in Arkansas.

A third casualty that night was Hillary's Methodist con-science. She had learned that to win in Arkansas one had to have the stomach for bending, and breaking the law. And if she was to win with Bill, she would have to stand by a man she couldn't trust. While Hillary railed against Bill's unfaithful-ness, she did, in the end, accept it. In the years to come, Hillary defended him in election after election. When Bill Clinton finally ran for president, Hillary went to Washington, sat and told stories of her wonderful husband at the "Sperling Breakfast" for prominent Washington journalists. She sat next to her husband on *60 Minutes* and shamed reporters for asking about Gennifer Flowers, by admitting they had pain in their marriage. Hillary made it sound as if there was a period in their marriage when they grew apart, perhaps that Bill had temporarily strayed. Hillary characterized it as a momentary bad time between them, but certainly not a pattern. In fact, of

course, Hillary knew differently. She knew that for the whole
of her marriage she accepted, supported, and even encouraged
a compulsive philanderer in his—and her—quest for power.

There would in the course of this arrangement, be anger,
tears, recrimination. After several terms as governor, Bill's
humiliation of Hillary was so public and so flagrant that they
almost divorced. Like the Secret Service in the future, the
staff at the governor's mansion would cower at the words of
abuse—and occasionally dodge objects—that the Clintons
hurled at each other.

But in the end, nothing happened. The basic deal
remained intact. The other women remained, on the outside,
an enormous distraction and the source of great pain and
immense risk, but ultimately used and discarded. Only Hillary
was the first lady. Only Hillary had the ring. Only Hillary
could count on a husband whose political instincts and abili-
ties were so fine that his White House staff would one day call
him their "racehorse." Only by staying married could Hillary
have a husband who could win power and would be willing to
fully share power with her.

One constant of their relationship, from the early days in
Arkansas to their most recent summer vacation on Long
Island, is a devotion to reading history and biographies.
Scattered among murder mysteries, light fare about faith or
self-improvement, is almost always the latest biography on
Franklin, Eleanor, Jack, or Jacqueline.

They are steeped in history, often to a degree that is
counter-productive. Bill, according to Dick Morris, consciously patterns his marriage after FDR's marriage to
Eleanor Roosevelt, seeing in Hillary a wife who is his intellectual equal. "Sunday-morning Clinton felt no hypocrisy in

marrying Hillary Rodham," Morris writes. "Indeed, he probably saw marrying for brains as a notch above marrying for
glamour as Kennedy had done. It mimicked more closely the
behavior of his other role model, FDR, who betrothed to
Eleanor but tarried with Lucy Mercer."[38]

Hillary, for her part, willingly plays the role of Eleanor,
obsessing on her predecessor to the point of imaginary con-
sultations with Eleanor in the White House. In return, she is
given access to power and the ability to make decisions that
Eleanor could only have wished for.

The morning after losing to Hammerschmidt, Bill Clinton
cheerfully went about Fayetteville shaking hands, in effect
campaigning for his next election.

For Bill, the campaign had been a strenuous workout, a
chance to establish himself with voters and gear up for the
next race, a statewide race he'd have to win.

For Hillary, it was a lesson on life in Arkansas and life with
Bill Clinton. Years later, in the aftermath of Hillary's publicly
revealed "seance" with Eleanor Roosevelt's ghost, Hillary told
the *Washington Post*, "When the inevitable crap comes, which
it will, in anybody's life, and, not just once but several times,
there is a cushion of capacity there, and there is a structure
that gets you up in the morning."[39]

Part of that "structure" is her religious belief, her ideological zeal, and her persistent identification with a former
first lady and her travails. Another is the knowledge of what
she gets out of the basic terms of the deal she has made.

Hillary worked out this deal with Bill, just as Eleanor and
Franklin did after she learned of his numerous affairs as a
rising young dandy in Washington.

Over time, the union between the Clintons became, as it did for the Roosevelts, a marriage of the mind, a political convenience for two ambitious people who inhabit—or often don't inhabit—the same bedroom. Of course, the Clinton marriage takes the equation to lengths that ultimately makes the comparison utterly untenable. Bill Clinton seems unable to contain his vociferous appetites, and repeatedly sublimates his presidency, his nation, his political party, and his family to his personal wants and needs. Hillary knows that he has done so, and knows that he will continue to do so. But she stays, and she supports him because she knows that he is her ticket to the fulfillment of her own equally intense needs. They are partners. They both know that if they are to survive—and to prevail—they will do so linked inseparably together.

FIVE
VILLAGE SOCIALISM

"The human spirit glows from that small inner light of doubt whether we are right, while those who believe with complete certainty that they possess the right are dark inside and darken the world outside with cruelty, pain, and injustice. Those who enshrine the poor or Have-Nots are as guilty as other dogmatists and just as dangerous."

— SAUL ALINSKY, *RULES FOR RADICALS*

The president-elect, William Jefferson Clinton, and his wife arrived in the capital before the inauguration to attend a glamorous fund-raiser at the National Building Museum. But Hillary, not the president-elect, gave the keynote address. The evening and the cause were Hillary's. The fund-raiser was for the Children's Defense Fund (CDF).

In her quarter-century of attention to "children's issues," Hillary focused most on the subject of children's rights. She radiates enthusiasm when she speaks on the subject, yet she does so without a trace of Alinsky's inner doubt. "There is no such thing as other people's children," Hillary often tells her adoring crowds.[1] Another favorite quote of hers is from John Wesley: "Do all the good you can, by all the means you can, in all the ways you can, at all the times you can, to all the people you can, as long as you ever can."[2] To paraphrase her husband, it depends on the meaning of the word "good." For Hillary, children are the levers by which one forces social change.

Hillary found an outlet for her social agenda in the CDF, and through her long association with its founder Marian Wright Edelman, a leading civil rights activist and longtime FOH. Edelman's group was well-funded, well-staffed, and well-connected long before one of its leading advocates became the first lady. Its donor base is generously sprinkled with Fortune 500 patrons.

In 1973 it dawned on Edelman that the "country was tired of the concerns of the sixties. When you talked about poor people or black people, you faced a shrinking audience.... I got the idea that children might be a very effective way to broaden the base for change."[3] A convenient, sympathetic, photogenic, and maleable cause—how perfect. Hillary agreed.

Edelman's great insight was to put children squarely in the front of almost every domestic policy debate. This is central to the CDF's mission and a marvelous marketing tool. Throughout the Carter, Reagan, and Bush years, the CDF used a combination of shrewd inside lobbying and outside activism to protect and expand the welfare state. The CDF has browbeaten lawmakers for such programs as Head Start or the nutrition program for Women, Infants and Children, as well as expanding welfare and public housing programs, guaranteed employment, and higher minimum wages.

When critics argued that America's welfare program was subsidizing illegitimacy and creating a culture of government-dependent poverty and victimhood, the CDF countered that any attempt to reduce the welfare state was a direct assault on children.[4] This kind of high-profile political warfare brought instant status to the CDF and Marian Wright Edelman.

Named after Marian Anderson, Edelman had earned her law degree at Yale, was the first African-American woman to pass the Mississippi bar, and was a hero of the civil rights movement, organizing voter registration drives and protests against segregation.

It was Edelman's husband, Peter, a former aide to Robert F. Kennedy, who first contacted Hillary after reading about her Wellesley commencement speech in *Life* magazine.

Later, as a Yale law student, Hillary read a profile of Marian Wright Edelman in *Time* magazine. In the spring of 1970, "in one of those strange twists of fate that enters all our lives if we're open to hear and to see them," Hillary recalled that she noticed that Edelman was returning to her alma mater to give a speech. Hillary was in the audience and experienced the kind of minor epiphany that seems to strike her with some regularity. "I knew right away that I had to go to work for her."[5]

It was easy to see the attraction. By 1970 Marian Wright Edelman had become a central figure of the mythic left. She used her growing clout to establish the Washington Research Project, the forerunner of the CDF. Hillary secured a small civil rights grant to go work for her. As part of her summer job, she performed research for a Senate subcommittee chaired by Walter Mondale. She traveled to migrant labor camps and interviewed workers and their families, documenting the conditions and their effect on children.

Later, Hillary worked as a volunteer in family custody cases in New Haven. Hillary, by then living with the gregarious third-year law student who would become her husband, took a fourth year to study child development at the Yale Child Study Center. There she researched her now well-known legal writings on the rights of children for the *Harvard Educational Review*.

After Yale, but before she went to work on the House Judiciary Committee, Hillary moved to Boston to serve a stint as a lawyer for the CDF. She joined the CDF board in 1978, and eventually served as its chairman for six years.[6]

To understand Hillary's politics today, it is not enough to review her resume and her rapid assent through the then-chic liberal advocacy groups. One must read her writings from this period. It is in these samplings from her past that Hillary finds a fully developed, albeit superficial, political philosophy. All of this was set before her husband's political ambitions forced her to retract, disguise, or repackage in more benign wrapping her radical critique of society and the family.

Marian Wright Edelman opened other doors for her bright young acolyte. She helped Hillary win a coveted research position with the Carnegie Council on Children. At the Carnegie Council, Hillary worked as a research assistant on a panel chaired by Yale psychology professor Kenneth Keniston. Kenneth Keniston opened up the world of social sciences and psychology to enrich Hillary's legal agenda.

Keniston ran the Yale Child Study Center and supervised

Hillary's work drafting guidelines for abused children at the Yale New Haven Hospital. More importantly, Hillary assisted Keniston with several chapters of the Carnegie panel's report on children's rights, *All Our Children*. This report became a kind of compendium of left-wing, pie-in-the-sky wish list, one in which Keniston advocated a national guaranteed income, a universal entitlement state, and greatly expanded procedural rights for children. Issued in 1977, this report quickly became the conventional wisdom of the time, that adult life-style choices would inevitably create different kinds of families. Moreover, rather than resist this deconstruction of the American nuclear family, the report advocated that society had best find ways to encourage, supplement, and support single-parent families.

If anything, the Carnegie Council's report took a sanguine view of the rising divorce rate and single motherhood, a view that Vice President Dan Quayle would later assail in his "Murphy Brown" speech. What would matter in the future of children, the Carnegie Council stated, was not the family structure, but the larger village of teachers, pediatricians, and social workers who would socialize the task of raising, supporting, and nurturing children.

The time had come for society, we were told, to see the rearing of children as less of a parental task than as a social one. It was here that the full panoply of Hillary's beliefs can be seen in microcosm, from generous family leave to universal health care. Most utopian and ultimately insidious of all were the council's proposals to develop "public advocates" who could intervene between parents and children on the latter's behalf, reducing parents to subunits of the state. There would even be "child ombudsmen" who would represent the rights of children in public institutions, helped by a new class of public interest lawyers to advocate the rights of children.[7] Thus the parents would be subordinate to judges, social workers, and bureaucrats—the real experts in the raising of children.

Hillary, ever rigorous, explored the idea of children's rights to their utmost limits.

THE CHILDREN'S CRUSADE

During the 1992 campaign, sympathetic journalists and campaign image-masters claimed that right-wing demagogues had grossly mischaracterized Hillary's academic writings on children. Columnist Eleanor Clift informed her *Newsweek* readers that "The Republicans had great fun at their convention last month ridiculing Hillary Clinton as a radical feminist who promotes left-wing causes that undermine traditional family values." She complained that Hillary was hysterically accused "of comparing marriage to slavery, and of favoring the rights of children to sue their parents over such mundane matters as taking out the garbage. Clinton's critics say her husband may be a moderate, but that she has a secret liberal agenda and the Rasputin-like influence to implement it."[8]

Hillary, of course, was particularly anxious to put the Republican characterizations to rest. "There is no way that anybody could fairly read the article and say I was advocating that children sue parents over taking the garbage out," Hillary told *Newsweek*.[9]

John Leo wrote in *U.S. News and World Report* that "The Republican attempt to demonize Hillary Clinton is shameful." Leo added, "She is not a radical feminist. She did not say that marriage is like slavery or the Indian reservation system."[10]

These articles, and others like them, served as a firebreak against further criticism.

Hillary completed her image-makeover on children's issues as first lady with the 1996 publication in her name of *It Takes a Village*. The book was breezy, folksy, and moderate in tone, vacuous, but middle of the road on substance, stressing the importance of the larger community of adults taking responsibility for child rearing. *It Takes a Village* was seasoned with Tipperesque critiques of Hollywood culture and moralistic quotes from Bill Bennett before the Christian Coalition.

The 1992 campaign criticism of Hillary as a dangerous ideologue is now long forgotten, swept away with all the campaign bunting and failed rhetoric of President Bush's unfocused and discursive reelection campaign. But in fact, a careful reading of her work reveals a not-ready-for-primetime Hillary as radical as the Republicans said she was. Hillary's writings reveal a leftist ideologue, dedicated to centrally directed social engineering, dismissive of the traditional role of the family, and interested in children primarily as levers with which to extract political power.

"The phrase children's rights is a slogan in search of a definition," she declared in the opening sentence of her opus on the subject in a 1973 issue of the *Harvard Educational Review*. That term "does not yet reflect any coherent doctrine regarding the status of children as political beings," she said. She started with the unremarkable proposition that children already had limited rights as parties in lawsuits, as legatees under wills, as intestate successors. Older children had additional legal rights based on some recognition of their growing competence—including the right to drive, to drop out of school, to vote, to work, to marry.

Between the late 1940s and late 1960s, successive rulings by the U.S. Supreme Court extended procedural protections afforded adults (against self-incrimination, the standard of reasonable doubt) to children in juvenile court. The court also ruled in favor of limited First Amendment rights for children, allowing them to refuse to salute the flag if it offended their religious beliefs, and protecting their right to wear black armbands to protest the Vietnam War.

But, Hillary argued, the only way to give children real power was to make their needs and interests enforceable as constitutional rights. Her solution was to use the alchemy of the law, to melt all arguments in the furnace of adversarial argument, and, as she saw it, to separate the base from the pure.

She made several assertions that still have the power, many years later, to cause jaws to drop—statements that reveal the contours of Hillary's better world.

She writes: "The pretense that children's issues are somehow above or beyond politics endures and is reinforced by the belief that families are private, nonpolitical units whose interests subsume those of children."

Charting the fallacies in this one sentence is quite an undertaking, but a useful one. The word "pretense" indicates that somehow there is a conspiracy at work in the treatment of children, which the rest of the sentence indicates is somehow political. In a condescending, academic way, she snidely ridicules the belief that families are "private, nonpolitical units" indicating that she does, in fact, reject the notion that the family is a traditional institution that has arisen organically and stood the test of time. In her view, families are essentially low-level public entities dedicated to explicitly political ends. If they are subunits, what is the larger unit but the state, its public programs and prevailing ideology?

Her contemptous tone toward the family unit continued throughout her paper with her conviction that the interests of a family—its culture and beliefs—unfairly subsumed, and thus undermined the best interests of children. Taken one way, this is Jeffersonian individualism on 1960s recreational drugs. Taken another, it is a pointed denigration of families steeped in religious tradition or a particular culture, whether they be Hassidim, evangelical Christians, or recent refugees from Kosovo.

Another passage was so damning that it became the focus of damage control in the 1992 election:

> The basic rationale for depriving people of rights in a dependency relationship is that certain individuals are incapable or undeserving of the right to take care of themselves and consequently need social institutions specifically designed to safeguard their position. It is presumed that under the circumstances society is doing what is best for the individuals. Along with the family, past and present examples of such arrangements include marriage, slavery, and the Indian reservation system.

John Leo's subsequent rationalization of this passage was based on a quick dismissal of it as a piquant, but fair, description of the evolution of the legal concept of dependency. But Hillary herself is not so easily disguised. Children's helplessness in society must be seen, she wrote, "as part of the organization and ideology of the political system itself." It is not enough to say that between the give and take of powerful interests like business and labor, children get left behind. She saw a more sinister conspiracy at work—a theme which is an indelible part of her hard-drive. She perceived the hidden hand of ideology, a power elite that for whatever reason is actively anti-child. In other words, the opposition is not just wrong, it is morally perverse and out to repress good and maintain the rule of the suppressive elite.

Her early writings are also shaped by a radical academic Marxism and feminism. Christopher Lasch, one of the few intellectuals to take her writings seriously enough to criticize them, wrote a trenchant article on these Hillary essays in *Criticism* on the eve of the election. "Though Clinton does not press the point," Lasch writes, "the movement for children's rights, as she describes it, amounts to another stage in the long struggle against patriarchy."[11]

One of Hillary's legal models was a 1972 opinion by Supreme Court Justice William O. Douglas. Douglas dissented when the Supreme Court upheld the right of Amish parents to exempt their children from compulsory schooling, on the basis of religious freedom. Douglas noted, somewhat mildly, that there were two parties with stakes in such decisions, the parents and the child. Given that the "education of the child is a matter, on which the child will often have decided views," and he or she may want to "be a pianist or an astronomer or an oceanographer," it is reasonable to seek the view of the child. This is a relatively modest step, given that the law recognizes the child as a person (a consideration that neither the late Justice Douglas nor Hillary Clinton has ever conceded to the unborn).

It is a huge leap, however, from the judicial consideration of the child's needs and desires, and the litigation of these needs and desires *by the child*. Yet Hillary has been anxious to make that leap. The same woman who later forbade her daughter Chelsea from piercing her ears would advocate giving children the same rights in court as adults.[12]

"Ascribing rights to children," Hillary wrote, "will not immediately solve these problems, or undermine the consensus which perpetuates them. It will, however, force from the judiciary and the legislature institutional support for the child's point of view."

Using children to force judicial mandates and legislative change is at the core of her phiosophy. That goal would have to be accomplished, of course, by adults acting on the children's behalf. But what is the "child's point of view" and who will determine it?

Hillary qualified and defended her views in her 1978 essay "Children's Rights: A Legal Perspective." "The fears," she wrote, "that many people have about the formulation of children's rights arise from their concern about increasing government control over such intra-family disputes. A letter sent out several years ago about the Child and Family Development Act urged persons to oppose the proposed bill because it would, according to their writers, allow children to take parents to court if they were ordered to take out the garbage."

The real issues, Hillary argued, are far more important, and were already embodied in legal doctrine. "There are, for instance, a line of cases in which a child either wished or required a certain medical procedure that his or her parents refused to provide." Hillary cited cases in which courts allowed minors to receive abortions without parental consent, and the rulings of courts to override the refusals of Jehovah's Witnesses to allow their children to have surgery and blood transfusions.

"I prefer that intervention into an ongoing family be limited to decisions that could have long-term and possibly irreparable effects if they were not resolved," she states. "Decisions about motherhood and abortion, schooling, cosmetic surgery, treatment of venereal disease, or employment, and others where the decision or lack of one will significantly affect the child's future should not be made unilaterally by parents."

In other words, don't get so worked up. Children's rights will be invoked only for the serious stuff, like terminating pregnancies, which school to attend, breast implants, whether to work in a saloon, the things that really matter; not for taking out the garbage or any other frivolous dust-up between parent and child. In Hillary's world judges, social workers, and other "real" experts will only play a decisive role in the things that matter, the parents can still be involved in the little things.

Set aside the whole abortion issue. Set aside the fact, which Hillary herself presents, that courts will not hesitate to override the rights of parents to advance their perceptions of the health and safety of the child. The larger issue is that given the sort of lawsuit-crazy society in which we live—and I write as a lawyer myself—we know the answer is, yes, children *will* sue their parents over taking out the garbage, how late to stay out, and what clothes to wear and there *will* be lawyers who will argue that taking out the garbage is involuntary servitude.

Hillary seems utterly oblivious to the fact that in our legal system, any new right that is created is certain to be explored to the farthest frontier of absurdity. This, after all, a legal system in which suits have been filed on behalf of children against Disneyland over the trauma of being taken on a backstage tour, only to see that their beloved cartoon characters are really people in costume.[13]

This is a legal system in which a girl sued a county school board for $1.5 million after being allowed to play football, only to be injured in the first scrimmage.[14]

This is a legal system in which a teenager won a $50,000 award from his school when he snagged his teeth on a basketball net while making a slum-dunk, losing two teeth.[15]

This is a legal system in which a California law allows children to live on their own as adults, and a Florida judge granted an eleven-year-old the right to "divorce" his parents.[16]

Whatever the extenuating circumstances, all too often law that addresses human tragedy ends up as social farce. If children were given full rights to sue, parents would become the targets of the suits of the future. Hillary also seems to have no concept that the adversarial process of lawsuits will turn parent and child into defendant and plaintiff, and bitter life-long enemies.

Although she may have a better appreciation of the civil justice system now than when she wrote these things, Hillary also seems to have been oblivious to the reality that the cost alone of a lawsuit is enough to sink most family budgets, forcing parents to sell their homes or liquidate their retirements to fight their own children in court, or just to keep them in the family. Nor does she seem cognizant that lawsuits are ill-suited to resolve disputes over a parent-child issue because of the months or years of bitter wrangling a suit can eat up. It is not unusual for suits to drag on for years before final resolution. By the time a suit can finally be resolved in a child case, the original issue will be often moot. Many children will be well on their way to independence.

Hillary's kiddie rights solution builds on the extension of adult rights to children made in 1967 by the U.S. Supreme Court *Gault* decision. *Gault*, however, involved the rights of juveniles charged with serious crimes. (Hillary obliquely criticized the Court's refusal to require jury trials for juveniles. Unanswered is whether she would empanel a jury of adults, or true peers. If children have rights, why not a jury of other kids, perhaps a jury of twelve-year-olds?)

The courts, even while extending procedural protections to children, have always recognized the limits of treating kids as adults. Hillary does not. She notes that children's rights are enforceable only vicariously, dependent as they are "on adults to represent them in claims to achieve their rights."

It is at this moment that Hillary puts her philosophy of family socialism on parade. "Although there are difficulties attached to making the law more discriminating, they do not seem to be any greater than the problems lawmakers confront in many other areas. Deciding what kinds of crop aid should be given for a particular year to various regions affected by different weather, pests, and prices is not easy either, but it gets done."

It is astonishing that any parent could believe that raising a child is as simple as deciding on aid to farmers, but Hillary and her husband have been politicians and wards of government most of their adult lives. Perhaps it is understandable that she would have such a warped and disconnected view of families and normal life.

In a 1977 *Yale Law Review* critique of *The Children's Cause*, by Gilbert Steiner (on which she bestowed mild approval, though registering disappointment with it for having a "cautious attitude toward government involvement in child-rearing"), Hillary called for a series of national experiments.

"If Albert Shanker wants the teachers to control day care programs, let him have an experimental grant for a few years…. The Children's Defense Fund might be given financial support to coordinate programs under varied community control models."

Why not experiment with a few children? Hillary expresses complete openness toward experimentation with children in a variety of ways—with the exception, perhaps, of any program that would lessen the dependency of families and children on public programs, such as school choice. (Though, of course, the Clintons would later send their own daughter to the same expensive *private* school attended by the children of Senator Bill Bradley and *Washington Post* reporter Bob Woodward.[17])

What comes through in these essays is the arrogant voice of the social engineer, the activist who believes that reshaping the most intimate of human relationships is as simple as rotating crops. There is more than a little foreshadowing here of Hillary's future effort to centralize the management of Arkansas education from the governor's office in Little Rock, and of her great socialist health care debacle in President Clinton's first term.

In a 1978 article Hillary wrote that the federal school lunch program "became politically acceptable not because of arguments about hungry children, but because of an alliance between children's advocates and the association of school cafeteria workers who seized the opportunity to increase its membership." Children, she concludes, deserve similarly "competent and effective advocates." It doesn't seem to matter to her that the cafeteria workers were not interested in the children, but the power of their work force. Children and their real interests don't seem nearly as important to Hillary as the power of the political lever they represent.

Just who will the children's advocates be? It is doubtful the field of kiddie rights would attract the likes of a Johnny Cochran. There would be no money in it. Who could afford such a practice? Those "interested adults" who would answer Hillary's call to arms could only be a certain type of self-professed public interest attorneys, inspired, sustained, and directed by groups like the Children's Defense Fund. Or if class actions or punitive damages could be added to the equation, perhaps the contingent fee trial lawyers, who have been such good friends to Bill Clinton throughout his political career, could be incentivized.

These advocates, to the extent not motivated by high fees, would come to each case not essentially as representatives of the child-client, but as activists looking to see how this little boy, or that little girl, fits into a greater strategy to expand an entitlement or control how a government agency functions.

"The notion," Christopher Lasch commented in his criticism of Hillary's writings, "that children are fully capable of speaking for themselves makes it possible for ventriloquists to speak through them and thus to disguise their own objectives as the child."

Hillary wrote in a 1978 book review for *Public Welfare*, "Collective action is needed on the community, state and federal level to wrest from machines and those who profit from their use the extraordinary power they hold over us all, but particularly over children."

The idea that power must be wrested from "machines" is peculiar, ignoring that, at bottom, Hillary's children's crusade is a hard-nosed exercise in expanding power in a different direction, in the direction of public interest trial lawyers with a social engineering agenda. Children are useful, just as migrant workers and the indigent elderly are useful, as tools to pry loose the controls, to get into the guts of the machinery of law and governance. Children are the rhetorical vehicles she still uses as first lady, whether pressing for national health care or to get Congress to pay UN dues. She writes: "Since many of its [the Carter administration's] top policymakers are reportedly inclined favorably towards children's programs, saving the 'family' may become the justification for, rather than remain the nemesis of, those programs." Her use of quotes are telling. The future of the family makes for a good propaganda point.

"Apparently we share so much apprehension about potential harm to cherished, albeit fantasized, family values that programs for children must demonstrate immediate success or risk extinction."

"Fantasized family values." The meaning is unmistakable. The government is the real provider of values, and the real source of necessary change against traditionalist "cherished," "fantasized" family values.

When the 1992 presidential election came, Hillary's radical stance had been blurred by her own election-motivated moderated rhetoric and by the friendly treatment she received from sympathetic members of the liberal establishment press. She was able to take what should have been an embarrassment in her past and transform it into a point of pride. As the wife of a presidential candidate, Hillary, the child advocate, took on Vice President Dan Quayle.

Shortly after Quayle's "Murphy Brown" speech, Hillary attacked the vice president's observations before a San Francisco audience, saying, "I wonder if he lives in the same America we live in, if he sees the same things we see. He's trying to blame the Los Angeles riots and blame the social problems in this country on a TV sitcom."[18]

That wasn't it at all. In attacking values disseminated weekly by the producers, writers, and directors of the *Murphy Brown* program, Quayle took to task a popular emblem of Hillary's own philosophy. He pointed to a growing body of empirical evidence that children raised by single parents—by a *nontraditional* family structure, in other words—are exposed to higher risks for everything from drug abuse to suicide and teen pregnancy.

Quayle had the full weight of social science and the facts on his side. Hillary had a sympathetic press and Saul Alinsky's tactics. She had picked her target, frozen it, personalized it, and polarized the debate, crushing Dan Quayle like a can of Tab.

Sören Kierkegaard foresaw Hillary's political tactics—of achieving radical aims under moderate-sounding New Democrat rhetoric—with an almost uncanny prescience. "A passionate, tumultuous age will overthrow everything, pull everything down," Kierkegaard wrote, "but a revolutionary age that is at the same time reflective and passionless leaves everything standing but cunningly empties it of significance."

Hillary would likewise empty the oldest of human relations—the family—of its significance and its independence. Her crusade is not rooted in Blackstone or even John Wesley. It appears principled, but it is really tactical. It has a spiritual appeal, but it is really about the temporal achievement of power.

It is Saul Alinsky to the core.

SIX
WATERGATE TO WHITEWATER

---

*"Ethical standards must be elastic to
stretch with the times."*

— SAUL ALINSKY, *RULES FOR RADICALS*

In 1988 and 1991 the *National Law Journal* included among its list of the one hundred most influential lawyers in the country one Hillary Rodham, partner in the Little Rock law firm of Rose, Nash, Williamson, Carroll, Clay and Giroir.

This was an astonishing development for a young lawyer in Little Rock. After all, most lawyers on that list were rainmakers or heavy-hitting partners of powerhouse firms, renowned legal scholars from the Harvard Law School, and attorneys general of the United States.

When *American Lawyer* actually researched Hillary's career, it found little—aside from her husband's political office—to explain how she could have become one of the nation's most influential lawyers. She had tried only five cases in fifteen years at the Rose Law Firm. Court reporters said they had seen little of her. It seems that much of her work revolved around copyright infringement for songwriters.[1]

One case given to her by Vince Foster was to defend a canning company against a consumer's claim that the hindquarters of a mouse had been found in his can of pork and beans. The cogency of her defense was highly praised by Foster. But Webb Hubbell claimed Hillary was "amazingly nervous" before the jury.

"She won the case," Hubbell wrote, "but began steering her practice toward nonjury matters."[2]

Hillary's lack of litigation skills or aptitude did not go unnoticed. Even though she had been assigned to the litigation division at Rose with Hubbell and Foster, Hillary's colleagues were only too happy to tell journalists from *American Lawyer* that they were surprised by her ranking among the top one hundred. Some doubted she was even among the top one hundred lawyers in Little Rock.[3]

How, then, did Hillary get on the list? She was married to a governor who was a rising luminary in the ranks of the centrist Democratic Leadership Council. It was mostly, however, her own growing national reputation not as a lawyer, but as a leading female lawyer *activist*. Hillary had established herself as a national figure in liberal circles at Wellesley and Yale, then as a bright up-and-comer who had secured one of the coveted spots on the House Judiciary Committee's investigation of Watergate.

Hillary maintained her visibility on the East Coast the entire time she was in Little Rock, spending several days a month in New York and Washington in the service of a variety of liberal causes.

As the head of the Legal Services Corporation—appointed by President Jimmy Carter—Hillary wielded power on a national basis, ultimately seeking to undermine the policies of the incoming Reagan administration.

She would, however, occasionally have to drop her duties at Rose and her leadership of the liberal lobbies to rescue Bill Clinton from himself, first to get him back into office after losing the governorship following a disastrous first term, then to guide him through a series of policy initiatives that were really part of a perpetual reelection campaign.

The young woman who had disdained the spreading of "walking around money" during her husband's failed 1974 run for Congress had changed. Now she unhesitatingly used tax-payer funded Legal Services dollars to support political campaigns. The young woman who had once held "the corporate power structure" in contempt had become a part of it, sitting on corporate boards and parlaying her meager holdings into a tidy nest egg. The young woman who had expressed her dismay at the ethics of her elders arranged to make a quick and highly lucrative killing in cattle futures with the guidance of a lawyer connected to a tycoon famous for his hatred of organized labor and his willingness to dump tons of chicken excrement into the rivers and streams of poor communities.

Hillary Rodham had seen what was needed to win, to gain power, and if that meant enriching herself and doing whatever it took to enrich Democratic campaign coffers, so be it.

The transformation of Hillary Rodham had begun *before* she came to Little Rock. The seeds of change in her life, sowed by the Reverend Jones and Saul Alinsky were nurtured, unwittingly, by Richard Milhous Nixon.

WATERGATE: LESSONS LEARNED

Hillary was twenty-six years old when two leading liberal lawyers singled her out for a remarkable assignment.

One of them was her old civil rights professor, Burke Marshall, a former assistant attorney general for civil rights. Burke was deeply involved in the Democratic establishment. He is best remembered as one of the first to receive a call from Ted Kennedy after the senator weaved off the Chappaquiddick Bridge and needed help explaining how and why he had left Mary Jo Kopechne to drown in his car.

Another was John Doar, liberal Republican, a civil rights firebrand who had worked for Burke in the Kennedy Justice Department. Doar was a hero of the civil rights movement, having nudged George Wallace out of a schoolhouse door and having once put himself in harm's way to stop a riot.

Doar now found himself center stage in a very different kind of political struggle. Watergate had descended upon the nation, with obscure names suddenly becoming the background patter of the times: Haldeman, Dean, Ehrlichman, Segretti. A political firestorm had erupted after Nixon fired Archibald Cox, and fresh oxygen was added to the blaze when Vice President Agnew resigned in disgrace over a bribery charge from his days as governor of Maryland.

Doar had been impaneled by Representative Pete Rodino, Jr., to serve as special counsel in charge of the House Judiciary investigation of the president. The investigation, ostensibly, was to be impartial and nonpartisan. Yet Doar had made private references to the investigation as "the war," and "the cause" against Nixon. The choice of a staff, almost uniformly liberal (including a few liberal Republicans like young William Weld of Massachusetts), belied the investigation's supposed impartiality.

One of these choices was a young woman Doar had come to know through the Barristers Union at Yale, Hillary Rodham. Hillary's activities, as campus activist and outspoken critic of Nixon and his "illegal" bombing of Cambodia, were familiar to those in anti-Nixon circles. Doar had seen Hillary perform at the Prize Trial at Yale and listened with interest to Burke's strong recommendation of her. Hillary planned to become a staff attorney with the Children's Defense Fund (CDF) in Cambridge, Massachusetts, but was captivated instead by Doar's proposition that she join his team of forty-plus lawyers who were to handle the committee's inquiry into the possible impeachment of Richard Nixon. She quickly accepted.

Hillary threw herself into the Nixon investigation with enthusiasm, passion, and intense determination. She put in twelve- to twenty-hour days, seven days a week, at a desk in a cramped office—permeated with the odor of mildew—in the Congressional Hotel. At night, she went home to a small bedroom rented from Sara Ehrman, a colleague from the McGovern campaign. A close associate was Bernie Nussbaum, then a right-hand man to Doar, who was later rewarded by Hillary with his appointment to become White House counsel to President Clinton.

Hillary's work with the committee began in January 1974. She was only one of two women lawyers on the staff. Her primary assignment was to make sure that the inquiry conformed to legal and parliamentary procedure.

Two years later, an article appeared in the *Atlantic Monthly* by Renata Adler, a journalist close to Doar and part of his circle of informal advisors. In this remarkable piece, largely overlooked by other journalists and historians, Doar confided that he had meant to use his legal team, dubbed "the faceless forty," as mere legal window dressing.

Their primary mission was to deluge the committee in a blizzard of documentation, Adler revealed, to create the appearance of great diligence. Meanwhile, Doar would work with a few select members of the team, a group within the group, to make sure that they reached the only acceptable objective, the removal of Richard Nixon from the White House.

Hillary Rodham's single-mindedness and ideological zealotry made her a natural member of the inside group. Supported by Doar and Nussbaum, she proposed a gag order on Judiciary Committee members, a measure that would have prevented them from cross-examining witnesses or drafting their own articles of impeachment; all power, in other words, would rest with Doar's staff. The elected committee members would be mere marionettes in a Doar-Rodham show trial.

The Judiciary Committee members were stunned.

William Dixon, a member of the committee staff, later told Joyce Milton that Hillary "paid no attention to the way the Constitution works in this country, the way politics works, the way Congress works, the way legal safeguards are set up."[4]

Hillary's protocols were so poorly conceived and drafted that Representative Jack Brooks, the populist Democrat from Texas, had no choice but to line up a committee vote to strike them down.

Was Hillary really so incompetent, so ill-suited to the scholarly role assigned to her? It is doubtful that Doar, who did not tolerate messy desks, would have tolerated scholarly incompetence. It seems instead that Doar and his protégés were driven by a secretiveness that rivaled that of the Nixon

White House itself, with similar antipathies toward democratic processes. They seemed to believe that an open inquiry could not be trusted to come to the proper conclusion. It would have to be orchestrated by smart young people like Hillary Rodham and her general, John Doar.

One staffer who saw through this gambit was Jerry Zeifman, chief counsel for the Judiciary Committee, who had every reason to feel he was being shut out by his special counsel, Doar. Zeifman later concluded: "It seems to me that Haldeman and Ehrlichman are crude amateurs at arrogance in comparison to the more polished and sophisticated arrogance and deceit of some of Doar's assistants."[5]

Whatever embarrassment Hillary might have felt, she retained Doar's confidence. If anything, Doar's reliance on Hillary grew. Hillary was one of the few researchers allowed to hear what the staff would call "the tape of tapes."

"It was Nixon himself listening to the tapes, making up his defenses to what he heard on the tapes.... You could hear Nixon talk and then you'd hear very faintly the sound of a taped prior conversation with Nixon, Haldeman, and Ehrlichman... and you'd hear [the president] say, 'What I meant when I said that was'.... It was surreal, unbelievable."[6]

Tom Bell, a Watergate colleague of Hillary's, told David Maraniss that Hillary's opinion of Nixon "was more a result of the McGovern campaign and Vietnam and those kinds of issues. I saw him as evil because he was screwing with the Constitution. She came at it with more preconceived ideas than I did...."

"She saw the work as absolutely the most important thing in the world," Bell continued. "I saw it as important but also as a job. To her it may have been more of a mission."[7] Some might say a jihad.

Hillary tracked the voices on the tapes with the comings and goings of staff and visitors on the White House logs. She reconstructed who spoke to whom, and where. She carefully sifted the evidence and extracted that which was the most incriminating.

Another aspect of her job was to write a scholarly background piece on the law of impeachment, encompassing four centuries of English and American law. She was to examine the scope of impeachable conduct, from the parliamentary trial of Warren Hastings, to the intent of the American founding fathers, to the impeachment of ten federal judges.

Her specific task was to find an extra-Constitutional rationale for impeaching Nixon over the secret bombing of Cambodia.

Hillary concluded in her report to Doar that "to limit impeachable conduct to criminal offenses would be incompatible with the evidence concerning the constitutional meaning of the phrase... and would frustrate the purpose that the framers intended for impeachment." These words have an ironic ring years later when her husband's squadrons of lawyers would have to make—and sell—the opposite case to save him from impeachment.

It is likely that Hillary's Watergate experience, shaped directly by Doar and indirectly by Richard Nixon, influenced much of her future approach to politics. It is hard to fully appreciate the degree to which she had become a close-in witness to history now that excerpts from the Watergate tapes can be heard on cable channel documentaries. In 1974, being one of the few select investigators allowed to listen in on the Nixon Oval Office, she must have felt as if she were there, hovering over Nixon and his aides, a witness to sinister conduct by an unsavory and distasteful man. She heard Nixon's dissembling, his private mutterings, his banal obscenities and often coarse characterization of others, sensed his suffering through the long sweaty hours of defense, denial, and counterdenial.

In the end, Nixon was his own worst accuser, a man who condemned himself in his own words, with his own voice. Nixon was trapped by his actions and in many ways prosecuted by his conscience. John Connally, the most trusted member of the Nixon cabinet, told Nixon to gather the tapes in the Rose Garden and proudly burn them.

From the standpoint of Machiavellian tactics, of course, Connally was right. Had Nixon burned the tapes he would have been seen by his supporters as standing up for the rights of the presidency, and daring his tormentors to impeach on the remaining evidence.[8]

From an amoral perspective of power politics, Nixon made two other critical mistakes. In the last days of his administration, he opted to put the country before his own personal legacy, to resign rather than force the ordeal of an impeachment upon America. But before that, his big mistake was thinking that he could survive by admitting half of the truth.

Hillary witnessed firsthand that such a path could only lead to ruin. As she and her husband were later to demonstrate, the final lesson of Watergate is that any compromise with a criminal investigation is fatal. They were to prove that if one stonewalls, denies the undeniable, destroys evidence, and attacks the accusers, one may be risking going to prison for the sake of political survival, but if prosecution can be avoided, political viability is also possible. If one cooperates, one may escape prison, but is certain to face political ruin and a lifetime of shame.

For Hillary, her husband, and their defenders, when faced with an impeachment of their own two decades later, this choice would be a no-brainer. As they learned in Arkansas, as they refined during the first campaign for the presidency, and as they perfected during the Kenneth Starr investigation and the impeachment proceedings, when accused, go for broke— and destroy the accuser.

SHELL GAME AT LEGAL SERVICES

As her husband won the office of attorney general, and then governor, Hillary burrowed into the legal establishment, winning her partner-track position with the prestigious "white-shoe" Rose Law Firm. She helped found and chair the Arkansas Advocates for Children and Families. More important, she was appointed to the board of the Legal Services Corporation, becoming its chairman in 1978.

Bill Clinton was close enough to President Jimmy Carter's political operation that he was given control of patronage in Arkansas. Yet it was likely Hillary's dedicated work as a deputy field coordinator in Indiana in 1976 that brought her to the attention of the Carter White House. Lacking a sufficient number of political volunteers, she came up with an ingenious idea: she worked with local bail bondsmen to get local felons to operate the phone bank.

One of her rewards was an appointment to the Legal Services Corporation (LSC), a federally funded nonprofit organization established by Congress, was an ideal platform for a young lawyer indoctrinated in the ways of Crit activism. Though LSC was born as a Great Society concept, the Ford administration tempered it into a means to equalize access to justice.

Under President Carter, it was transformed back into what many of its founders had intended it to be in the first place, a mechanism for growing and strengthening the social welfare state. Such an assignment might have been invented for Hillary Rodham. It replicated her thinking on children's rights on a grand scale, allowing her to put together a cadre of committed activist lawyers who, by mau-mauing the system, could use individual cases as levers with which to broaden mandates for social welfare spending, to create new rights needing new programs and public expenditures.

On the House Judiciary Committee, Hillary had shown a mastery of the Crit philosophy, interpreting law as she wished in order to advance a political goal. The LSC was the ultimate playground—and laboratory—for this philosophy. She was in a perfect position to manipulate public policy into a useful weapon to further her political causes.

It is not hard to see how she accomplished her goals. In the words of Warren Brookes, conservative muckraker and chronicler of the failures of the welfare state, LSC had become a grossly illegal "$300 million liberal political action committee."

Hillary Rodham's Senate confirmation after her recess appointment was initially jeopardized by controversy. As Bill Clinton rose on the state political scene, Hillary became the source of many conflicts of interest for the Rose Law Firm. During the confirmation hearings she was asked if Rose would recuse itself from business with organizations funded by the LSC. Hillary refused to say "yes." In control of another political party, Hillary may have had more trouble but the Democrats controlled the Senate. Thus, the senators reluctantly voted to confirm her.

At a staff retreat at Airlie House in Virginia, Chairman Hillary Rodham wasted no time in putting her stamp on the LSC. It was made clear that while showing a moderate public veneer, the LSC's activism would be expanded and made more aggressive. Under her leadership, the LSC budget grew from $90 million to more than $321 million.

What she did with the money was a serious scandal, but one which she managed to brazen her way through—like scandals to come. The LSC used public funds to print political training manuals to show "how community organizations and public interest groups can win political power and resources." The LSC contributed taxpayer dollars to a mayor's campaign in Georgia, as "a project to educate clients about their rights in the legislative process."[9] It held training programs that taught political activists how to harass the opposition, from nailing dead rats to an opponent's front door, to the black arts of private investigations and dirt digging.[10]

The LSC became heavily involved in the referendum politics of California. In 1980 Proposition 9 proposed cutting California's state income taxes in half. Without a hint that it recognized the irony of using taxpayer money to prevent a tax cut, the LSC illegally diverted public funds to a campaign by five hundred attorneys, led by LSC board member and certified FOH Mickey Kantor, to defeat the ballot initiative. During the campaign, the LSC doled out a special $61,000 "special needs" grant to hire campaign coordinators. The LSC paid for clerical staff, travel, printing, and postage for the campaign.[11]

The LSC also sought to return two-thirds of the state of Maine to Indians.[12] It paid Marxist orators and folk singers to try to galvanize oyster collectors who had a grievance with the

Louisiana Wildlife Commission.[13] It went to bat in Michigan to define "black English" as a separate language.

The LSC saw drug addicts and alcoholics as "handi-capped" and gave a grant for a suit against the New York City Transit Authority to force it to hire former heroin addicts. The reason? Discrimination against former addicts consti-tuted discrimination against minorities.[14]

While most of these cases remained local stories, the LSC's exploits were starting to attract national attention. One occurred in 1981, when the LSC joined the case of a trans-sexual welfare recipient who demanded that Medicare pay for a sex-change operation.[15]

Hillary could have used the LSC to make sure that poor minority—mostly black—men accused in murder cases received better counsel than the inadequate, court-appointed lawyers they were often stuck with. Instead, she made sure that LSC funds went toward political causes and expanding rights to create new law, to change the system through judi-cial activism. The activities of the LSC had gotten so out of hand that two leading politicians from Arkansas, Democratic Senator Dale Bumpers and Republican Ed Bethune, joined together in a complaint to the Carter administration that the LSC looked "for too many cases which can effect an economic or social outcome."

When challenged from the left, Hillary went on the attack with a vehemence that astonished many of her allies. She vig-orously and successfully opposed so-called "judicare," a pro-gram in which lawyers would offer discounted services to poor clients and receive reimbursement from the government.

But it was in former California governor Ronald Reagan that the LSC saw its most deadly opponent and the coming end of its freewheeling reign. As Reagan began to overtake Carter in the 1980 election, the LSC diverted funds from cases and threw its resources into a frantic effort to use indigent clients in a letter-writing campaign against Reagan.

In a later investigation, Republican Senate aides were astonished to see videotaped training sessions in which staffers spoke openly about how they were organizing the LSC's national network to defeat Reagan.

As soon as Ronald Reagan was elected, the LSC laundered its money into state-level agencies and private groups. By the time Reagan had taken the oath of office, the LSC had hidden its budget in cookie jars throughout the country. In the last days of the Carter Administration, some $260 million was disbursed so that it would be kept out of the hands of the eventual Reagan-appointed board.

As it turned out, that board would be a long time coming.

When President Reagan set out to appoint a board of his own through recess appointments, Hillary masterminded a lawsuit arguing that such recess appointments were illegal (though she, herself, had been appointed in just this way). Meanwhile, a successful, dirt-seeking opposition research campaign had tarnished the Reagan appointees, accusing them of overcharging their expense accounts and of racial bias. Though the Reaganites would later be cleared, the smear tactics achieved their intended effect, derailing the confirmation process.[16]

In 1983 the General Accounting Organization (GAO) investigated the LSC and concluded that the LSC's activities "and many of the people associated with it are uniquely reprehensible...." Strong words from a bipartisan, congressionally-controlled government watchdog. Indeed, the GAO said that the LSC "has itself engaged and allowed its grant recipients to engage in lobbying activities prohibited by federal law...."

The creators of the LSC, however, had carefully drafted its charter, including language that would have made the prosecution of Hillary Rodham difficult. There is no doubt, however, that she had spearheaded a deliberate, national plot to undermine the political process with millions of dollars worth of staff work and the diversion of taxpayer money into political campaigns.

As she did on the House Judiciary Committee, Hillary manifested a fierce commitment to the ends she had chosen and showed a remarkable indifference to the rule of law if it stood in the way of undermining "the system" or kept her from fighting the Nixons and the Reagans, who had become the *bête noires* of her politicized imagination.

LIBERAL LIONESS

Hillary had kept herself at the fore of liberal activism by flying East to lead many other causes and programs, and by creating miniature versions of those programs in her home state of Arkansas.

Some causes to which she directed money were in the liberal mainstream, from the National Association for the Advancement of Colored People (NAACP) to the People for the American Way. And she focused much of her activist energies in her new home state. While Bill served as attorney general, Hillary was helping to found the Arkansas Advocates for Children and Families, meant to be a state version of the CDF. Serving as president of the group's first board, she lobbied for and won more state financing for Head Start and other programs.[17]

On a vacation in Miami, she read a newspaper article about an Israeli child development program that worked with parents, usually mothers, in role-playing exercises to stimulate preschoolers' cognitive development. Within a short time, the Home Instruction Program for Preschool Youngsters, or HIPPY, had reached five thousand Arkansas children.[18]

Other causes took her farther afield.

Hillary chaired the New World Foundation from 1982 to 1988, during which time she awarded $15,000 to Grassroots International,which funneled the grant money to the Union of Palestinian Working Women's Committees and the Union of Palestinian Medical Relief Committees, both branches of the Palestine Liberation Organization (PLO).[19]

The public seems to have forgotten that before the Oslo Peace accords, the PLO had outsavaged the Baider Meinhof Gang, the Irish Republican Army (IRA), and the Red Brigade as the leaders of global terrorism. These were the bloody years of Munich, airport massacres, and laughing terrorists tossing an elderly, wheelchair-bound Jew into the Mediterranean. This was a time when the PLO was committed to the extinction of Israel and excelled in the arts of assassination and mayhem to press its claim. As a lawyer with the Department of Justice in 1989, I volunteered to fly to New York to serve papers to shut down the PLO "embassy" there to remove a terrorist foothold from our shores.

Other left-wing recipients of Hillary's largesse included the Committees in Solidarity with the People of El Salvador, or CISPES. CISPES unabashedly sought to bring a Communist revolution to Central America.[20] A grant of $15,000 went to the National Lawyer's Guild, a Communist front organization. Grants were given to groups with ties to the most extreme elements in the African National Congress.

Hillary also directed a grant of $20,000 to the Christic Institute, the looniest fringe group in the loony left, which publicized a number of bizarre conspiracy theories in which virtually every ill on earth could be traced to "secret teams" at the CIA involved in the narcotics trade.

It was not enough for Hillary to support causes dear to the Democratic Party and the American left. While her husband built an image as a moderate, centrist Democrat, Hillary rolled up her sleeves and made sure that American taxpayer dollars were disbursed to people dedicated to terror, disinformation, and violent revolution. She has never expressed a single word of regret for her support for these organizations and causes.

Hillary had also risen in the ranks of her favorite cause, the Children's Defense Fund (CDF). She spent considerable time back East on behalf of the CDF, chairing the organization from 1986 to 1992 (though many of her colleagues privately complained to the press that she should have resigned as soon as her husband announced for president).

Throughout this time, Hillary sought to hone a reputation as an East Coast liberal while living in Arkansas. She succeeded to a remarkable degree. She also succeeded in passing money and moral support to some causes that were ill conceived, others that were inimical to democracy, and some that were conduits to terrorists.

GOING YUPPIE

In the 1992 election, the Clintons went out of their way to demonize the Reagan-Bush years as a "gilded age of greed and selfishness, of irresponsibility and excess," and promised to deliver "the most ethical administration in the history of the Republic"—a boast that soon would become far worse than a bad joke.

For a brief period before and after winning the presidency, Bill Clinton seemed determined to force the American people into apologizing for having tolerating such a pair as Ronald Reagan and George Bush. He portrayed their years in office as a tragic interregnum, one in which the nation lapsed into an orgy of selfishness. His speeches honed the theme that we had lived through a time when the civic tone was set by Gordon Gekko, the unforgettable investment banker portrayed by Michael Douglas in Oliver Stone's *Wall Street* who crowed, "Greed is good!"

Clinton eventually had to drop this line when it boomeranged after the media investigated the full extent of his wife's aggressive pursuit of corporate connections and money; and we don't hear that theme much any more as the Clintons take $1,375,000 in cash from a wealthy friend to finance their post-presidency New York home. But there is always an excuse, a ready and sweetly packaged explanation whenever the Clintons get caught with their hand in one or another of the cookie jars into which they have dipped over the years.

"It was Hillary who decided that she wanted them to be financially secure, and took the steps to accomplish that," according to FOH and former chief of staff Betsey Wright. "Those decisions you wouldn't expect Bill Clinton to make, he doesn't care about those things. Bill Clinton would live under a bridge as long as it was O.K. with Chelsea. He just doesn't care. But Hillary did."[21]

This is the official spin: Bill Clinton, that loveable, goofy, absentminded professor of a public servant, just doesn't give a hoot about money. It is therefore perfectly understandable why Hillary, forced to live on her husband's paltry $35,000-a-year governor's salary, would want to provide for her family.

Roy Drew, who managed some of the Clintons' investments, offered another perspective in a *Business Week* interview. "She was doing the same thing as all those yuppies who she said represented the decade of greed.... Money was extremely important to the Clintons."[22]

The extent of Hillary's involvement in a spectrum of investments, corporate relationships, and high-risk deals is nothing short of breathtaking. The woman who had so recently and publicly "indicted" Corporate America was busy consorting with the enemy, drawing down a small fortune in director's fees.

Alinsky often said that he could persuade a millionaire to subsidize a revolution on a Saturday out of which he would make a huge profit on Sunday even though he was certain to be executed on Monday.[23] His young female understudy would prove the point, although in the end it was her ostensible principles that were massacred.

In 1990, Hillary joined the board of the French chemical giant, Lafarge, controversial for its toxic waste disposal contracts.[24] She joined the board of TCBY Enterprises, Inc., the yogurt franchise housed in the tallest building in Little Rock. A client of the Rose Law Firm, TCBY paid the firm up to $750,000 when Hillary served on TCBY's board.[25] The chairman of TCBY was one of Bill Clinton's most frequent and enthusiastic donors.[26]

And of course, no Arkansas resume would be complete without a spot on the Wal-Mart Corporation board, the

Arkansas big box superstore retailer that made Sam Walton the richest man in America. Owning $80,000 of Wal-Mart stock, Hillary served on its environmental committee, and launched an environmental education program and a company recycling program.[27]

Finally, Hillary served on the board of the southern Development Bancorp, described in a *New Republic* exposé as a "holding company created to give development loans in rural Arkansas." This outfit paid Rose between $100,000 and $200,000 in fees.[28]

In 1991 she earned $64,700 in director's fees. Her Rose firm salary was about $110,000. In all, she earned about $200,000 in director's fees at the conclusion of the "decade of greed," while at least two of those companies directed almost $1.3 million in legal fees to the Rose Law Firm.[29]

But there was more, much more.

In the context of her growing earnings, her husband's $35,000 salary and government financed home and transportation may be seen as more like a nice supplement to the family income stream than a ticket to the poorhouse. And, of course, being a governor, he had numerous other perks and special funds on which to draw, including state troopers to help him live a spirited social life.

One of the perks was a $51,000 "food allotment" fund. And Lisa Schiffren, in a brilliant investigative piece in the *American Spectator*, reported that a 1981 audit of the payroll of the governor's mansion showed that a nurse was employed at the governor's mansion from 1980, the year Chelsea was born, until Bill Clinton was voted out of office in 1981. The nanny was officially listed as a "security guard."[30]

Of course, the mansion with gardeners and servants was

free. When he wasn't jogging, the governor prowled around town in a chauffeured limousine.

Little wonder that by 1990, a family described by Betsey Wright as being in danger of living under a bridge had reached $212,000 in annual income, not to mention all the other benefits. Not at all bad for Little Rock. Hillary had established about $75,000 in stocks for Chelsea. And she had amassed a fortune in excess of $1 million in shares in Wal-Mart, TCBY, and her partnership in Value Partners, Ltd.,[31] a Little Rock "hedge fund." When her investment fund shorted its $1 million portfolio of pharmaceutical stocks at exactly the same time Hillary was in the White House pushing her national health care plan and publicly running down pharmaceutical companies, causing their stocks to drop by as much as a third, Hillary's $97,500 stake in the fund soared.[32]

Sometimes politics worked as her investment strategy. Sometimes it was no consideration at all. In 1981 Hillary reported a capital gain from the sale of stock in DeBeers, the South African diamond consortium. Hillary's determination to oppose apartheid and support the African National Congress apparently did not extend to her portfolio.[33]

Hillary also made a killing in cellular telephone franchises. In 1984, she joined seventeen other investors, a Who's Who of Little Rock business leaders and lawyers, in a scheme run by adman and future White House aide—and whipping boy—David Watkins.

Hillary bought a 1.15 percent share for $2,014. Of course, the investors never intended to build a local cellphone network. Instead, they sold the license to McCaw Cellular Communications, Inc., four years later.[34] In this one deal, for simply having the right friends, Hillary made $45,998. Of course, her friends could do even better. The return on the cellphone franchise pales in comparison to the biggest, sweetest deal of all time—in the form of cattle futures.

CATTLE QUEEN OF ARKANSAS

"The market was going up dramatically at that time," Vice President Al Gore said in loyal defense of the Clintons when Hillary's neat little cattle futures profit came to light. "That time" was October 11, 1979, three weeks before Bill Clinton was elected governor of Arkansas. Ten months later, Hillary Rodham Clinton and Governor Clinton made $100,000 in profit on a $1,000 investment. Eat your heart out Bill Gates.

When the story broke of how lawyer and commodities trader Jim Blair helped Hillary Rodham make a fortune in cattle futures, the first response of the White House was to react with feigned indignance.

"Hillary and Jim were friends; he gave her advice," said aide John Podesta, later to become White House chief of staff. "There was no impropriety. The only appearance is being created by the *New York Times*." Consider the chutzpah of that defense. The mean old *New York Times* making up nasty things about Hillary Clinton.

"Do they have to go weed their friends out and say they can only have friends who are sweeping the streets? "Podesta asked rhetorically, without a hint of the embarassment he must have felt in making such an absurd statement." They have friends who are high-powered lawyers. They have friends who write books, who write poetry."[35]

In other words, what should we expect among members of the meritocracy? How unfair to deny the Clintons the friendship of poets and commodities traders.

Jim Blair was certainly no street sweeper. He had made millions of dollars himself trading in commodities. The White House could only defend Hillary by adopting an Arkansas perspective on the whole deal. In the end what did it matter if Blair helped a friend make a little of her own?

The story intensified in April 1994, when the first couple was forced to pay an additional $14,615 in back taxes and interest after it was learned that the first lady had made more money on commodity trades than had been revealed to the public or to the IRS.[36]

After trying to hold back the details of the deal, the White House released the facts one by one.

At first, we were told that Hillary "consulted with numerous people, and did her own research," an aide to the first lady explained.[37] The American people were left with the image of Hillary, shrewd investor, thumbing through the *Wall Street Journal*.

Then the White House acknowledged that she had indeed received a small helping of advice, "but not on a specific date or specific trade."

The White House next conceded that Jim Blair—Springdale lawyer, former Fulbright aide, major figure in the Arkansas Democratic party, and the man Bill Clinton later married to Diane Kincaid—was one of several people who had given Hillary some advice in dealing with the market. When that story would no longer hold, Dee Dee Myers—always one of the most forthright, and therefore routinely humiliated, members of the Clinton team—said, bluntly, "I think it's become clear that [James Blair] placed most of the trades."[38] But surely he had been guided by the *Wall Street Journal*.

Blair, of course, also worked for Tyson Foods, the poultry

giant and largest employer in Arkansas, and a major Clinton donor. He bought land and made deals on behalf of the corporate giant. He would later become the company's general counsel.

The company is run by "Big Daddy" Don Tyson—a man who wears a khaki uniform, which is required of all employees, with his name stitched on its breast; a political kingpin; a wheeler-dealer and corporate egoist. In keeping with his oversized persona, and perhaps the helping hand his general counsel gave to the president-to-be, Tyson's office is a replica of the Oval Office.

"It would be irresponsible to my company and my industry if I didn't have any influence," Tyson said in a speech in Alabama. "Clinton understands the needs of business. There were several times in our company's growth that we could have taken opportunities outside of the state, but we chose to stay in Arkansas because he understands the balance between economic development and environmental issues."[39]

Hillary's cattle futures were purchased through Robert L. "Red" Bone of the brokerage firm of Refco, Inc. It was Jim Blair who had put her in touch with Bone—who had previously worked for Tyson for more than a decade. Bone was an inveterate gambler, a high-profile, high-stakes poker player well known to the pit bosses of Las Vegas. He was a gambler at the office as well. The year before, Bone's sharp practices had led the Chicago Mercantile Exchange to accuse him of allocating trades to investors *after* determining the winners and losers, a practice known as "straddling." Bone was punished by having his license to trade pulled for one year.[40]

The deal was arranged in the following way. All Hillary had to do was put $1,000 of her own money into a block of cattle futures at a time when her husband, then the attorney general, had a thirty point lead for the governorship.

How did Hillary make out?

From her initial investment of $1,000, she came away with $99,537. Among the community of experts, there is general agreement that between 75 percent and 90 percent of commodity players lose. And no one turns $1,000 into $100,000. "The average retail customer has about as much chance of that kind of success as I have of driving to Hawaii," one Chicago-based investment advisor noted.[41]

At one point in the trading, Hillary was $60,000 in the hole, with less than $40,000 in her account. Typically, an investor would be asked to pay the margin. Hillary was not, and she held on to the commodities until she hit pay dirt. (Later, the White House would explain that she quit at that point because she was pregnant with Chelsea, and just did not need the additional stress of investing.)

On July 12, 1979, Hillary's relationship with Refco remained intact even though she owed more than $100,000; but poor Stanley Greenwood, a fellow Refco investor, had his investments terminated when he failed to post $50,000 to cover his losses.[42]

By way of comparison, had Hillary instead invested $1,000 in the first offering of Microsoft stock in 1986, she would have made $35,839 by March 1994. The premier technology investment of our times, therefore, pales in comparison to what she had made on the world's oldest commodity: livestock. Hillary's cattle future investment gave her a 9,987 percent profit.[43] Later, when asked of her incredible success as a novice in the tough world of commodities trading, Hillary denied any preferential treatment with the illuminating statement: "I was lucky."

Unless you believe in good fairies, luck had nothing to do with it. It is pretty obvious that Hillary had something better than luck. She had well-placed friends who wanted her to have $100,000. The likelihood of such a return on such an investment was close to lottery odds, twenty-four chances in a million.[44] This was in a decade in which no speculator made more than $400 profit a day with one contract of cattle futures. Yet Hillary managed to make $5,300 a day. Such a return would have required her holding thirteen contracts, involving 232 tons of beef with a value of $280,000.

The *New York Post* explained, "There is no way that the commodity exchange or a broker would permit a novice speculator to control $280,000 worth of cattle with a skimpy investment of $1,000. Not, that is, unless a friend, guardian or partner guaranteed her investment."[45]

It seems unlikely that Hillary could have been unaware of the magnitude of this straddle or that her wins were at the expense of others. (Blair himself was a designated loser, losing millions on the cattle deals.) Many commodities traders suspected Hillary of allocated trading—an illegal procedure in which a broker buys block trades, waits for the win, then allocates it to favored customers after the fact. Just a few months after Hillary's "lucky" day in commodities trading, Refco—specifically Hillary's broker Red Bone—was disciplined by the Chicago Mercantile Exchange Board for "serious and repeated violations of record-keeping functions, order-entry procedures, margin requirements and hedge procedures."

One person who has done well during the Clinton years is the man who provided the nexus between Red Bone, Jim Blair, and Bill Clinton. That man is Don Tyson. During the Clinton-era, Tyson's company benefited from millions of dol-

lars in state loans, tax breaks, and the relaxation of environmental regulations. He received $8 million in tax concessions
for plant and workforce concessions, as well as $900,000 in
state grant monies to build roads and upgrade sites for a $40
million processing plant in Pine Bluff.[46] What was especially
extraordinary was the kid glove treatment Tyson received
from a governor who at least affected a tough and uncompro-
mising stance on protecting the environment.

Before Clinton was elected, the state had reissued a
license for a Tyson plant with the proviso that the company
had to work out a plan with Green Forest city officials to treat
its wastes, tons of chicken feces that the plant dumped into
nearby Dry Creek. With Clinton in office, it soon became
clear that nothing would have to be done to clean up the plant
and save the river. Unfortunately, the runoff of chicken feces
ultimately filtered into the town drinking water, sickening
local residents and forcing Governor Clinton to declare the
locality a disaster area.[47]

Tyson was not only an overt financial contributor to the
Clintons. As reported by *Time* magazine in 1994, allegations
of envelopes of cash coming from Tyson's headquarters to the
Clintons in the governor's mansion had surfaced by
Independent Counsel Donald Smaltz. These allegations were
never pursued, however, because Smaltz's request to widen his
probe was shot down by Attorney General Janet Reno.

However murky the background, what is clear is that
Hillary and her husband did quite well during their personal
decade of greed. But one could not say that they were *entirely*
uncharitable. Journalist Lisa Schiffren learned that Hillary
donated to the less fortunate. Dozens of bags of old clothing
she, Chelsea, and Bill had worn were given to charity, and

Hillary valued these donations between $1,000 and $2,300 each year for tax deductions. She meticulously listed each item, and gave a value for them, including $10 for Bill's old running shoes and $1 for each pair of Bill's and Chelsea's old underwear.

THE LEADING MAN AND THE ROSE

A key figure in the Clinton rise to power was a childhood friend of Bill Clinton—and Hillary Rodham's Rose Law partner— Vince Foster. Before he had been old enough to go to school, Foster played cowboys and Indians with little Billy Blythe in Hope. Later Foster and Thomas "Mack" McLarty III—future president of Arkla (Arkansas Louisiana Gas Company) and White House chief of staff—attended "Miss Mary's kinder- garten," as Miss Marie's School for Little Folk was known around Hope, with Bill. Virginia soon moved Bill off to Hot Springs, and the two lost track of each other.

It was Hillary, not Bill, who drew Vince Foster into the Clinton orbit. Hillary and Vince Foster developed a long- standing relationship, complex, intellectual, touched with sparks of romance and intrigue, that would ultimately prove fatal to one of them, and devastating to the other.[48]

In the fall of 1976, Foster, handsome and dignified, a graduate of Vanderbilt Law School, chaired the Arkansas Bar Association's meeting on legal aid clinics in Northwest Arkansas, where he heard the impassioned testimony of Hillary Rodham.

Over the course of these Fayetteville meetings that went on and off for several weeks, a deep connection was estab- lished. Foster came back from Fayetteville singing the praises of the young law professor, arguing that it was time for Rose to open its door to women and determined that that woman should be Hillary Rodham.[49] This was a big break for a brash, Yankee lawyer who was so new to Arkansas—a woman who once outraged Arkansans by sitting next to her husband at a Razorback game—engrossed in a book. When Foster, with some help from Hubbell, brought Hillary on as an associate, it was a move viewed with decidedly mixed sentiments at Rose.

Bill Clinton was well known and intensely disliked by at least one partner. Some partners were Republicans who did not like the growing identification of Rose with Arkansas's one-party state. All shared some apprehension about possible conflicts of interest that could be generated by making the attorney general's wife an associate. In many states, this would have been an impediment fatal to Hillary's career. In Arkansas, the attorney general handles criminal cases and acts as a consumer advocate in rate cases before the Public Service Commission.[50] But because Rose was a civil firm that did no utility business, there were no immediate conflicts. Foster and Webb Hubbell pressed the case for Hillary hard so that no partner would stand in their way. The offer was extended.

Concerns about conflicts of interest intensified, however, after she was hired, and it became clear that Bill Clinton was moving further and faster than many expected—becoming the "boy governor" in 1978. By then, however, Hillary was entrenched, and there was little that could be done. One of the governor's responsibilities was allocating state bond work to law firms. Now, some of the partners saw Hillary as a potential ticket to increased fees.

If greed kept her in her job, fear almost lost it for her, after her husband was defeated in the 1980 gubernatorial election by Frank White, a Republican. Webb Hubbell was asked to persuade Hillary to resign if her husband's defeat cost the firm business, or to make up any potential loss in the state bond business by billing more hours and attracting other clients. Hillary was not the resigning type.

The partners at Rose had been disturbed by something else about Hillary. Her office attire of casual clothes, her utter lack of concern for cosmetics, and her frumpish appearance were not the look Rose Law Firm wanted to show its clients. She had a framed speech on the Equal Rights Amendment from the *Congressional Record* in her office, a political stance that made some wonder at the likely reaction of Rose's more conservative clients, not to mention partners.

For her part Hillary believed that sexism was pervasive at Rose. A secretary confided to Hillary that her boss, a partner, said she'd get a raise if she'd wear tight jeans more often.[51] Of course, Hillary's jeans were another matter. One day Hillary was caught by a senior partner wearing jeans to the office, a sight that threw him into a quiet fit.

But there were likely other reasons why Hillary was so controversial.

If the men were traditionalists, the women of Rose were downright catty.

"When Miss Rodham came, she gave me all this personal work," Carolyn Cruce, one former secretary assigned to Foster, told the *Tallahassee Democrat* in a 1993 interview. "She was very political even then."

One day, when Foster demanded to know why Cruce took so much time to process his work, Cruce told him of Hillary's demands. Foster immediately walked into Hillary's office and ordered her not to heap personal work on his secretary. Within a few moments, Rodham came out of her office and ripped into Cruce.[52] A former Rose Law Firm colleague told the *New Yorker* about Hillary's temper: "It's not so much that she screams—it's more the tone in her voice, the body language, the facial expressions. It's *The Wrath of Khan*."[53] Hillary gave Cruce the full *Wrath* treatment. By her account, Cruce responded coolly: "I just looked at her and said, 'Is this what the woman's movement is all about? So a few of you can get ahead and then lord it over the rest of us?'"[54]

The continued ascendence of the Clinton family ultimately took the Rose firm on a wild ride. Like so many others who found their fates intertwined with the Clintons, the Rose partners had an opportunity to rise to the very top, even opening a Washington office to take advantage of their solid Clinton connections. Ultimately, however, the Clinton touch dragged them back to the bottom, and the firm was forced to disband.

This was an ironic outcome, for until the 1970s, Rose advertised its character by staying in a drab, nondescript location at Third and State, the message being: In this colorful sea of crooks and characters called Little Rock, we are a bastion of low-key competence and integrity.

The history of Rose reads more like that of a distinguished liberal arts college than a law firm. The oldest law firm west of the Mississippi, Rose was older than Arkansas itself, founded in 1820 by Chester Ashley, a contemporary (and rival) of Stephen F. Austin.

The firm had been renamed for U.M. Rose, a delegate to the Hague Peace Conference, whose likeness stands in Statuary Hall in the U.S. Capitol.[55]

Rose was a hushed place, where young lawyers worked under the watchful gaze of oil portraits. Law degrees from the most prestigious universities were common and several of the older partners had been Rhodes scholars.

Until the early 1970s, Rose had succeeded in keeping itself small and discreet. There were ten partners and six associates. Its small size also allowed it to operate in a collegial, democratic manner, one in which the distinctions between partners and associates were glossed over. It took a majority vote to make a major decision. It took a unanimous vote to admit a new member.[56]

Given its aura of history and discretion, it was a mysterious place, almost sepulchral. In his memoirs, Webb Hubbell described Rose in poetic terms.

"It was as though that big glass-top table was the tip of some unfathomable iceberg, and as these men sat in their morning meetings in their fine suits and cufflinked shirts, their hands on that cool surface connected them to something very deep and broad and hidden," he wrote.[57] He added that any close connection to politics was frowned on.

But Arkansas began to change, and Rose to change with it.

The firm grew from sixteen lawyers to fifty-three. The partners moved out of their humble, but historic, office and into a renovated downtown YWCA, an elegant red brick building with hardwood floors and an indoor swimming pool.

Inside the walls of Rose, the older, mannered elders of the firm were entering their *emeritus* phase. Young bulls had entered the partnership, determined to remake the place in their own image.

Leading them was Joe Giroir, smooth, elegant, cultivated, and tough as nails. He soon became the firm's top rainmaker in the financial services division. In time, he established a separate compensation structure within Rose, one that rewarded those who worked with him on the extremely profitable bond deals. This, in turn, gave Giroir the power to eventually shove aside Rose tradition and egalitarian sensibility to have himself declared the first chairman in the law firm's history.[58]

It was Giroir who successfully lobbied the legislature to loosen the state's usury laws and restrictions on bank holding companies. Giroir soon became less of a lawyer and more of a financial tycoon, buying four banks and selling them to a holding company owned by one of the Stephens brothers from Stephens, Inc., the Arkansas banking family, and the billionaire Riady family of Indonesia, owners of the LippoBank of Los Angeles. Giroir, as deal-maker, pocketed tens of millions of dollars, as well as stock in the new holding company, Worthen.[59]

When Worthen (and by implication, the Riadys) became a major client of Rose, it did not take long for the money culture to invade the inner workings of the firm.

In time, Giroir would be on the outs with his partners. The Worthen deal went south on a bad loan, costing Giroir himself tens of millions of dollars. Giroir's Worthen partners accused him of taking illegal profits in a stock deal, forcing him off the Worthen board. It was only a matter of time before the Stephenses cut Rose loose as well.

Giroir was besieged from within. The dual system of rewards at Rose had destroyed the last vestiges of collegiality, sowing widespread resentment. A triumvirate of litigators, Foster-Hubbell-Rodham, forged an alliance with Giroir's lieutenant, William Kennedy III. When Kennedy—a future Rose chairman—agreed to betray his mentor, the ouster of Giroir was as good as done.

Webb Hubbell, Vince Foster, and Hillary Rodham became first among equals (under Kennedy), making more deals and cutting more corners than ever before. Of the three, Hillary was the least active at the firm. She was deeply involved in her East Coast causes, managing the perpetual Clinton campaign, and last (and perhaps least) raising Chelsea.

She was not so busy, however, as to be a minor player in the triumvirate. When the time came for Vince Foster to ask Joe Giroir to give up the title of chairman, it was Hillary who bucked Foster up for the task. When a shared secretary had to be fired, Vince left the job to Hillary.

She was equally tough in managing the few cases she had. The legacy of one such case was to dog her for years.

In 1980 Hillary represented one Barbara Joyce, who was planning to relocate to Missouri with her eight-year-old daughter. When Joyce's ex-husband, Larry Nichols, learned of this, Nichols threatened to seek a court order enjoining her from leaving the state.

"I called Hillary and talked to her about it," Joyce said in a sworn deposition in 1994. "And that's when she told me I should leave as soon as possible, which I did." Lisa Caputo, Hillary's press secretary, claimed that the first lady had no memory of the case.

Nichols had been a longtime FOB and had produced Clinton's political ads. Perhaps fearing what he would say in a national campaign, the Clinton machine moved in to discredit him. In 1988 Nichols was fired from his job as marketing director with the Arkansas Development Finance Authority for using state phones to make calls to Adolfo Calero and other friends in the Nicaragua Contra movement.

In January 1992, according to the tabloid the *Star*, Larry Nichols tried to achieve his revenge by alleging that while governor, Bill Clinton had used state funds to conduct adulterous affairs with five different women, including Gennifer Flowers. Led by the *Star*, Flowers became the focal point of media investigations of Clinton's background. It was this journalistic investigation that pushed the Clintons to confess on national television that there had been "pain" in their marriage in the celebrated *60 Minutes* interview that saved their presidential campaign from its first big "bimbo eruption."

THE PROTECTORS

In her Arkansas years, Hillary drew strength from her friendship with the two mentors who fast became her protectors, Webb Hubbell and Vince Foster. Webb Hubbell had been a young man on a break from his Arkansas bar exam when he first met Bill Clinton and Hillary Rodham.

He claims to have been momentarily spellbound by Clinton's hold on a small group of admirers. He describes his most unusual first impression of Hillary: "Under the wild hair and behind the glasses, there was something oddly attractive about her. She was quiet, and there was a power in that. At one point she reached over and gently tugged at Bill's sleeve. She didn't look up, didn't implore, she simply tugged at his sleeve as if to say, 'Okay, time to stop talking and start studying.' In a minute or so, he did just that."[60]

Later, a friend explained to Hubbell that Bill Clinton was a Rhodes scholar and Yale law graduate. When he asked who Hillary was, his friend laughed, and said, "The rumor is, she's his brains."[61]

Long before the ouster of Giroir, the litigation team of

Hubbell, Foster, and Rodham had solidified into a fast friendship, one that would ultimately be dissolved by the death of
one and the imprisonment and disgrace of another. The three
held a regular lunch together, although in the formal environment of the South both Webb Hubbell and Vince Foster were
said to have had to get permission from their wives to be seen
in public with another woman. Even then, they went to their
lunches at a local greasy spoon, or at an intimate Italian
restaurant, usually arriving at one o'clock, after the capital's
early lunch hour, to minimize the gossip.[62]

Hillary also joined her two comrades at lingerie style
shows, ostensibly held so businessmen could select clothes for
their wives, in reality so the men could ogle the models.
Perhaps this was the beginning of Hubbell's mysterious
Victoria's Secret bills. Hillary proved to be a good sport, going
along if for no other reason than to make fun of "the
Neanderthals" she worked with.[63]

Vince Foster and Webb Hubbell had worked together for
twenty years, forming a brotherlike bond. But for all their
closeness, they were as different as two men could be. Webb
Hubbell, appointed mayor of Little Rock and then appointed
by Clinton to a brief term as chief justice on the Arkansas
Supreme Court, craved the respect and admiration of his fel-
lows no less than Bill Clinton. Now a felon convicted by
Kenneth Starr for padding his hours, stealing from Rose and
his clients, and cheating on his taxes, Webb Hubbell is
remembered in Washington as a disgraced former associate
attorney general. But in his prime, Webb Hubbell was a Little
Rock power player, a man who could, through his powerful
father-in-law Seth Ward, open doors to inside deals.

Vince Foster was a vision of the kind of man Hubbell

wished to be. Women noticed Foster. The women on the
White House staff later voted Vince Foster the man they
would most like to have an affair with.[64] Tall and handsome,
his graying hair and austere manner were offset by a crinkly
smile and sly twinkle about the eye. Foster was the soul of discretion, a charismatic introvert who could keep a secret and be
trusted to carry out critical assignments.

Hubbell projected power through a kind of gregarious,
back-slapping amiability. Foster attracted power through
gravitas, his personal code of silence and decorum. (Hillary
jokingly called him "Vincenzo Fosterini," and he did, in fact,
have something of the aura of the classic peacetime con-
sigliere from *The Godfather*.)

Lisa Foster was as outgoing as her husband was silent, a
voluble woman dedicated to her Catholic faith and more than
a little jealous of her husband's close relationship with Hillary
Rodham.

When Hillary came to Arkansas, drinking cronies of the
Stephens brothers spread the rumor that Hillary was a lesbian.
Now another inevitable rumor circulated, that Hillary and
Vince spent entirely too much time together, that he had a
mysterious way of appearing at her doorstep whenever the
governor was out of town, and that she noticeably brightened
when Vince came into the room.

If so, who could blame her? Bill Clinton, though scared
off from heavy drinking by the alcoholism of his stepfather,
had become a nightlife afficionado just like his mother, a fix-
ture of cabarets, honky-tonks, and holes-in-the-wall from
Texarkana to the Missouri line. His affairs were the stuff of
legend. Rare was the person who had not seen or heard a first-
hand account of the governor living it up, surrounded by a

bevy of beauties, a girl from a state agency, a former beauty
queen, a new television news reporter, or a cabaret singer
named Gennifer Flowers.

If Hillary had her fling, people asked, who would blame
her? Barbara Walters would later ask Hillary point blank if she
and Vince were lovers.

"I miss him very much. And I just wish he could be left in
peace, because he was a wonderful man to everyone who knew
him."[65] The artful dodge was truly a Clinton trademark; as in
other instances it spoke volumes.

L.D. Brown, then a state trooper serving the Clintons, speaks
openly of having become a kind of alter ego for Bill, often
arranging trysts for the young governor and himself.

He remembers the Fosters and the Clintons going with a
third couple to a Chinese restaurant operated by Charlie Yah
Lin Trie, now a key figure in the scandal concerning Chinese
political donations to the Democratic Party.

"Bill, Hillary, and I had met at a residence near the restaurant where everyone converged for the night out. It would be
a night that would demonstrate just how the understanding
worked. It would also serve to confirm in no uncertain terms
who Hillary's significant other was." Later that evening,
Brown says, "Vince and Hillary [looked] like they were in the
back seat of a '57 Chevy at a drive-in. Hillary was kissing
Vince like I've never seen her kiss Bill, and the same sort of
thing was going on with Bill" and the wife of the third couple.
"Vince, good looking, tall and suave obviously knew what he
was doing, but Hillary looked awkward and unbalanced."[66]
Excited by this taste of the forbidden, Brown says the
Clintons parted from their friends and made love in the back
of their limo while he drove them home.

L.D. Brown's falling out with the Clintons would later lead to titillating stories of the governor living a frat-boy quest of easy sex, using his troopers as retrievers. It was one such escapade—one that did not involve L.D. Brown—that led to the recruitment by another trooper of a low-level state employee, Paula Jones. It was an encounter that went badly for Bill, and felled a legal domino that caused a train of disasters leading to his impeachment as president.

While Bill Clinton may have the most documented sex life in human history, Hillary's personal life is more opaque.

Whether sex was or was not part of the equation is less relevant than what Hillary shared with Vince over the years. Whether or not the story from Charlie Trie's restaurant is true, the Foster-Rodham relationship was surely less carnal than any of a thousand little interludes initiated by Bill. It was not a tryst, but a confidence between people who felt shut out from being themselves by marriage, by the need to make money, and by circumstances.

In many ways, it was a typical small-town romance, the kind that develops when two people become utterly sick of living in full view of their neighbors. It was a touching side to both of their lives, but one doomed by the dynamics of Washington. In time, Hillary would become FLOTUS—the First Lady of the United States—and Vincent would become her knight-protector as deputy White House counsel.

The terms of their relationship changed. In Washington, Lancelot would not only be under constant attack from without, he would also face stinging criticism from within, often from Guinevere herself. Of all the people in the Clinton circle, Foster was perhaps the most idealistic, a man with a deep sense of obligation to his friends, a low threshold for public embarrassment, and a brittle ego. He was a good man poorly suited to the challenge of being a defender of the Clintons.

WHITEWATER

Saul Alinsky wrote of the bishop who "bootlicks and politicks his way up, justifying it with the rationale, 'After I get to be bishop I'll use my office for Christian reformation,' or the businessman who reasons, 'First, I'll make my million and after that I'll go for the real things in life.' Unfortunately one changes in many ways on the road to the bishopric or the first million...."[67]

In the 1992 presidential election, it was former California Governor Jerry Brown who was independent enough, and indiscreet enough, to identify publicly the extent to which upward mobility had changed Hillary Rodham Clinton. He condemned the business practices of Bill Clinton's wife in a debate just before the Illinois and Michigan primaries. "You ought to be ashamed of yourself for jumping on my wife," Clinton shouted back. Clinton won applause for standing up for his wife in a way that Michael Dukakis had failed to do for Kitty. He also made Brown look like a cad. In fact, Brown had performed a public service few in the press, or even the Republican opposition, were willing to do.[68]

THE DEAL

The tangle of deals, blunders, and mutual backscratching called Whitewater would not be understandable without reference to its mastermind Jim McDougal. He is now remembered by most people as he appeared in his last days, when McDougal was rail thin from disease, with a bald Lex Luther dome and a dandyish preference for ice cream–white suits and watch fobs.

In his prime, McDougal was a man to be reckoned with. In a small state like Arkansas, any number of talented and ambitious men can reasonably imagine themselves getting elected to office, perhaps to the highest office in the state, perhaps the land.

There is little doubt that McDougal, who came to know Bill Clinton as a junior campaign volunteer for Senator Fulbright in 1968, shared the younger man's vision of himself as a man destined for greatness. At age twenty, he had been a leader of John F. Kennedy's presidential campaign in Arkansas. He had served on the staffs of two southern giants, Senators J. William Fulbright and John McClellan, and had become an important behind-the-scenes player in Arkansas politics.

McDougal revered FDR, quoted him often, and sprinkled his observations with the great man's witticisms, his quips about Republicans and the president's dog, Fala. He combined a quick mind and a flamboyant temperament with a sense of humor right off the porch of a general store. A recovering alcoholic, McDougal had the personality of a country trial lawyer or a politician.

Politics, however, did not pan out for him. Business was his metier.

Once he reconciled himself to that reality, he devoted his considerable skills of persuasion to making a fortune the Arkansas way: wheeling, dealing, and back scratching. Early in his business career, McDougal had lured Fulbright himself into a partnership in a real estate deal. In the end, practicing business in Arkansas was just another form of politics.

Jim McDougal first met his future wife Susan while teaching a political science class in a small college in Arkadelphia.

She was the classic southern type, the stylistic opposite of Hillary. Posing in a television ad, Susan showed off a good figure with a bust that pressed tight against her shirt, wide girlish hips poured into tight shorts, long flowing black hair, and big luscious eyes. She possessed a demure but coquettish look, an attractive and sexy facade, over a steely ambitious interior.

The McDougals were small-town versions of their more powerful friends, the Clintons. The McDougals had access to money, something Bill and Hillary wanted very much. The Clintons had growing access to power—the ability to ease restrictions, cause a regulator to wink, or keep a sticky matter at the bottom of a state auditor's pile—which would be helpful to the McDougals.

That is how things are done in Arkansas, so it was completely natural that before he became governor, Bill and his wife would meet the McDougals over dinner at the Black-Eyed Pea and decide to do a little land deal together.

McDougal had considerable credibility then as a developer with a green thumb. Bill and Hillary had already made a tidy profit from a previous deal that had included Senator Fulbright. McDougal's description of his new land development as a kind of Ozark Valhalla for the retired set struck a chord in the young politician's acquisitive wife. "Let me tell you this about Bill Clinton," McDougal later said. "If you ever tried to discuss finances or anything but politics with Bill, his eyes would glaze over.... Whatever we had to discuss, I discussed it with Hillary."[69]

Big dreams were shared among the foursome. They would even set aside plots of their own, a place for the Clintons to go for weekends, perhaps a place to retire when

Chelsea was gone to college. McDougal solemnly promised Hillary that there would, in fact, be enough money to send Chelsea to college in style.

The land deal was, of course, White Water Estates. It was 1978 and Bill Clinton was already attorney general. Hillary was just beginning to cash in on various deals. Bill was making only $6,000 a year. But McDougal had plans for how Clinton could help him. So, despite the Clinton's meager finances, McDougal gave them sufficient assurances—and incentives—to get the Clintons to sign up. The Clintons put up no money, co-signing a mortgage note with the Citizen's Bank of Flippen that held them liable for a mortgage of about $200,000.

The plan was simple. Retirees were discovering the Ozarks. A gentle rise overlooking the confluence of the White River and Crooked Creek would be an ideal spot for affluent retirees to live. And, of course, this being Arkansas, many wealthy friends and contributors in Little Rock or Springdale could buy into the property, whether they intended to retire there or not. Having Bill Clinton's name on the deal was a great way to secure the loan for such a bold investment, and a good way to attract customers.

But the devil jumped into the details. Interest rates soared to their highest level since the Civil War. Money was tight during the last Carter years, and southern land values plummeted during the Reagan years. It soon became painfully clear that Whitewater was destined to be largely undeveloped, and what little of it would be developed would become a shabby trailer park.

McDougal, being a man of immense pride, could not bring himself to tell his friend, now the governor, that their real estate had turned into dirt. He depended on Bill for many things. He had even served for a spell as an advisor on "economic development." At the very least, he was supposed to be developing the Clinton family economy, and he was failing at that job.[70]

Perhaps to keep his early venture afloat, Jim McDougal went into a far more lucrative business, the savings and loan (S&L) industry. He bought a rural S&L and dubbed it Madison Guaranty. The practices during these heady days of Charles Keating were loose: money could be stashed in anything or anywhere, or given to anyone for any reason. The magnitude of the malfeasance by the S&L sector would not be apparent until the failure of institutions across the South and West threatened the liquidity of the entire United States banking system.[71]

McDougal supercharged Madison, raising its deposits from $6 million to $123 million within three years.

By 1984 Madison was warned by federal regulators to tighten its practices, strengthen its management, and add $3 million to its capital base. McDougal did strengthen management—by hiring the federal regulator as Madison's vice president.[72]

Still, McDougal found himself in an increasingly tight spot. Like all managers of a pyramid scheme, he convinced himself that if he could just get a reprieve, everything would balance out in the end. A momentary break came in January 1985, when Governor Clinton replaced the state securities commissioner with Fayetteville friend and longtime supporter Beverly Bassett. As a lawyer for a Little Rock firm, she had done work in the past for Madison. In March the governor squared the circle by appointing Madison's chief executive officer to the state S&L board.

In April, Hillary became the official representative of Madison before the state securities commission. By now, the Clintons had managed to create a parade of friendly faces all along the way for their business partners. Six days later, Hillary contacted Bassett on behalf of Madison.

Around this time, McDougal wrote an overdraft in the form of $30,000 from a Whitewater account at Madison. Then he raised a like amount of money—$35,000—to "retire the deficit," as the young governor put it. The deficit in this case was a $50,000 loan Clinton had taken out from the Bank of Cherry Valley to buy a battery of television ads to fend off a challenge in the 1984 election. McDougal generously held a fund-raiser in the Art Deco lobby of Madison Guaranty.

McDougal later paid himself a similar amount as a "bonus" from Madison. Given the spotty records from the fund-raiser, and conflicting accounts (Fulbright's signature was on one check, but he said he never attended), it is likely that McDougal simply made most of Clinton's contributions himself, repaying his overdrawn account from the Madison coffers.[73] This was one of several enormous favors, saving the governor from having to pay the Cherry Valley loan he had personally guaranteed.

In May, Bassett informed Madison's attorney in a "Dear Hillary" letter that the legal opinion she had written on a McDougal proposal to recapitalize Madison by issuing preferred stock was acceptable. The recapitalization plan, selling stock that was essentially worthless, was approved. McDougal was cleared to add another layer to his pyramid.

Another part of this tangle of needs and interests was Hillary's need not just for money, but to show her Rose partners that she could bring in clients. In one 1993 account to the

Los Angeles Times, McDougal said the governor jogged by his
office one humid morning in August 1984 and asked
McDougal to send business to Hillary. This story rings true,
complete with a novelistic detail about a quietly seething
McDougal listening while the governor's sweat-stained thighs
ruined an expensive leather chair. By another account, Hillary
came to the McDougals in April 1985 and asked for their
business. It is likely that Hillary had sent Bill. When he did
not succeed, she made the appeal herself. "One lawyer's as
good as another," McDougal concluded, and started paying
Hillary and Rose $2,000 a month.

By 1986 the fact that Madison was a house of cards could
no longer be disguised. Federal regulators acted to remove
McDougal. Madison ultimately collapsed, costing U.S. taxpayers $60 million.

Given such a record, one would think that Madison and
related work would have been considered radioactive by
Hillary and her partners. In fact, Vince Foster solicited business from the Federal Deposit Insurance Corporation (FDIC)
for S&L work, including Madison. The work was only
secured after Foster (or perhaps someone close to him) wrote
a letter denying conflicts of interest to the FDIC. "The firm
does not represent any savings-and-loan association in state or
federal regulatory matters," it said. Unstated was the fact that
the firm had had such representations in the recent past.

In this way, Hubbell would earn $400,000 for Rose, lead-
ing the FDIC to sue Madison accountants. When they
learned of the deception, federal regulators were astonished
and outraged.[74] They had been duped by a simple semantic
trick, like Bill Clinton's later denial of a sexual relationship
with a White House intern on the ground that the affair was

no longer ongoing ("it depends on what the meaning of 'is' is").

Whitewater is often presented as an impenetrable morass. In truth, it is quite simple. Hillary's law career had been helped by McDougal's business, and Clinton had been personally rescued by McDougal's willingness to pay down a Clinton political debt. Once Hillary became Madison's lawyer, she helped obtain approval of McDougal's own rescue plan—a recapitalization based on stock sales that were but another layer of McDougal's pyramid scheme. She represented McDougal before a state regulator who had, herself, done legal work for him. The only way the arrangement could have been tighter would have been for all participants to have been cousins.

The great irony is that much of the subsequent scandal and embarrassment over Whitewater could have been avoided if Hillary had accepted a generous offer from McDougal in 1985. By then it had become clear to all that Whitewater was a failure. The Clintons, along with their partners, were liable for tens of thousands of dollars in interest payments on the original loan. And the inability of the development to pay property taxes had created a potential embarrassment for the governor. The Clintons seethed over a newspaper listing of their names as citizens who were delinquent on their taxes.

McDougal, however, gallantly offered to assume all remaining obligations and pay all taxes if the Clintons would sign over to him their half of the investment. The governor recognized a good deal when he saw it. McDougal was offering to take a small fortune in debt in return for a piece of paper.

Such generosity was not understandable to Hillary. It trig-

gered her greed, and then suspicions—then made her angry.
After all, she was still counting on the proceeds from the
Whitewater deal. According to James B. Stewart's account in
Blood Sport, Hillary shouted, "Jim told me that this was going
to pay for college for Chelsea. I still expect it to do that!"[75] In
another account told to *Time*, Susan McDougal recalled
Hillary's saying, "We own half of it, and we are not getting out
of it. It's incredible that partners would be asked to sign over
their stock."

"This is Jim McDougal's project, his idea, his money!
Don't you understand that I don't want anything," Susan
pleaded. "It's all going to Jim. It's morally wrong for you not
to give it to him." Susan broke down. "You're terrible people,
after all he would and did do for you, that you wouldn't do
this."

Hillary told Susan she would not be "blackmailed."[76]

THE W FILES

Hillary would also do everything she could to avoid being
called to account when Whitewater became the subject of a
Congressional investigation. Shortly after the Whitewater
investigations had begun, two college students were hired to
shred piles of materials from the Rose Law office of Vince
Foster. Foster—then six months in his grave—had been in
charge of the Clintons's personal legal affairs once they moved
into the White House. His files could not conceivably have
been shredded without the Clintons' consent.[77] Investigators
cannot prove, but do not have any doubts, about who ultimately ordered the shredding of those files.

Then there were Hillary's own papers. In the move from
Little Rock to Washington, Hillary took great care that her
papers were personally guarded by someone she trusted.

This collection of files had started as part of the "Betsey files," part of the vast compendium of private intelligence and personal papers held by Governor Clinton's chief of staff, Betsey Wright. For a while, Webb Hubbell kept them for safekeeping in the basement of his house. Later they would be transferred to private attorney David Kendall.

Some papers, whether from the Betsey files or somewhere else, years after they had been subpoened, made a mysterious appearance in the White House in January 1996. Carolyn Huber, who had worked as a clerk for Hillary at Rose, and then came to Washington with her to handle correspondence, suddenly discovered the records in a White House residence "book room."

I deposed Huber during congressional investigations into the White House Travel Office firings. Huber testified that in the course of transferring correspondence between her office and the first lady's, Huber took a stack of papers from the third-floor living quarters of the White House, just off from Hillary's office,[78] and returned them to her East Wing office. Huber didn't look at them again until several weeks later. What she saw forced her to call Hillary's lawyer, then her own lawyer.[79] They were Hillary's itemized legal work for Madison Guaranty, under subpoena for several years, the existence of which had been repeatedly denied by the White House.

Hillary had told investigators that she had ordered all Whitewater records and Madison records shredded in the mid-eighties. This had been done "to save money by reducing the number of closed, stored files," Hillary had written to Whitewater investigators.[80]

Now, like the ghost of Christmas past, these records had reappeared, almost at the foot of her bed, to accuse her.

Moreover, Huber said she was certain the papers had been placed there recently—which suggested that Hillary had been reviewing the papers all the while she had been denying their existence.

Hillary told investigators that she had done virtually no legal work on the Madison account. Now the billing records showed that she had performed sixty billable hours for Madison with state regulators. She had discussed legal matters with Madison executives on sixteen occasions, holding twenty-eight conferences or phone calls with Rose lawyers on Madison accounts. Also included in the billing records were details of her involvement with Castle Grande, a failed development that wound up costing taxpayers $4 million.

Castle Grande had been structured in such a way as to encourage low-income customers to buy swamp land with Madison loans, with no cash down. Most buyers would eventually have to default, something all participants were in a position to foresee. These defaults, in turn, would take almost $4 million from the taxpayers who were the ultimate guarantors of the S&L. Hillary played a role in Castle Grande, arranging a complicated payoff deal to Webb Hubbell's obstreperous father-in-law, Seth Ward.

"I don't believe I knew anything about [Castle Grande]," Hillary said in 1994 to federal investigators from the Resolution Trust Corporation. Now her own billing records showed that she had done thirty hours of legal work on that very development.

Harold Ickes, tough New York lawyer and iron-fisted warrior for the Clintons, sought to get the word to Arkansas securities commissioner and FOB Beverly Bassett Schaffer to stay on the same page as the White House. "If we fuck this up, we're done," he said.[81]

Hillary had sworn that she had done no work on Castle Grande. When presented with irrefutable evidence, she said that she had known the project under a different name, IDC. She was refuted again when David Hale, a municipal judge who had loaned $300,000 to Susan McDougal, swore that he had spoken to Hillary about Castle Grande.

The burst of revelations left the White House reeling, the staff anxious to learn from the Clintons what land mines were on the path ahead. But the Clintons told their own defenders as little as necessary, leaving the White House staff on the defensive. The White House spin strategy quickly became to dismiss as "old, recycled, rehashed news" on a "failed land deal" all the new exposés of Hillary's denials. The records, even with Hillary's fingerprints on them, ultimately proved nothing, the spin doctors said. David Hale was a felon and a proven liar. It was his word against the first lady's.

"Perjury takes intent," said White House spokesman George Stephanopoulos. "Simply describing plots of land by a different name when both names were in common usage is not perjury by any stretch."[82]

The idea of sending a first lady to prison on obstruction of justice charges was so distasteful that it proved the final defense against federal investigators.

The matter was dropped. Hillary won the day, and the story of the mysterious records became a part of White House lore.

HILLARY'S SECRET POLICE

In the tangle of Arkansas business and political interests, if one pulls at a thread, even the unlikeliest string, it can unravel much of the whole ball. One of these threads is Larry Nichols, the father slighted by Hillary in a child custody case. Nichols is often characterized as disgruntled, an understatement akin to saying that Brutus was disaffected from Caesar. Like so many other Clinton critics, his claims were undermined by a scandal of his own—the more than six hundred "contra calls" he made on a state line. Even in his disgrace, however, there is something to learn about the power of the Clinton machine and what ex-Clinton confidant Dick Morris calls its "secret police."

What is remarkable is not that Clinton accusers themselves have feet of clay. It is that they are so swiftly exposed and attacked the moment they speak out against Bill or Hillary Clinton. In this respect, the fate of Nichols greatly resembled that of Steve Clark, who followed Clinton into office as attorney general and attempted to follow him as governor. Clark, tired of waiting for Clinton to leave office, prepared to challenge Clinton's hold on the governor's mansion, charging that members of the Arkansas Development Finance Authority (ADFA) were being offered six-figure bribes. His accusations threatened to throw a spotlight on a sweetheart deal many in the capital preferred to only whisper about— how William Kennedy III at Rose had brokered an ADFA deal in which this public entity financed the sale by Stephens, Inc., of thirty-two nursing homes with an $81 million tax-exempt bond.

Clark alleged that the nursing home chain had been sold for an inflated price, which resulted in higher costs eventually being passed on to aged residents.[83] Not long after launching his attack, Clark himself came under assault. It was revealed that he had made personal charges on his state charge card, a scandal that led to his arrest and disgrace.

This is a now familiar pattern for Bill and Hillary Clinton.

As president, when facing a trial in the Senate on impeachment charges, Clinton's accusers in Congress saw the full force of the Clinton counter-assault. Sexual secrets were revealed by a troika of private detectives, disseminated by professional smear artists (like Sidney Blumenthal), and paid for by pornographers (like Larry Flynt). The strategy has been replayed over and over—Nixon's "enemies list" strategy played at a thermonuclear level, with no holds barred: Take on the Clintons, and you're in for a world of hurt.

In the case of Nichols, despite his damaged credibility, he did reveal unpleasant truths about the governor and his relationship to the ADFA.

The ADFA was conceived as an agent of regional industrial policy. Using the pension money of state workers, it was intended to act as a development bank to bring businesses and jobs to Arkansas.

About a tenth of the fund was to be invested in the state, and this being Arkansas, it was often invested in dubious ways. Nichols's lawsuit alleged the governor used ADFA as way to launder money to bond kingpin—and convicted cocaine dealer and Clinton supporter—Dan Lasater and other high-rollers, as well as a personal slush fund to pay for fun-time pursuits with women, including Gennifer Flowers.

The money-laundering charge was potentially fatal to Clinton. Lasater, who had made a fortune selling the Ponderosa steak house chain, was a one-man emblem of the excesses of the 1970s. Fast horses, fast women, and fast times were his hallmarks.

He won the admiration of Virginia Kelley, Bill's mother, for his thoroughbred races in Hot Springs. Not yet thirty, Lasater would back the right horse in the political arena as well.

THE COCAINE CARTEL

The relationship between Bill Clinton and Dan Lasater began in earnest when Clinton was out of office and down on his luck. Losing to Republican Frank White in 1980, Bill visited Lasater at his Quapaw Towers apartment and forged a relationship that he would use to partially offset the indifference and outright opposition of the Stephenses (they had little use at the time for the boy governor and had supported White in his bid to oust him).

Bill had to have known that Lasater was a dealer of drugs as well as bonds. The very apartment he visited was widely known as the e-ticket to euphoria, the scene of legendary parties that rivaled the groupie rock scene for its outrageousness, with ashtrays brimming with cocaine, and young women and high school girls offering themselves as party favors. Lasater's private jet, which he had used to fly the Clintons to the Kentucky Derby, was another Arkansas legend, truly a place to get high in the sky. If Bill had not heard about this from the Little Rock rumor circuit—which alone is hard to believe—all he had to do was to ask his half-brother.

Roger Clinton had grown up, haunted by his late father's legacy of booze and wife beating, yet doomed by genetics to repeat some of his father's ways for at least part of his life. A poor student, Roger was moody and wild, a braggart who was not shy about telling near-strangers about how he could use his brother's connections.

By the 1980s, Roger was in the grips of a heavy addiction to cocaine. By his own account, Roger coked up many times in the bathrooms of the governor's mansion, and even threw coke parties for his friends in the mansion during Hillary's absences. Presumably the governor knew nothing of these

parties, or if he did, maintained an uncharacteristic stoic ability to stay away from a good time. (Roger had been caught on
tape by a Hot Springs narcotics officer. After snorting coke
for a buy, he said, "I've got to get some for my brother, he's
got a nose like a Hoover vacuum cleaner!")[84]

It was only natural that Bill would ask his friend and ally
Lasater to look after his little brother. Roger had worked for
Lasater as a driver and at a horse farm. But that was just his
day job. His work for Lasater likely had more to do with
"mules" than horses, assisting with his drug connections
between Little Rock and New York. (Roger carted cocaine to
the East Coast on at least one trip with his brother.)

In a sense, Bill had offloaded the role of big brother and
protector to Lasater. One day a terrified Roger Clinton came
to Lasater saying that drug dealers to whom he owed money
were threatening his life as well as threatening to kill his
mother and brother. Lasater settled $8,000 of Roger's $20,000
drug debt and sent him to work at a stable in Florida where he
could hide out. In short, there was a two-way street between
Lasater and the governor, and it was becoming a major Little
Rock thoroughfare. Lasater furnished Clinton with a list of
possible appointees to the Arkansas Housing Development
Authority, which chose underwriters for the state bond business. Between 1983 and 1986, Lasater's company was involved
in $637 million worth of state bond offerings.[85]

Bill knew that Lasater was under investigation for distrib-
ution of cocaine. After all, Lasater had been named in court
testimony as a target of a police sting operation. Nevertheless,
Clinton awarded a contract to handle a $30 million bond issue
to Lasater to upgrade the Arkansas state police radio network. Aside from the obvious irony of buying police radios

with laundered drug money, the deal was doubly unusual. Bonds are usually issued for major infrastructural projects, for schools or highways, not for police equipment. And it was rare, even in Little Rock, for a governor to personally lobby the legislature to steer a bond deal to a specified firm. Clinton's largesse allowed Lasater to rake in three-quarters of a million dollars in underwriting fees on that one deal alone.

Tommy Goodwin, lieutenant colonel in the state police, would later tell the Senate Whitewater committee how Clinton had come to him asking about the progress of the drug investigation against Lasater. The committee reported: "Colonel Goodwin agreed that Governor Clinton's focus was not on Lasater's use of cocaine [which Clinton knew of]; rather it was directed toward determining whether he was going to be arrested for such use while his company was handling the police radio transaction."

Not long after Lasater collected the take on the police radio deal, he was sentenced to prison. So was Clinton's stepbrother.

Clinton himself would earn public esteem by seeming to sign off on the very sting operation that sent his brother to prison. The truth is, he was alerted to the sting by the state police and acted as the sting's apparent supporter in order to close off an investigation that could have led to the governor's mansion.

Bill and Hillary saw to it that Roger was well taken care of. His lawyer was William R. Wilson, a criminal defense attorney with whom Hillary had worked on several cases and who would later be appointed to a federal judgeship by Clinton. In the 1984 trial, Wilson put on a masterful defense of Roger Clinton that resulted in a remarkably light sentence for someone who possessed and sold cocaine by the pound. He would get out of prison within a year.

Of course, getting busted meant that Roger was forced to turn on his old patron, testifying about the drug debt Lasater had settled and adding other damning details. But governor Clinton repaid Lasater for his friendship, and took the steps necessary to see that a man who undoubtedly knew a whole lot too much would not take his anger out on his former patron. The last act of the Clinton-Lasater connection occurred in 1990 when the governor reached into his heart, saw all the greater good that Dan Lasater had done for the world, and found it necessary to pardon him. All debts had been paid in full. In fact, Lasater's top aide—who actually ran his affairs while he was in prison—was Patsy Thomasson, later to become the Clinton White House's Director of the Office of Administration. Ironically, she was put in charge of the White House's drug testing program.

STEPHENS, INC., AND THE
EARLY CHINA CONNECTION

Bill had thrown in his lot with the likes of Lasater because the big players in Arkansas, Witt and Jackson Stephens, were adamant in their dislike, even disgust, for Clinton. In time, however, their mutual needs and ambitions would bring them together.

Once again, the ADFA, whose charter had been drafted by Webb Hubbell, was the genesis of a major political relationship. In many states, such official bodies like the ADFA share appointment power with the governor and the legislature. In Arkansas, the governor had the power to appoint all ten of its board members. To make sure that his control would be total,

Hubbell also saw to it that the bond proposals approved by the rubber stamp board also had to have the signed approval of the governor. (This was in keeping with the tenor of the times. Webb Hubbell had also drafted the state's ethics-in-government act, which exempted the governor and his appointees from having to report conflicts of interest.)

Hubbell's influence over the ADFA paid handsome dividends. For example, ADFA bond issues provided almost $3 million in loans to Park-O-Meter, a parking meter company owned by Hubbell's irascible father-in-law, Seth Ward. (Hubbell, as the father of the Arkansas Ethics in Government Act, was never one to worry too much about appearances; he was both the certifying attorney for the ADFA and Park-O-Meter.)

It was only natural and initially not suspicious that Stephens, Inc., a major off–Wall Street investment banker, would become a major ADFA underwriter. But eyebrows were raised when Governor Clinton appointed to the ADFA board two executives from Stephens-controlled concerns, one from the Worthen Bank and another from a Stephens-controlled nursing home chain.

Bill Clinton's arduous courting of the Stephens brothers paid off when the Worthen Bank rescued Clinton's floundering presidential campaign in New Hampshire with a $3.5 million line of credit. Clinton would return the favor again, making sure that his $55 million in federal campaign funds was deposited in Worthen.[86]

What was Hillary's role in all of this? Rose handled much of the legal side of the ADFA business. She did not take payments or commissions, but Hillary was paid in a different currency. Doubts about her value to the Rose firm had disappeared. She had been elevated among her peers to the role of rainmaker. Bill Clinton was remunerated in other ways as well. When he ran for governor, beneficiaries of ADFA loans or business contributed $400,000 to his campaign. When he ran for president, they kicked in millions.[87]

Perhaps the biggest favor of all did not take the form of active support of Bill Clinton, but the prevention of what could have been a major headache. This favor occurred in the mid-1980s, when Worthen lost $52 million in state pension money on a bad loan. Despite loopholes that could have spared Worthen the losses, Jack Stephens and another investor agreed to cover them, sparing Bill Clinton a major political embarrassment.

The other major investor was Worthen kingpin James Riady, son of Mochtar Riady, owner of the LippoBank. A CIA report to the Senate investigation led by Senator Fred Thompson divulged that through their extensive holdings in China, the Riadys are intimately connected to elements in the Chinese military and likely act as agents of influence on behalf of Chinese intelligence services.

It was through the largesse of the Riadys that Bill Clinton was spared a setback, one that could have cost him his career. It was through the Riadys's good offices that a Riady executive named John Huang escorted Bill and Hillary around Hong Kong on a leg of their 1985 Asian trade mission.

John Huang later became a key figure in the Clinton Commerce Department—and in its lax oversight of technology transfers to Communist China. In fact, there is evidence that Huang himself was affiliated with Communist Chinese intelligence services.[88]

Hillary had gone from Watergate to Whitewater in the span of twenty years, accomplishing feats of financial and political aggrandizement Richard Nixon would never have dared. And unlike Nixon, her opening to China was not the diplomatic coup of a world-class statesman, but the beginning of a Communist Chinese penetration of the Clinton White House with campaign cash.

SEVEN
THE CAMPAIGN MANAGER

"Let nothing get you off your target."

— SAUL ALINSKY, *RULES FOR RADICALS*

"Hillary's keeping her own name," Bill Clinton informed his mother Virginia over coffee the morning before his marriage. Virginia wept, hurt that her soon-to-be daughter-in-law did not want to carry the Clinton name.[1]

The reaction of many of Hillary's legal colleagues was not much more measured. She explained that she needed to maintain the Rodham name to keep her own identity distinct from the public identity of her husband. In the South of the 1970s, older lawyers and judges regarded a "lady lawyer" as an oddity. The fact that she didn't want to use her husband's name struck many tradition-bound colleagues at the Rose Law Firm as the statement of a 1960s bra-burning feminist.

The public was not much more understanding, despite

the approval of her husband. Bill Clinton patiently explained to the *Arkansas Gazette* that Hillary "had quite a career for herself as a lawyer," and was "nationally recognized as an authority on children's legal rights."[2]

SERVING THE CANDIDATE

The fourteen years between 1978 and 1992 witnessed an array of challenges and setbacks for Bill Clinton. His political career and personal life took on the qualities of a *Perils of Pauline* movie. Bill and Hillary have always moved swiftly from success to disaster, from the heights of power to the edge of ruin and back again. He won the governorship in 1978 at age thirty-two, only to be soundly rejected by the voters two years later.

Even before the Clintons were evicted from the governor's mansion, Hillary took control of his reelection campaign and planned his comeback. As Bill then held onto the governorship for a decade, Hillary remained ever ready to take a leave from the Rose Law Firm, to step away from her work with liberal lobbies, to keep alive Bill Clinton's shot at the presidency.

Campaign managers and political operatives came and went. But it was Hillary who managed the perpetual campaign. This achievement, however, had a price. A very stiff price.

In order to keep her husband's chances alive, Hillary had to sublimate her ambitions, even her identity, to his. In time, she could no longer be Hillary Rodham, activist and attorney-at-law. She became what she said that she despised and sought to avoid at all costs: Mrs. Clinton, the cookie baker and supportive wife.

GETTING STARTED

Bill Clinton has run in every race like a prime marathoner with a thirty-pound pack on his back. From his very first race, a third of the electorate always had an immediate, visceral reaction against him. Bill Clinton has always excited the greatest passion not among his supporters, but among his detractors. His casual way with the truth, his ability to transform his scandals into badges of honor and his setbacks into victories, and his cavalier approach to morals and principles infuriate opponents.

When Clinton ran against John Paul Hammerschmidt, a story circulated around Arkansas that a longhaired protestor at the university who outraged many in the state with his antics while sitting in a tree had, in fact, been Bill Clinton. Twenty years later, a story in the *Star* tabloid magazine alleged that he had fathered an illegitimate son with a prostitute. Other stories described sexually transmitted diseases hidden in his medical records.

A check on Bill's whereabouts showed he had been at Oxford when the protestor in the tree was arrested. A DNA test ruled out Clinton's paternity of the prostitute's son. And his medical records remain sealed. Hillary refers often to such incidents, especially the tree incident, relishing the false attacks because they give her the chance to suggest that everything said about her husband is equally false, the imaginings of jealous detractors.

The truth is somewhat more problematic.

Bill Clinton, from his very first race, had to hide the deceitful way he dealt with the draft board and hoped that the maudlin, desperate, and self-congratulatory letter he wrote

about maintaining his "political viability" would never surface. Bill Clinton may or may not have had sex with the
mother of the illegitimate child, a prostitute who lived in a
run-down complex a few blocks from the governor's mansion.
His neighbors, however, had seen the young governor's
digressions on his morning jogs, which were characterized as
more like the prowlings of a predator than the outings of a fitness enthusiast. As a result, few were able to dismiss the paternity story as categorically untrue.

With Bill Clinton, rumor is the penumbra of fact; the
boundary between the two is indistinct. This is the continuing
threat that constantly must be managed by his campaign advisors, from Paul Fray to Paul Begala. When the *Star*'s prostitute story hit the headlines, the White House was notably
muted in its denials. No one on President Clinton's or
Hillary's staff wanted to go out on that limb.

For most campaign aides, treading this line between trust-
ing the candidate and checking up on him is a difficult enough
task. For Hillary, the manager of the perpetual Clinton campaign, explaining Bill has been more than a cross to bear. It
must seem like a perpetual purgatory. But it is the price that
she has willingly assumed to affix herself to the Clinton roller-
coaster. She must have decided that it is worth it.

THE WAKE-UP CALL

Bill Clinton handily won the governorship in 1978, arriving to
take the oath of office with ink-stained hands from the final
edits he had made on his inaugural speech in the car. The
inaugural party that evening had a 1970s mock-elegant,
mock-country theme, "Diamonds and Denim." Planeloads of
friends came from the East, luminaries from the days of
Oxford, Wellesley, and Yale.

It had been a rapid ascent in five years—from being a law student to being the chief executive of a state. It happened because Bill Clinton had shrewdly chosen a path that others had ignored in their quest for federal office. But it was an ascent that came too fast for Bill and Hillary's own good.

From his perspective, it must have seemed more like a coronation of charm and intellect than an election. Bill Clinton arrived in the governor's office with sweeping ambitions to remake the state in his own image, with little appreciation of the obduracy of the bureaucracy, the legislature's appetite for flattery, and the need always to listen to the people.

At that time, the governor of Arkansas served only a two-year term, allowing for a miserably brief period to make a mark on policy before launching a bid for reelection. The brief cycle of a governor's term ensured that a successful chief executive would be forced to wage a constant campaign.

A mature politician would have realized that given such a short term and with such stubborn legislators, the best agenda would have been the shortest. A governor could hope to achieve one—at best, two—big items.

But Bill Clinton, like his fellow governor Jerry Brown of California, set out to change the world by making his state the shining example of what a farsighted, liberal government could do. Rather than control the bureaucracy, Governor Clinton created new departments for economic development and for energy (as though a state of two million people could set its own energy policy). In a region rich in petroleum, coal, and natural gas, the governor's advisors envisioned solar panels proliferating around the state like daffodils.

The young governor and his wife also had a plan to

remake Arkansas's system of health care. Governor Clinton and Hillary sought to reorganize school districts and change teaching methods.

His thirst for reinvention extended to the governor's office itself. The young governor had no need for a chief of staff. Instead, the governor's office was run by a troika of bearded young idealists who often liked to show up at the capitol in T-shirts and ragged cutoffs. Two of them, Rudy Moore, Jr., and Steve Smith, were self-styled Young Turks who had served in the state legislature, where their most notable achievements had been to antagonize and bewilder their older colleagues. They had earned the contempt of the Little Rock political community, baggage Governor Clinton readily assumed by hiring them.

Steve Smith was an American Civil Liberties Union (ACLU) activist and was openly dismissive of the Little Rock business community, referring to them as "suits." In a state where jobs and economic growth depended on attracting factories and manufacturing jobs, Smith argued for state subsidies for quaint cottage industries. One such example was a $500,000 payment by the state (that is, the taxpayers) to train fifty people to chop firewood. An ardent and outspoken critic of timber practices, Smith quickly made powerful enemies for Bill Clinton with major state employers like International Paper and the Weyerhaeuser Corporation.

Nor was Bill Clinton the only one to blame for his personnel selection. As has been the case ever since, Hillary's fingerprints were all over Bill Clinton's staff. Another aide, John Danner, was the husband of Hillary's Wellesley friend Nancy "Peach" Pietrafesa. A Berkeley lawyer, Danner outraged the legislature by spending federal money on staff seminars on such inane topics as "How to Tell What Turns You On." He astonished the state's civil servants by tacking butcher's paper to the wall during meetings and scribbling his stream-of-consciousness ideas as fast as he could write. Like Smith, Danner extolled a naive environmentalism that seemed to rule out the twentieth century.

It wasn't long before the Arkansas capitol crowd started referring to Clinton's office as the "children's crusade" and the "diaper brigade." Danner and Peach were too outrageous to last, even in the Clinton administration. They were gone in fourteen months. But under the Young Turks Steve Smith and Rudy Moore, the staff operation still remained out of control, and most everyone knew it except Bill and Hillary.

On the outside looking in was Dick Morris, an Alinsky protégé and New York street organizer turned political consultant. From the start, Bill Clinton was impressed by Morris's ability to spot the essential challenge of a campaign and chart a strategy. Over the years, his quick mind, acerbic expressions and talent for intrigue have made Morris scores of enemies among Clinton loyalists (most notably Harold Ickes, a long-time rival from New York politics). Also, Morris was suspect among many Clinton friends for his willingness to help Republicans like Ed King beat Michael Dukakis in Massachusetts, or help Congressman Trent Lott win a Senate seat in Mississippi.

Morris recalls Clinton as his first and best client. The truth is, in the long political relationship between the two men, Dick Morris may have been the Clintons's most perceptive political consultant.

Morris had imported the Hollywood technique of using polling and focus groups to sharpen a story line. He taught the young politician and his eager wife that polls could not be read as static points, but as indicators of dynamic trends in constantly shifting public opinion. He would eventually teach the Clintons the efficacy of the continuous campaign, one in which governing and politics were inseparably fused and in which a candidate had to be ever on the lookout for a defining moment or an issue that would polarize a majority and keep it on his side.

In his first term, Bill Clinton listened but did not learn. Once in office, he ignored Morris and grew bored with his polls. When Morris showed the boy governor poll results that contradicted one of his cherished policy goals, Governor Clinton fired him.

The issue that Morris brought to Bill and Hillary's attention, an increase in fees for car and pickup registration and a hike in the fees for transfer of vehicle title, seemed trifling to a governor engaged in widespread social revision. Morris recalled in his book that Clinton reacted, "It's such a small amount of money, and why shouldn't the motorists pay for the roads?"[3] What Morris had tried to explain and what Clinton was unwilling to hear was how people felt about the whole system—how people felt about having their earnings eaten away at every turn by new taxes for everyday necessities.

"You went to the revenue office and took a number and waited through an interminable line—and then the lady told you you were missing one vital piece of proof," Webb Hubbell wrote. "She said you'd have to get in your car and drive over to the county clerk's office, where you would wait in another line to get a piece of paper that would entitle you to drive back to the revenue office and take another number."[4]

Nor was the doubling of the registration fee a trivial

A first lady such as Arkansas had never seen before.

On the campaign trail in New Hampshire, 1992.

Campaigning for first lady of the United States, with a new look—and her own
microphone.

Of one mind—inauguration day, 1993.

Taking charge on health care...

...and reading out her enemies.

Warding off reporters—jokingly here, but also with serious new restrictions on their access to the White House.

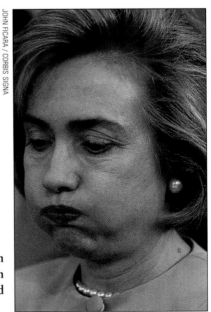

Exasperation has struck Hillary often in her roller-coaster White House years with so many of her pet projects, like socialized medicine, going down in defeat.

Beating the drum for children—and government's role in child-rearing.

Campaigning as a demure housewife in a pink dress.

Triangulation at work—co-opting religion. In Arkansas...

...and with the Reverend Schuller at the State of the Union address in 1997.

Wife, counsel, co-conspirator. Hillary gives advice while President Clinton denies having had a sexual relationship with White House intern Monica Lewinsky.

Global reach. Traveling in Slovakia...

...and addressing the World Economic Forum in Davos, Switzerland.

Surprise, surprise. Hillary and Bill Clinton respond to a suggestion by Democratic Senator Chuck Robb that Hillary might run for the United States Senate.

expense to many Arkansans subsisting on minimum wage jobs. Worst of all, the increase often came as an unpleasant surprise. Motorists often did not learn about the increase until they were already standing at the window. It was later publicized that the Clintons themselves had not had their car properly assessed. This alone was enough to crystallize the image of the young governor and his Yankee wife as arrogant and out of touch. At dinner conversations in every home around the state, a price tag could be placed on the costs of allowing Arkansas to be run by a bunch of activists from the ivory tower. The car tax issue underscored that Clinton had become a world-class talker and a third-rate listener.

Clinton made matters worse by appearing on the local bar scene, often with his brother Roger in tow. As "Saturday-Night Bill," to use Morris's unforgettable phrase, made the rounds with his constituents of the night, more and more people remarked that his nose was positively glowing. Little Rock began to whisper that the governor's brother was a cocaine abuser, and that maybe the governor was, too.

The ridicule of the local press that had been directed at the governor's staff was now being heaped on the governor himself. Editorial cartoons from this period often depicted Bill Clinton as a petulant baby.

The car tag blunder may have been survivable, but was soon coupled with another toxic issue. From Bill Clinton's days as a volunteer in 1976, he had sought to ingratiate himself with President Jimmy Carter and had been delighted to take Hillary to a state dinner at the White House. As the 1980 presidential reelection campaign approached and Carter found himself duped by Fidel Castro, President Carter was forced in turn to betray his young protégé in Arkansas.

The issue was refugees from Communist Cuba. At first, Americans welcomed the Cuban "freedom flotillas." It soon became apparent, however, that among the "boat people" expelled by Castro was a deluge of hardened criminals and violent mental patients.

President Carter could not afford to let these murderers and rapists loose on America. Nor could he humanely return them to the dictator from whom they had ostensibly fled. In a panic, the Carter Administration twisted the arms of governors to house these refugees at detention centers within their states. Clinton, promised by Carter that this would be a temporary measure, willingly took his share of Cubans at a center just outside of Fort Smith, Arkansas. Clinton later had to call out the National Guard after hundreds of refugees escaped, panicking local residents and stoking a white hot fury in the more Republican western edge of the state.

The governor's fortunes suffered a final catastrophic slide when Carter broke the pledge to send no more refugees. The political arithmetic was simple: Big states like Florida had more electoral votes than Arkansas did. Carter closed refugee detention camps in other states and consolidated them in Arkansas.

HILLARY AND DICK

Another issue was Hillary's decision not to take Clinton's name—a decision she eventually realized had become a political liability for her husband.

"To her, it was an act of self-worth," her old Wellesley chum Eleanor Acheson told *People* magazine. "Many people felt she was one of those pointy-headed, overeducated Yale types who had come to Arkansas to spread the word to the uninitiated. There was an attitude of 'Who the hell does she think she is?'"[5]

Now the signs of calamity had become unmistakable. Hillary made an urgent call to Dick Morris in Orlando. According to Dick Morris, she pleaded, "Bill needs you right now, and you've got to help him see how he can get his career back on track."[6]

At the time, Morris was sealing a victory for Paula Hawkins, a Republican riding high on the wave of anger over the Cuban refugee crisis, to become a United States Senator. Morris dutifully came to Little Rock, reviewed the numbers, and declared the campaign hopeless.

Bill Clinton was confident, despite having lost a third of the primary vote to a septuagenarian turkey farmer protest candidate. Governor Clinton's opponent in the general election was Frank White.

Many Clintonites believed that White simply could not win. White had switched to the Republican party in a one-party Democrat state. He was not a particularly attractive candidate: a homespun banker with a pot belly and bulging eyes. The polls consistently showed Clinton ahead. White simply was not taken seriously by the Clinton camp.

But White had several potent weapons. One of them was his wife, Gay, an evangelical Christian, a gracious and polite woman with red hair and ruby red lipstick. Among Arkansas voters, she compared favorably to Hillary, the first lady who kept her own name and refused to shave her legs or arm pits. White conspicuously introduced Gay as "Mrs. Frank White," while Bill Clinton received stacks of letters demanding to know, "Doesn't your wife love you?"[7]

Another weapon in White's arsenal was a keen under-

standing of the building anger against Clinton. White's ad
campaign was based around the simple negative message of
"car tags and Cubans."

"We've got to hit back!" Hubbell remembers Hillary
saying. "We can't let those charges go unchallenged."[8]

But perhaps the ultimate weapon in White's arsenal was
the befuddled and ineffective Jimmy Carter, a Democrat in
the White House who was the perfect impetus for the powerful Republican surge led by Ronald Reagan.

A photo from election day shows a haggard-looking
Clinton between the parted curtains of a poll booth, gamely
trying to smile and not succeeding at it. The boy governor
went to bed that night declared a winner. He woke up in the
morning to find out that he had, in fact, lost the governorship.
The Clintons would soon move out of their mansion and into
a modest frame house to one of the few houses ever paid for
without taxpayer dollars where the former governor would
complain about having to do his own laundry.

RECLAIMING THE LEGACY

The day after his defeat, the governor was puffy-eyed and
fragile appearing on the balcony of his mansion, where he
glumly received well-wishers who came by to give their con-
dolences. Always susceptible to bouts of self-pity, Bill Clinton
slid into a deep depression. He managed to go through the
motions of moving into an office in a law firm with Bruce
Lindsey, his future right-hand and fix-it man in the White
House.

For much of the time, however, the former governor
walked about in a funk, wandering the aisles of grocery stores
and challenging strangers to tell him why he lost.

Hillary was devastated but stayed on a more even keel. She dealt with the loss not by grieving but by acting. While Bill hashed and rehashed what had happened to him, Hillary put together the comeback plan. She started by ruthlessly weeding out the weaker members of their circle. Hillary's scorn was like "walking into a revolving air fan," one early Clintonite told the *New Yorker* magazine. "Her attitude about Bill's old friends is, 'Why are you hanging around with these losers? They're not successful, not rich.'"[9]

Hillary's campaign to retake the governor's mansion began even while they were still living in it. She organized strategy sessions in the living room and kitchen. Betsey Wright, Hillary's old feminist McGovern colleague from Texas, was persuaded to move from a good job as political director of a government union to live in Little Rock and manage the campaign to retake the governorship.

Betsey arrived in Little Rock before Bill and Hillary had even left the governor's mansion, taking up residence in the guest house. She organized the files of the governor's supporters, creating a system of index cards in which the candidate only had to glance down to see the essentials of his past dealings with the person on the other end of the line.

"It was always important to me that strong political feminists have relationships with strong male politicians," she said later. "And Bill Clinton has no problem with strong women."[10] In Betsey Wright's case, it led to airing the idea that Hillary would be a better candidate and a better president than Bill.

Now, in order to win, Hillary and Bill would have to do something neither had a knack for doing. They had to humble themselves. How this happened in Hillary's case is a matter of dispute.

"Hillary's gonna have to change her name, and shave her legs," a powerful legislator had advised during the losing campaign.[11] As president, Bill Clinton told Connie Bruck of the *New Yorker* that he had never requested that Hillary change her name. In fact, Bill Clinton claimed he was dead set against it. "Hillary told me she was nine years old when she decided she would keep her own name when she got married. It had nothing to do with the feminist movement or anything. She said, 'I like my name. I was interested in my family. I didn't want to give it up.'"

According to Bill Clinton's account, Hillary came to him and said, "We shouldn't lose the election over this issue. What if it's one percent of the vote? What if it's two percent?"[12]

Whether Bill and Hillary did or did not have such a conversation, the president's account, as usual, falls short of the truth. In fact, it was such a testy issue between the two that Bill had to go to others to lobby his wife to change her name. He buttonholed Webb Hubbell on a golf course, and persuaded him to talk to Hillary about what everyone knew as "the name issue."[13]

When Bill announced his bid to retake the governorship in late winter 1982, Hillary Rodham was introduced as "Mrs. Bill Clinton." The press noticed and questions followed. "I don't have to change my name," Hillary demurred with typical Clinton disingenuousness. "I've been Mrs. Bill Clinton. I kept the professional name Hillary Rodham in my law practice, but now I'm going to be taking a leave of absence from the law firm to campaign full time for Bill and I'll be Mrs. Bill Clinton."[14] The Clintons seemed to be learning that a lie was easier than the truth and the public were willing accomplices.

To compete with Gay White, Mrs. Bill Clinton ordered a

total makeover, from the wisp of hair at her crown to her polished toenail. When it was complete, Hillary looked more feminine, more like a traditional first lady. Her hair had been lightened and she had a new wardrobe provided by a fashion consultant.[15] "I had been trying to wear contact lenses since I was sixteen," Hillary said. Suddenly, she was miraculously able to make the change, liberating her face and eyes from the owlish frames.

Hillary's makeover continued for the next twenty years. Hillary read the autobiography of Prime Minister Margaret Thatcher, who wrote that some women should lighten their hair after a certain age. Soon thereafter, Hillary's hair became lighter and lighter. In fact she experimented with so many hair styles that in the 1990s, a Website was dedicated to tracking them all.

As first lady of the United States, Hillary Clinton even went so far as to make fun of her past frumpish appearance. She took an old hippie headband and gave it to the hosts of *The Regis & Kathie Lee Show*, saying, "I don't need them anymore and thought you might want it for Halloween."

From the start, Arkansans appreciated the efforts Hillary made to accommodate their idea of what the first lady of the state should be. It was, in part, because of her willingness to remake herself in these ways that Hillary Clinton was able to preside over a second inaugural in 1983. In perfect character, Mrs. Bill Clinton wore an elegant beaded inauguration gown with Chantilly lace over charmeuse silk.[16]

Bill Clinton had other amends to make. He had to make the rounds of the state, apologizing to business leaders for allowing his aides to refer to them as "corporate criminals." Candidate Bill Clinton promised to advance their interests in the future. He also had to apologize to the voters, to publicly admit that he had been arrogant in his first term and had learned from the experience.

Clinton, however, is a fast and facile learner and the studied apology (and, as we later saw, repentance) comes as naturally to him as slick evasions. Dick Morris persuaded the Clintons that Bill needed to make a formal apology to the people of Arkansas. Clinton bridled but agreed to appear in a commercial designed to win back the voters. They flew to New York City, where Clinton looked into a camera, extemporizing much of his script. He spoke of the car license and title-transfer fees, admitting they had been "a big mistake" because "so many of you were hurt by it." Bill Clinton skirted using the "a" word—he could not bring himself to an outright apology.

But he came up with something even better, something only Clinton could devise.

"When I was a boy growing up," he said, "my daddy never had to whip me twice for the same thing."

Morris marveled at the ingenuity of Clinton's phrasing. The immediate reaction to the ad, however, was negative. Bill Clinton plunged in the polls. Morris bucked him up, arguing that the commercial was like being immunized. "You get a little sick, but you don't get the disease when you are exposed to it for real," he said.[17]

In a few months it was apparent that Morris had been right. When White got around to attacking him "for real" on the car tags and the Cuban refugee issue, the voters' reaction was negative—against White. Bill Clinton had already apologized for this, they felt—why beat a dead horse?

In this way two classic Clinton techniques were born.

First, conventional political wisdom has always held that advertising should be done late, when voters are paying attention and impressions are sure to last to election day. Bill Clinton aired his first campaign ads ten months before the 1982 election. In 1995 he successfully repeated this early and often technique, airing his first commercials to kill the Dole campaign before it even started.

The second classic Clinton technique was to speed up the burn rate of a negative issue, making critics look mean-spirited and petty for continuing to harp on it.

White was unable to gain any traction in his attacks on the chastened young man who had seemed to open his heart to the people of Arkansas.

HOLDING PATTERN

Dick Morris, Betsey Wright, and the Clintons coalesced into a team to keep the governor's mansion until the time was right to run for president of the United States. Of the four, Hillary was clearly the team leader.

"After he came back, she was going to make sure he never lost again," a Clinton cabinet officer observed.[18]

Morris did the polling. Betsey Wright, who had brought her organizational skills to managing the database of supporters, now managed the governor's office and his legislative agenda as chief of staff. Bill, of course, was the candidate and front man. But Hillary was much more than just a front; she was the other principal, the behind-the-scenes candidate calling the shots on broad strategy. She often brought the foursome together to work on scripts, on paid media, on earned media, and on mass mailings.[19]

Hillary managed some of the trickiest issues for her husband during the 1980s. She worked out a compromise on a sticky school desegregation issue that, had it not been resolved, could have harmed Clinton politically. Behind the scenes, she saw to it that the Rose Law Firm represented the Public Service Commission in its dispute with the powerful utility Arkansas Power & Light over who should pay for costly electricity from the Grand Gulf nuclear power plant in Mississippi. She saved her husband from political embarrassment while earning her law firm a cool $115,000 in state business.

Frank White exploited this blatant conflict of interest in a bitter 1986 rematch. A Rose Law Firm press release explained that these fees were "segregated" from Hillary's income—it was as though a partner would not benefit in ways other than monetary from bringing in a major client. White was never able to make his charges stick. He never capitalized on the fact that the real conflict wasn't the money, it was the way in which Hillary used her law firm to defuse a dangerous issue for the governor.

When White pressed his attacks, the Clinton campaign fired back with a bumper sticker that said, "Frank White for First Lady." Hillary and her people were becoming masters at the martial art jujitsu—of turning the force of an opponent's attack back on himself—a skill they were to refine and perfect against George Bush, Newt Gingrich, Bob Dole, and Ken Starr.

A change in the state constitution had lengthened the governor's tenure to four years, giving the Clintons a margin of comfort. Bill Clinton's comfort level with strong women, however, was soon to be tested. The three women—Hillary, chief of staff Betsey Wright, and press secretary Joan Roberts—were satirized in a cartoon by a local wag as

Valkyries. For a spell, they ran Bill Clinton's office and they ran his life. Betsey Wright, fearful of the governor's tendency to expose himself to dangerous situations, tenaciously controlled his schedule. It was reported that their fights grew so loud and bitter that the Clintons were forced to move Wright out of the governor's office.

Another key challenge during the long holding period in the governor's mansion was to neutralize John Robert Starr, the managing editor of the *Arkansas Democrat* and the former chief of the Associated Press's Little Rock bureau. Starr not only edited the news, he commented on it daily with a column that was keen, sharp, and caustic. In the small state, constant pounding from Starr did significant damage to Clinton. His frequent and bitter attacks were one reason Clinton lost his first reelection race. (One is forced to wonder whether any fortune-teller ever warned the Clintons to watch out for men named Starr.)

In the first term, the Clintons ignored Starr. But in 1982 Hillary launched a "charm offensive," taking Starr to lunch. She worked to flatter him in the age-old way politicians have always flattered journalists—by soliciting his opinions and appearing to hang on his every word. Back in the office, Betsey Wright instructed Joan Roberts to make her first priority to keep Starr happy.

The offensive worked. "I decided any man married to that woman couldn't be all bad," Starr said. "The deal he and I cut after I reassessed him was that I would not remind everyone what a bad governor he had been and would give him a new chance as long as he kept his campaign clean."[20]

In their regular lunches, Starr recalled, "one of Hillary's frequent sayings was 'Now, John Robert, you and I may disagree on this'—and I would say, 'Hillary, the only thing we disagree on is the worth of your husband.'"[21]

MONKEY BUSINESS IN ARKANSAS

Bill Clinton had served as governor of Arkansas for eight years by 1988. His was a rising luminary in the Democratic party, seen as a centrist southern Democrat with a Kennedyesque flair. The usual route for a sitting governor would be to move on to the United States Senate. However, that route was blocked for the Clintons by incumbents Dale Bumpers and David Pryor.

The time had come to consider going for broke, to go ahead and make a run for the White House. A serious bid to challenge George Bush was studied and debated among the Clinton team. Bill Clinton flew to New Hampshire, where he shared a stage with the Democrat front-runner, Senator Gary Hart of Colorado.

Hart and Clinton shared much of the same appeal. Young and charismatic, they both emulated John F. Kennedy and sought to win over a new generation of voters with a "third way" agenda that eschewed the old machine politics of the Democratic Party. In 1984, Hart had come close to wresting the nomination from Walter Mondale, a prospect that had worried Reagan campaign advisors.

Now it was Hart's turn to be knocked out of the saddle, this time by his own behavior. He had not appreciated the extent to which the rules of the game had changed since the Kennedy era. After foolishly daring the press to catch him in infidelity, the *Miami Herald* newspaper reporters took him at his word. The reluctance of the press to report on politicians' private lives, the factor that had protected John F. Kennedy so well, evaporated with this blatant challenge. The *Herald* staked out the senator's apartment, ultimately reporting the married senator's affair with Donna Rice. Tabloid photos of Hart and Rice on a Caribbean cruise aboard the *Monkey Business* left little doubt that the senator was a liar and a cheat.

It was over when the American public watched Senator Hart try to regain his viability while ignoring the humiliation he was heaping upon his victimized and helpless wife. Years later, the Clintons learned from this debacle and successfully had Hillary out front to defend Bill's affairs. She never let the American public feel that Bill had humiliated her to the point of silence. She was always front and center as his staunchest defender.

Hart's campaign fell apart and he soon had a brighter future as an entertainment lawyer than as a politician. These events posed an interesting dilemma for the Clintons as Hillary busily assembled a campaign, bringing in Susan Thomases and Harold Ickes from New York to create the nucleus of a presidential campaign. With Hart out of the race, the pressure grew on Bill Clinton to run. Yet he knew what Thomases and Ickes did not know. Bill Clinton knew the full range of his own indiscretions, and how much reason he had to fear exposure and national embarrassment.

Arkansas-Democrat editor John Robert Starr spoke to Bill Clinton about what was often referred to as a potential "Gary Hart problem." Clinton matter-of-factly confirmed that he did have such a problem.[22]

No member of his top team was more aware of the liability Clinton faced than Betsey Wright, who had observed his compulsive and irresponsible promiscuity including his use of state troopers to procure women and cover his tracks. Betsey had often called the governor in the middle of the night just to see if anyone would answer. Often, of course, the phone would just ring into the night. When the governor mused about the prospect of seeking the presidency, Betsey forced him to make a list of the women. All of them. When and where. Clinton did and Betsey looked at the list and told him flatly to stay out of the race.

Hillary, who apparently did not know the breathtaking extent and frequency of her husband's philandering, urged him to run. Betsey, who knew all, promised him he would be slaughtered if he did.

On a summer day in 1987, Bill Clinton called a press conference, alerting the networks to break in on daytime programming. As he spoke, Hillary's face was a mask of stone.

"There are many whom I treasure who have urged me to run again," the governor said, "who say that is the thing to do for the state and who are obviously worried about at least one of the alternatives. There are others who say with a great deal of conviction that ten years is a long time. And I can see that there is an argument for that proposition.... And then there is the whole question of the personal toll which is taken on every family, on every life in the public. The things that make it so wonderful also make it quite difficult from time to time. Ambition always takes its price sooner or later."

Governor Clinton concluded by saying he would stay in Arkansas for the good of his family, especially his seven-year-old daughter.

As Bill Clinton delivered his letdown, Hillary's stony composure broke and she wept openly. These were tears of fury and humiliation, and of ambition publicly failed.

Hillary seemed to have been surprised by her husband's

announcement. She had assembled their bid for national power and Bill Clinton's philandering stopped them cold. Before the 1992 race, Bill Clinton would have to come completely clean with his wife. This was because by then Hillary had thoroughly investigated her husband's life.

And she had come to terms with it.

NEAR DEATH EXPERIENCE

Once Clinton had bailed out, the way was open for another governor to take the Democratic nomination, Michael Dukakis of Massachusetts. At the Democratic National Convention in Atlanta, Dukakis offered the Arkansas governor a coveted spot. He was to give the nominating address, a chance to connect with a national television audience.

Nominating addresses usually do not last more than fifteen minutes. Their purpose is to build up enthusiasm for the main event and end in thunderous applause for the candidate. Clinton spoke more than twice as long as he should have, testing the patience of millions of people.

"We have to be here, too," NBC's Tom Brokaw complained. A red light flashed on the podium, which Clinton cheerfully ignored. The audience began to boo, shouting "Get the hook!"

As Clinton droned on, Hillary paced about, bitterly complaining about the bright floor lights and the Dukakis whips who egged on a rambunctious crowd to applaud whenever the nominee's name was mentioned.

The Dukakis people had "set Bill up," Hillary told Webb Hubbell and Vince Foster when she got back to Little Rock.[23] She said that Dukakis himself had urged Bill to give the whole speech. Nor did they dim the lights, a signal that would have told the speaker to wrap it up. In truth, Clinton's embarrassment did Dukakis no favors. The speech snafu was the kick-off of a notably incompetent campaign. But Hillary would hear none of these innocent explanations. As she would in 1992, and again and again thereafter, Hillary Clinton saw the hand of conspiracy in every misfortune.

Bill Clinton returned to Little Rock a national joke, the stuff of late-night monologue humor and cocktail party chatter. Ridicule can be deadly to a politician, and the jokes heaped on Bill Clinton were killing his career.

Hillary treated this setback as another challenge, as she had treated the loss of the governorship in 1980. She turned to Hollywood producers Harry Thomason, a former high school football coach from Arkansas, and his wife, Linda Bloodworth-Thomason. From their humble origins, this husband-and-wife team had risen to earning an estimated $300,000 a week with television shows like *Designing Women* and *Evening Shade*. Joining with Mickey Kantor and his wife, a television anchorwoman in Los Angeles, they persuaded Clinton that he could do more than survive this escapade, he could turn it into positive advertising. But he had to act quick. They helped book the young governor on the *Tonight Show*, where he appeared with Johnny Carson to make one self-effacing joke after another.

By showing that he could poke fun at himself, Clinton transformed an embarrassment into an image asset. The jokes ended. Hillary had once again helped Bill Clinton save his career. She would get the chance to do it again and again.

ATTACK DOG

Bill Clinton was only one of three Arkansas governors to have won more than two terms. Only two of his predecessors had served more than six years as governor. In 1990 Bill Clinton had spent a decade in the governor's mansion. Should he go for fourteen?

"My popularity was very high in the state at the time," he said. "But I was afraid people might say, 'Give this guy a gold watch, he's done a good job. Give him the gold watch!'"[24]

So they considered running Hillary. Bill was supportive. Having Hillary in office would keep him alive politically, while sparing him the very real possibility of getting "the gold watch" from the voters.

Hillary herself pined for the race, supported by encouraging noises from potential financial supporters like Jack and Witt Stephens of Stephens, Inc., the Little Rock investment firm whose connections to Mochtar Riady and the Lippo Group—and through them to Communist Chinese funds—would later prove embarrassing. Also supportive was journalist John Robert Starr. But she bridled at the thought that she would be seen as a Lurleen Wallace, a woman known only as a stand-in for a more powerful husband. Polls were commissioned, and they were not encouraging.

Bill Clinton decided that he had to run. The fact was, the mayors of a half-dozen cities have a bigger job than the governor of Arkansas. Without the prestige of the governor's office, Clinton would be cut loose from power, and have no base from which to launch a presidential bid. He needed to hold on to the governor's mansion if he was to keep the aura of a rising politician and keep his donor base active and interested.

Almost immediately, Clinton faced strong opposition in the Democratic primary. His opponent was Tom McRae, who had been director of the Winthrop Rockefeller Foundation, a wealthy think tank. To Clinton's surprise, McRae mounted a surprisingly strong campaign, with television ads that showed

Clinton at the Little Rock airport on his way to yet another campaign event for his coming presidential bid. Another ad showed the surrealistic, melting clocks of Salvador Dali, lampooning the stretching of time Clinton spent in office. In short order, McRae made major inroads among voters in the primary. If he defeated Bill Clinton, the governor's run for the presidency would be over.

As usual, Hillary had a plan. She explained it to her husband and to Dick Morris. They listened patiently, hashed it over, and agreed.

A short time later, McRae held a press conference in the state capitol rotunda, daring Clinton to debate. He was in mid-sentence when a loud voice interrupted him. "Tom, who was the one person who didn't show up in Springdale? Give me a break! I mean, I think that we oughta get the record straight...."[25] Hillary had crashed McRae's press conference. Local news teams zoomed in. Amid the flashing, whirring, and clicking of cameras she pulled out old reports McRae had written for the Rockefeller Foundation. "Many of the reports you issued," she charged, "not only praised the governor on his environmental record, but his education record and his economic record!"

Too shocked to respond, Tom McRae stood before her as still and mute as a mannequin. As with the 1982 ad in which the young politician had talked about being whipped by his daddy, the initial reaction was unfavorable. It doubled recognition of McRae's name among voters. The attack itself was illogical. If the charge was that Bill Clinton was afraid to debate, it was only underscored when he sent his wife out to debate his opponent.

In time, though, Hillary's shock therapy had its intended

effect. The line of attack from this arch feminist was to make a blatant appeal to the voters' sexism. If Tom McRae couldn't stand up to the governor's wife, he had to be a very weak man indeed. An effective series of ads, produced by David Watkins, defended the governor's travels as a way to bring jobs to Arkansas. The tagline was "Don't let McRae build a brick wall around Arkansas" as workmen built a brick wall.

Clinton won the primary. He was still, however, in deep trouble. He won with less than 55 percent of the vote.

The second crisis of the primary campaign occurred in the kitchen of the governor's mansion when a meeting between the governor and Dick Morris turned ugly, then violent.

"You got me into this race," Dick Morris recalls Bill Clinton screaming at him in his book *Behind the Oval Office*, "so you could make some extra money off me. That was the only reason. And now you give me no attention, no attention at all." He accused Morris of turning his back on his client, and screamed, "You're screwing me!"

Hillary tried to calm him down, but Morris responded in kind. "Thank you, thank you, thank you. You've just solved my problem. I'm getting shit from [Lee] Atwater and shit from [Trent] Lott for working for you, and now I can solve my problem. Go fuck yourself. I'm quitting your goddamn campaign, and now I'm a free agent. I can be a fifty-state Republican and don't have to take your shit."

Clinton apparently charged at him, wrapped his arms around Morris's torso, and they fell to the ground. The governor soon cooled down and then turned apologetic. Morris stormed out.

Hillary ran after Morris and put her arm around his shoulder. "Please forgive him," she pleaded. "He's under so much pressure. He didn't mean it. He's very sorry. He's overtired, he hasn't slept well in days."[26]

Hillary was instrumental in keeping the channel to Morris open through the election. Morris guided his client in beating Republican Sheffield Nelson in a tight race. Morris did his job, but remained aloof.

Dick Morris stayed away from Clinton's successful 1992 presidential bid, recommending the "ragin' Cajun," James Carville, for the job of campaign manager. When President Clinton needed rescuing again in the middle of a disastrous first term, it was Hillary who once more made sure that Morris's talent and strategic sense would be at the president's command.

GOING FOR BROKE

"You almost have to do it," Hillary said to Bill as he awakened one morning in his final term as governor.

The time had come to plan a run for the White House. At the time, George Bush was the victor of the Persian Gulf War, with a stratospheric approval rating. A race now seemed to Bill Clinton and most of his people as a warm-up bid for 1996.

At a morning meeting with their advisors around the kitchen table, the obstacles were discussed. How hard would it be to beat New York Democrat Governor Cuomo? How likely would it be to beat a well-liked incumbent president?

Bruce Lindsey asked the governor the unthinkable question, "What if we win?"

Hillary answered it. "Then, we serve."[27]

"She always thought that the right kind of Democrat would have an opportunity to be elected in 1992—always," Bill Clinton said. Hillary spotted the weakness of the Bush presidency from the moment he took office. "And when he got up to seventy percent and then ninety percent or whatever in the polls after the Gulf War, she never wavered in her conviction that 1992 was a good year for the right sort of Democrat to challenge the established orthodoxy of the Democratic Party, and also challenge the incumbent president. It was amazing.... That's one where her instinct was right and I didn't feel that way for the longest time."[28]

As the campaign staff was assembled, it was clear it would be Hillary's team.

One personnel choice that had a great deal to do with Hillary's good humor on the campaign trail was Brooke Shearer. Brooke had been a friend for twenty years, and was the wife of Bill's friend Strobe Talbott. She is the sister of Cody Shearer who was accused of trying to strong-arm Indian tribes into donating more campaign money to obtain presidential favors. Now she became a near constant companion, traveling with Hillary for nine months. Hillary recruited friends and volunteers from her days as a schoolgirl, her time at Wellesley and Yale. They all moved to Little Rock and shared efficiency apartments to work on the campaign. It was clear that they did this not for Bill Clinton, but for Hillary.

In time, this became a moving road show, sometimes referred to as Herc (derived from her initials HRC) and the girls, or more often as "Hillaryland." In dealing with the governor's staff, especially the state troopers, Hillary was often arrogant, dismissive, overbearing, and vulgar, with four-letter expletives being her all-purpose response. With her own handpicked staff, however, Hillary is described as relaxed and easygoing. Sing-alongs were common, as was the staff's amusement at Hillary's cruel and dead-on imitation of critics.

Another key selection to the campaign team was Morris's recommendation of James Carville. Carville had proven himself in the major leagues with Harris Wofford, who took down Bush's attorney general, Richard Thornburgh, in the Pennsylvania Senate race. Now Carville was ready to take on the president himself.

Mary Matalin, the brilliant and witty Bush campaign aide who later married Carville, knows all too well the intensity of her husband's determination to win. During any given crisis in the White House, James Carville would be up at 4 AM reading all the major newspapers' reporting on the facts and ready to join a conference call with George Stephanopoulos, John Podesta, and Rahm Emanuel. This allowed them to steal a beat on the day's news and prepare the Clinton rapid response. As soon as the call ended, every major political reporter would have his own anonymous "White House staff" tidbit to report and ample "off the record" spin to turn any negative story into a positive play of events. This routine was repeated seven days a week for as long as was needed.

This pace of business began during the campaign. The Bush people were well-mannered, genteel, professional, and so well versed in the law that they weren't inclined to break it. Many had young families, and they were not adverse to kicking back on the weekends. The people Hillary chose were hungry and obsessive. They had fire in their bellies. It was war and they were going to win, come hell or high water.

Two of the campaign regulars were the Hollywood power couple who rescued the Clintons in 1988, Harry Thomason and Linda Bloodworth-Thomason. They produced the campaign film *A Place Called Hope*, a distinctly Reaganesque portrayal of Bill Clinton's life. Harry created a series of whistle-stop tours that highlighted the Clintons's light-hearted interaction with people. Linda brought in hair and makeup stylists, lightening Hillary's hair even more, and making her look like an appealing middle-class housewife.

Another key campaign aide, first recruited for the aborted 1988 run, was Harold Ickes. Son of a reform-minded Interior Secretary in the FDR cabinet, Ickes is driven and choleric, a born hater and intriguer. An organizer of protests against the Vietnam War, Ickes forged a close relationship with unions and their underworld friends as a labor lawyer. "He has done more singlehandedly to destroy the Democratic Party than anyone else," a Clinton insider told Daniel Wattenberg of the *American Spectator*.[29] We never underestimated the force of Harold Ickes's determination to protect both Clintons during our investigations. I was the one to depose Mr. Ickes in the Travelgate investigation—alone. The other counsels asked to be excluded—one had children and the other a horse. I think they were kidding, but Mr. Carville's reputation had preceded him.

In 1972 George McGovern had tapped Ickes to select delegates. Ickes ignored party rules to push out traditional Democrats and stack the deck with far-left activists. Ickes had also served as the convention manager for Jesse Jackson's campaign in 1988. Now he took his place as the dark prince, this time in a "centrist" campaign that actually had a chance of winning.

Not only was he trusted by Hillary, but Ickes had a long and complex relationship with Hillary's most powerful staffer in the campaign: Susan Thomases.

Camille Paglia characterized Thomases in an effort to see something working beneath Hillary's attempts to soften and feminize her own image. "But her [Hillary] "steely soul remains, the butch substrate that can be seen in the baleful, bloodless face of lawyer Susan Thomases...."[30] This may be unduly harsh. Then again, it would be very difficult to be unduly harsh in describing the persona of Susan Thomases.

A successful New York lawyer, Susan Thomases seems to think of herself as brisk. In truth, she comes off as curt, rude, obscene, and unduly quick to dismiss any idea that didn't originate with her.

"She is the juice," a Clinton insider told the *Washington Post*. "She's the juicer too. The Braun automatic."[31]

Perhaps she is more like a semiautomatic, leveling people with staccato bursts of profanity. One reporter visited the primary campaign and saw a campaign aide holding a telephone in the air. The sound of Thomases's blue tirade and screamed obscenities was audible at a distance.[32]

Susan Thomases is often credited with having "masterminded" the last Senate race of New Jersey's Bill Bradley, in which a powerful and entrenched incumbent came within a hair of losing. To say the least, Thomases's high regard for her political talents is not shared by her colleagues.

Once let loose by Hillary, Thomases began to try to run every aspect of the campaign. She showed up at meetings and barked orders, and supervised polling, advertising, advance, and policy.

She sided with Hillary to keep the campaign based in Little Rock and not Washington, even after Clinton squeaked by in the critical New York primary and became the inevitable nominee. Had the move to Washington occurred, the campaign would have been flooded with centrist and conservative Democrats from the Democratic Leadership Council, which

Clinton had led. Hillary's personnel would have been shoved aside.

In June, Thomases finally overplayed her hand. She went to Hillary to kill a poll the political professionals had commissioned. The senior members of the campaign had had it. David Wilhelm, George Stephanopoulos, Eli Segal, and pollster Stanley Greenberg went to Clinton and promised to walk off the campaign if something wasn't done. Hillary's solution was to redefine Thomases's role, putting her in charge of Clinton's schedule. This was a job perfectly suited to Thomases's temperament, in which she could use her forceful manner to reject requests for the candidate's time.

Thomases retained her powerful influence, remaining the "Braun automatic" through Hillary's first four White House years. And she and Ickes fanned Hillary's ambitions by encouraging her to run for the Senate in New York.

As different as they are in temperament, Hillary's people have a certain combative quality in common. The sure way to be in Hillary's inner circle, a former White House spokesperson told Gail Sheehy, "is to show a balls-out, go-to-the-mat mentality about taking on their enemies. Anybody who has a hang-up about fairness is cast out as part of the enemy camp."[33] The result was the Clinton "war room"—an idea cooked up by Carville and warmly approved of and managed by Hillary.

The key players, the ones who had the will to win, would be brought together like generals in a bunker to mau-mau the Bush campaign, a rapid response brigade that would turn every attack into a counterattack. That "war room" has been reconstituted for Hillary's run for the Senate. It is clear that they will remain her "kitchen cabinet" and political allies—whether in the Senate, the World Bank, or back in the White House.

THE SEX WARS

Chelsea, whose interests were paraded forth as the excuse not to run in 1988, had to learn to live with the increasingly damaging revelations about her father. Ignoring his own role in creating the factual conditions that made the attacks on him inevitable, Bill Clinton piously intoned that Chelsea "is fully aware of what happens in politics. With it comes a lot of the worst that human nature has to offer. We've been telling her that since she was six."

Hillary and Bill had to brace themselves and their child against the impact of the disclosures that they knew were sure to come. Hillary knew how badly they could be embarrassed by revelations about their finances. Bill had other reasons to worry.

When the first revelations of Hillary's dealings with James McDougal became public in the campaign, Bill and Hillary's reflexive posture of indignance gave their denials a credible sound.

"They think of themselves as the most ethical people in the world," a White House aide would later say. "They think everything they do or say is above board and for the good of the country. Therefore they can't understand why someone would doubt their integrity."[34]

When, inevitably, details about Bill's reckless personal life began to leak out, their initial response was the same.

Hillary had kept tabs on her husband's indiscretions since the first campaign. One private investigator, Ivan Duda, told a tabloid that "Hillary wanted me to get the dirt and find out who he was fooling with."[35] Duda gave Hillary the names of six women—including one from the Rose Law Firm—as potential bimbo embarrassments.[36] Moreover, Duda said that

"Bill was extremely suspicious of Hillary's relationship with Vince. When confronted, she simply denied it was a romance and claimed they were just good friends." According to Duda, Bill hired a private investigator of his own who confirmed that an affair had taken place.

"Bill confronted her with the information and they had several explosive arguments—screaming, shouting, red-faced blow-outs," Duda said. "Hillary is not meek, and while she never confessed to cheating, she aggressively reminded Bill of his numerous affairs and how he not only humiliated her but nearly wrecked their own political career with his behavior."[37]

Perhaps an accommodation had been reached by the time Trooper L.D. Brown witnessed the makeout orgy at the Charlie Trie restaurant in Little Rock. In middle age, the Clintons had settled, if somewhat awkwardly, into Bloomsbury morality and open marriage. Now their arrangement was in danger of becoming more open than they ever intended.

In Little Rock, an aggrieved state employee filed suit after losing a job to Gennifer Flowers. As details about Clinton's long affair with Gennifer Flowers percolated in the tabloid press, Hillary decided the campaign would have to act vigorously to contain the damage. She rejected a bid to appear with the analytical and precise Ted Koppel on *Nightline*, opting instead to go with an exclusive offer to *60 Minutes*. It was agreed that interviewer Steve Kroft's questions would be cleared by the Clintons first—an unusual and generous accomodation from the usually hard-charging producers of the investigative news show. They even agreed to produce it for a special fifteen-minute slot after the 1992 Super Bowl. Once on the *60 Minutes* set, Hillary took charge of Steve Kroft and his crew.

"We fiddled around with who should sit on which side, and they fiddled around with chair heights and things like that," Kroft told Gail Sheehy. "If you didn't know she was his wife, you'd have thought she was a media consultant."[38]

Kroft's questions made softballs look like bullets. He did everything but get on his knees. The Clintons sat next to each other, close and supportive, while Bill admitted to having "caused pain in our marriage." There were several big lies told in that interview.

The first lie was Hillary's assertion that there had been a rough patch in their marriage that was now over. That was untrue. Bill, as she knew from her investigations, was a constant and prolific serial sexual predator.

Kroft framed the issue as adultery, but adultery was not the point. The issue, never pressed by Kroft, was whether Bill Clinton was self-destructively promiscuous, the sort of man who would risk his career and even endanger the security and reputation of his office and his country to satisfy his insatiable sexual appetite.

There was no hint of the Bill Clinton who sought a quickie from Gennifer Flowers in the mansion while a crowd waited outside for a speech. In the years ahead, Bill Clinton would bring more "pain" into their marriage. He would later bring a female Arkansas Power & Light executive to visit him in the basement of the governor's mansion four times *after* his election to the presidency, creeping down to meet her, while a state policeman stood watch against Hillary and Chelsea upstairs. He would bring it again by groping Kathleen Willey and turning his inexhaustible seductive powers on a twenty-one-year-old intern in the Oval Office.

The second lie was that Bill Clinton had never had an affair with Gennifer Flowers. Kroft, like so many interrogators, took it for granted that Clinton would answer him in good faith. When he asked if Clinton had had a twelve-year affair with Flowers, Clinton said no. Of course, Bill Clinton's way with the truth was not yet fully known. It probably never occurred to Kroft that he should have also asked if he had had an eleven-year affair with Flowers or quizzed him about his understanding of the meaning of the word "affair."

When Kroft tentatively began to press him, Hillary interrupted. "I don't want to be any more specific. I don't think being any more specific about what's happened in the privacy of our life together is relevant to anybody but us." Kroft meekly backed away.

Throughout the interview, every time Clinton started to wander into a dangerous digression, Hillary stepped and brought the interview back to rehearsed responses.

"Those who were there said that throughout the ninety-minute taping, the tension was so thick that it was not even broken when a row of heavy lights came crashing down, narrowly missing Hillary's head," recounted journalist Meredith Oakley.[39]

It was Hillary who won the day, orchestrating the interview and forcing Kroft to eat out of her hand while she appealed to Americans' natural horror of journalists prying into private lives.

"There isn't a person watching this who would feel comfortable sitting on this couch detailing everything that ever went on in their lives or their marriage," she said, "and I think it's real dangerous in this country if we don't have a zone of privacy for everybody." Kroft could only nod his head in agreement.

The interview saved Bill Clinton's career, and once again it was Hillary who was the one to pull him out of the fire.

There was only one slight skip in the record. Hillary told Kroft that she was not "sitting here because I'm some little woman standing by my man like Tammy Wynette. I'm sitting here because I love him and respect him and I honor what he's been through and what we've been through together, and you know, if that's not enough for the people, then heck, don't vote for him."

The second half of the statement, the "heck, don't vote for him," was a winning moment. She looked every bit the middle-class housewife Linda Bloodworth-Thomason had made her up to be. The first half of her statement was off message. For millions of stay-at-home women, whether they were Tammy Wynette fans or not, there was a hint of condescension in dismissing "some little woman standing by her man."

It was condescension that became more overt when she later told reporters "I suppose I could have stayed home, baked cookies, and had teas, but what I decided was to fulfill my profession...."

To many women it was deeply offensive to be told that running a household and raising children while their husbands were in the workplace made them simpleton cookie-bakers.

The Yale feminist Crit scholar had thrown away her disguise and Hillary would have to humble herself, once again, by baking cookies for a women's magazine.

The week after the *60 Minutes* interview, Gennifer Flowers, backed by a tabloid, released a tape recording of her phone conversations with Governor Clinton. Among other topics, there was admiring talk between the two of Bill's consummate ability to perform oral sex. The story led all three networks. Many wives would have been driven to hide. Hillary went to a pay phone at a campaign stop in Pierre, South Dakota, called her husband and coolly began to organize a counteroffensive.

Hillary once again saw the hand of conspiracy. She directed all her anger at the Republicans she believed were behind the assault. Hillary positioned herself to play coy defense.

"Well, I don't understand why uncorroborated rumors and all of the stories that are being promoted command as much attention as they seem to," she told the press. "So from my perspective, I am bewildered by the kinds of press attention they've generated."[40]

Then came the whopper: "I feel very comfortable about my husband and about our marriage."

She also played offense, throwing the war room into full gear. In 1988 both Clintons had expressed exasperation with Michael Dukakis's inability to respond to Bush's attacks. Now the Clintons were responding to the Bush campaign themselves.

Hillary set out to level the playing field by slipping into her interviews mentions of the unsubstantiated rumor that George Bush had had an affair with a former aide. "I don't understand why nothing's ever been said about a George Bush girlfriend," Hillary said in a *Vanity Fair* interview. "I understand he has a Jennifer, too," she said coyly.[41]

The war room kept up the assault on the Bush White House from every angle. Bill Clinton, the man of many shady deals, denounced the straightlaced George Bush as a trafficker of sleaze while promising to deliver the most ethical administration in history. Clinton attacked Bush's China policy while teaching the Democratic Party how to use John Huang and Charlie Trie and their Communist Chinese handlers as ATM money machines.

"The enemy," Alinsky wrote, "properly goaded and guided in his response will be your major strength."[42]

The Bush campaign was goaded into overreacting where it should have ignored attacks, underreacting when its vital interests were at stake. Under the thrall of the notoriously fickle Office of Management and Budget Director Richard Darman, the Bush people spent an inordinate amount of time worrying about their inability to acknowledge the existence of the recession, while hoping that Clinton's past would yield a silver bullet that would put him away for good.

In this way, Bill Clinton became the forty-second president of the United States. It was a presidency won and operated in large part by Hillary Rodham Clinton, one of America's shrewdest campaign bosses since Mark Hanna.

Hillary had reorganized Bill's comeback victory after he lost the governorship through sheer ineptitude. During his long tenure in office, she solved problems for him from the school desegregation order to the costly energy from the Grand Gulf nuclear plant. She neutralized enemies like John Robert Starr and helped her husband recover from his disastrous 1988 speech in Atlanta.

Hillary Clinton never shied away from putting herself on the line, ripping into candidate Tom McRae and now the Republicans. In her *60 Minutes* interview, Hillary explored new levels of public humiliation and victimhood.

In short, Hillary has enabled Bill Clinton to escape his fate, Houdini like, again and again. She has come through. Now it was time to collect. The gangly student activist wanted to become the co-president of the United States. It was only the beginning for Hillary Rodham Clinton.

EIGHT
THE BLUE LIGHT SPECIAL

"Effective organization is thwarted by the desire for instant and dramatic change, or as I have phrased it elsewhere, the demand for revelation rather than revolution."

— SAUL ALINSKY, *RULES FOR RADICALS*

During the 1992 presidential campaign, Bill Clinton showcased his ambitious and brainy wife as one of the advantages of electing him, saying, "Buy one, get one free."

Hillary would sometimes add, "People call us two-for-one. The blue light special."[1] At a campaign stop, Bill Clinton added: "I think what we will do if I am the nominee and if I am elected, we will try to decide what it is she ought to do, then discuss it with ourselves and then tell the American people, and give them time to get adjusted to it. It would be unusual, there has never been a...."[2] He never finished that thought. He didn't have to. The direction the candidate was heading was unmistakable. Bill would become the President of the United States, known by the acronym POTUS, and Hillary would become the Co-President of the United States (to be known, perhaps, as COPUS). On the morning after the election, Bill Clinton woke up, looked over at his wife, and they both started laughing. "Can you believe that this happened to us?" he asked. She told *Time* magazine, "A friend of ours said it's like the dog that keeps chasing the car and all of a sudden catches it."[3]

It did not take Hillary much time to settle into the role of co-president. By the time of the election, it was apparent to most economists that the 1992 recession had been relatively shallow and the country was building toward a recovery of massive proportions. This was a good news/bad news scenario for the president and co-president. An administration lives or dies by the economy, and the Clintons certainly did not want to meet the same fate as George Bush. Yet, in another sense, the timing of the recovery was politically inopportune. They needed to show that somehow the Bush people had almost driven America off the cliff and the new Clinton Democrats were the rescuers. They needed the recession to linger a bit longer if they were to portray the Bush years as a grim and dark depression, with George Bush cast as Herbert Hoover and themselves as the Roosevelts.

But the recovery was already under way. They merely had to jump in front of the parade and appear to be leading it. The Clintons quickly organized an economic conference in Little Rock, one that would position them to take credit for the economy.

At the economic summit in December 1992, Hillary signaled to the world where she stood in the administration. As the nation's leading economists came to Little Rock to offer their advice, Hillary sat at the table with her husband, diligently taking notes, showing the world that she would take a major role in shaping policy.[4]

This was not the first time a first lady had boldly exercised power. For a month after Woodrow Wilson's devastating stroke, Edith Wilson and the president's physician were the only people allowed to see him. Mrs. Wilson guided her husband's unsteady hand in signing major bills. She would disappear into his bedroom and come out, like a female Moses walking down from the mountain, to issue edicts. Whether the decisions came from Woodrow or Edith Wilson is still a guessing game for many historians.

Florence Harding was at least as instrumental in the rise of her husband, Warren G., as Hillary would be to Bill. Rosalynn Carter sat in on Jimmy Carter's cabinet meetings, stirring a great deal of resentment in Washington. During the Reagan years, Nancy Reagan kept a watchful eye on her husband's staff and was blamed for engineering the dismissal of Chief of Staff Don Regan. Even Barbara Bush, caricatured by the Clinton minions as a hopeless, antifeminist housewife, was known by insiders as a shrewd judge of character and a prescient unofficial political advisor to the president.

As with Rosalynn Carter and Nancy Reagan, though, some Americans did not like the idea of Hillary Clinton, an unelected official, becoming, in essence, a second vice president, and one of dubious constitutionality. "If Hillary makes a stupid suggestion, who's going to want to call her on it?" asked Ben Wattenberg, former aide to President Lyndon Johnson and an American Enterprise Institute fellow.[5] Hillary was

denounced by Margaret Thatcher's former press secretary Sir
Bernard Ingham as the "unacceptable face of nepotism."[6]

Still, for the most part the "blue light special" was tremen-
dously popular. It presaged a willingness—even a hunger—
among American voters for outward signs of equality. And this
aura of goodwill allowed the Clintons to make a dramatic
departure from the Wilsons and the Hardings. The Clintons
were open about the nature of their power-sharing arrangement. They advertised it and made a point of it among women
voters. It was only later, that some started asking whether Bill
was enthusiastically sharing power with a spouse whose intellect he respected or rather a dangerously exposed politician
making a craven deal with someone who had the power to
stop him cold.

Once in Washington, Hillary knew enough about the
White House to appreciate that physical proximity to the
Oval Office directly reflects political power. First ladies tradi-
tionally occupy an office in the East Wing of the White
House to be closer to the family residence quarters.

With the help of her friend Susan Thomases, Hillary soon
assigned herself prime space in the West Wing, strategically
located where she could keep an eye on the domestic policy
advisors running up and down the stairwell to see the president below. "We were looking at this floor plan," a White
House aide said, "and presto, she had a layout it would have
taken an industrial engineer weeks to figure. Not everybody
was happy, but she got it right."[7]

In an early bid to show the White House staff "who's
boss," her portrait was placed more prominently than Vice
President Al Gore's.[8] Even more pointed was her attempt to
relegate Vice President Al Gore to the Old Executive Building.

If there were going to be two vice presidents, *she* was going to be the senior one, close to the ear of the president. As recounted by Bob Zelnick in his book *Gore: A Political Life*, Hillary's advisor Susan Thomases "arrogated to herself the role of 'official office space designator' for the new administration. She suggested that Gore would be able to function perfectly well from a fine suite of offices in the Old Executive Office Building"—across the street from the White House—"leaving the one about eighteen strides from the Oval Office for Hillary Rodham Clinton." It was a power grab that would be thwarted, but not without a fight.

Even though she lost the office space battle to the vice president, she did secure a prime position in the office space pecking order at the West Wing. Her office had a bird's-eye view of the stairs and was across from Vince Foster's office.

"I can see [my husband] any time I want to," she told the *Ladies Home Journal* in 1993. "I can look out the window and see Bill." She boasted that her husband called her twelve times a day, leading everyone to presume it was for policy advice and direction on personnel.[9]

THE CO-GOVERNOR

By the time she had become first lady of the United States, Hillary had considerable experience sharing executive power with her husband. For the past four years in Arkansas she had virtually been co-governor of Arkansas.

"I was one of those who sincerely believed the wrong Clinton was occupying the White House," said *Arkansas Democrat* managing editor John Robert Starr. This was an opinion held by many in Little Rock where, from 1983 to 1987, Hillary Clinton dabbled in Arkansas government constantly, leading an education reform effort that became a prototype for the Clinton blitzkreig way of governing in the project to remake America's health care system.

The education reform effort began when the governor was ordered by the state supreme court to equalize funding of Arkansas's school districts. This ruling put him in extreme jeopardy. Clinton could either take money out of wealthier school districts or he could raise taxes for poor school districts.

Either way, it was an invitation to political suicide.

Another potentially fatal element was added to this toxic cocktail of issues: the state's abysmal reputation in education. Arkansas business leaders were horrified that Arkansas schools ranked nearly lowest in the nation, discouraging hopes for attracting new business to the state.

Governor Clinton had little choice but to undertake immediately education reform as the centerpiece of his agenda. In 1983 Hillary asked her husband to put her up front, in the glare of the cameras, as chairwoman of the state commission to fix education. It was the first time Arkansans had a chance to see her at work, and they had liked the picture they were shown.

Hillary made a great show of diligence. She visited every one of Arkansas's seventy-five counties, sitting in nine hours of committee meetings on a typical day.[10] While she made a drawn-out public drama of listening to the people, a "listening" game she was later to replay with the voters of New York, Governor Clinton worked the Little Rock power circuit, inviting business leaders, journalists, and key legislators to the mansion. Hillary charmed the Good Suits Club, a kind of Business Roundtable of Little Rock leaders, enlisting them in the cause of education reform.

In short, it was a textbook campaign. The Clintons spent a great deal of time "listening" to the people, from local educators to Fortune 500 CEOs. As with so many of their efforts, the town hall meetings and backyard shindigs were sheer public relations, window dressing for an agenda that was already decided. But Arkansas fell for it.

As with the Watergate House Judiciary staff under John Doar, there was an outside effort and an inside effort. The public tour was the outside effort. Since the court had left Clinton with no other option than to deal with the education issue, then the challenge of the inside effort would be to make it a winning issue. The Clintons used education to launch the booster phase of their perpetual campaign for the rest of their years in Little Rock and ulitmately to set the stage to run for the presidency.

Hillary's appearances before Arkansas legislators were full of virtual substance and self-depracating humor. She made frequent references to her small family and spoke with passion of Arkansas's future. Hillary wowed them, as she would do a decade later when testifying about health care before Congress.

When the recommendations of her commission were released, they were chock-full of the education reform ideas in vogue at the time. Class sizes would be reduced. The school year would be lengthened. Kindergarten would be made mandatory. In a state in which many schools simply did not teach foreign languages, such courses would become a requirement. Math, social studies, and science would be given greater emphasis. Students would be regularly tested and held back for remedial work if they failed to meet minimum standards.

The plan had teeth. If 85 percent of students failed in a given district, it would be decertified.

There were also two other requirements. One, predictably, was a penny increase in the state's sales tax. The other, announced by Governor Clinton on a statewide television address, was the result of a high-risk inside political calculation made by Bill, Hillary, and Dick Morris. This element—mandatory teacher testing—shocked the education bureaucrats.

In virtually every state, there is no lobby more powerful or more dedicated to protecting and advancing the liberal agenda than the teachers' unions. This time the Arkansas Educational Association (AEA), the Clintons's most loyal allies, were utterly and completely betrayed.

This would not be the last time the Clintons were to catch their natural allies off-stride. The Clinton solution to the court mandate was a work of sheer political calculation, an early version of the Clinton/Morris triangulation strategy.

At one corner of the triangle was a state electorate desperate to shed its image as a rural backwater. At the other corner were teachers, many of them unqualified.

The Clintons held their position at the apex of the triangle, appearing to taxpayers in one corner as reformers and to the educrats at the other corner as betrayers who might yet be willing to cut an inside deal. This put them in a position of great potential power. At a time when Ronald Reagan was starting to ride high late in his first term, and tax increases were about as popular as sour milk, the Clintons also took the sting out of their tax increase by linking it to a notably conservative proposal.

There was also a subliminal racial appeal in the strategy,

since the least qualified teachers tended to be found in the most poorly financed school districts, which tended to be black. It was an early version of Bill Clinton's 1992 harangue against Sister Souljah. He lost some allies and old friends, but Clinton solidified his hold on the electorate by seeming to stand up to a powerful special interest.

If the education reform campaign had all the trappings of a political campaign, that's because it was. A finance committee raised $130,000 for radio and television advertising. Another group raised funds to distribute a quarter-of-a-million brochures. Each brochure included a postcard that a presumably indignant citizen could mail to their state legislator in support of the reforms.[11] When the AEA recovered from its shock and fought back, Hillary was ready at every turn with crisp rebuttals.

The hostility aimed at the Clintons by the teacher's union was palpable. After she was hissed at, jeered, and booed, Hillary told friend Diane Blair that "it's heartbreaking, but someday they will understand."[12] Far from being a problem, the spirited opposition of a teachers' union extended and deepened the governor's popularity. The more the union attacked, the more support the governor received from around the state. He projected the image of being so committed to the well-being of the children of his state that he'd take on the most powerful element in his own party.

Winning in the legislature was a dicey proposition. It took late night arm-twisting and personal appeals from Hillary to get recalcitrant legislators to sign on the dotted line. In the end, most of the Clinton package passed, including the added one-cent sales tax that promised $185 million in new education monies. Bill and Hillary celebrated in the mansion with champagne. And when they finished the bottle, they opened another one. As a result of this early experiment in triangulation, Bill Clinton's 1984 election was the easiest victory he had ever won. The education campaign rolled throughout the rest of the new term, building steam for the elections ahead.

"For two or three years, he got rid of the special-interest groups, the AEA and the blacks," John Robert Starr told the *New Yorker*. "He told them to go stuff it. He called me once and said the blacks were on his ass. I told him, 'Don't worry, I'll go after the blacks—I'll get them so mad at me they'll forget about you!' I called them pipsqueak preachers."[13]

With the reform firmly in place, the state could dissolve or annex any school that failed to meet its standards. This forced schools to teach state-approved education guidelines, a multicultural curriculum that watered down American studies and Western civilization and extolled the virtues of African civilization.

Blair Hurt of the *Wall Street Journal* found that the twenty pages of the Education Standards report that the reform legislation was based on, included 124 "shalls." All school districts were forced to bow to Hillary's "shalls" including a multicultural agenda on history lessons. In 1984, eighty-four of Arkansas's 367 school districts facing the threat of dissolution were forced to bow in another way. They were forced to increase local taxes.

School districts remained under the constant threat of abolition if their students failed 85 percent of the Minimum Placement Test. The result, Blair Hurt reported in the *Wall Street Journal*, was widespread cheating—students left alone in a classroom with the answers or given the answers outright.

Worse was the onerous burden Hillary's reforms placed

on the schools that honestly chose to comply. Benny Gooden, superintendent of the Fort Smith school district, found that it took eleven pounds of paperwork to prove his district had complied with Hillary's bureaucratic, top-down standards. Some school districts were also forced to increase local taxes to avoid dissolution.

Nor was teacher testing the panacea that it had been advertised to be. Remedial training and a generous willingness to allow teachers to retake the test over a period of years kept 97 percent of Arkansas teachers in place. In time, the education establishment would "understand," just as Hillary predicted. They didn't like being used as a political piñata, but in the end they saw that not much had changed. In fact, they had reason to be delighted with Bill Clinton for raising hundreds of millions of additional tax dollars for education.

Eventually, everyone seemed to benefit on the surface. The governor burnished his popularity. Hillary got a chance to exercise power as a principal, not merely as an adjunct to her husband. The AEA got a payback in the form of tax money and teacher tests that were irrelevant. Everyone was better off except for the children of Arkansas and their taxpaying parents. In truth, the Clinton campaign did not improve Arkansas's educational standing. The *Wall Street Journal* reported that test scores for high school seniors on the American College Test (ACT) *fell* in 1986. The ACT test scores went up in 1992, but with a new test that inflated scoring. When adjusted according to the pre-1992 scoring, Arkansas students again came near the bottom of the twenty-eight states that use the ACT. In 1993, 57 percent of all Arkansas college freshmen had to take remedial classes in reading, writing, or math.[14]

For all the sound and fury, very little had changed. Very little had been accomplished, except for two things.

The Clintons maintained their hold on power. And Arkansans paid more of their earnings to their government.

After the Clintons left for Washington, Betty Tucker, wife of Clinton's successor Jim Guy Tucker, began getting calls from the state Department of Education asking her permission to make the most minuscule of decisions. Reportedly, the governor's office was asked by districts if it could hire a teacher or add a janitor's slot. "The suspicion was," David Brock was told, "that the department had been micromanaged out of the governor's bedroom."[15]

Hillary's education reform brought every district in the state under her thumb—and kept it there.

THE CO-PRESIDENT

Hillary's co-presidency began on a note of disappointment. She had wished to follow fully in the footsteps of Robert F. Kennedy. Being attorney general allowed RFK to be a presidential sidekick in whom enormous power and confidence would be invested. There was loose talk among Hillary's admirers about her serving as White House chief of staff, or perhaps holding a cabinet position.

It remained just that—talk. No one had bothered to research the possibility. An official appointment for Hillary would have been impossible. Call it LBJ's revenge. In 1967 Lyndon Baines Johnson, still miffed that Robert Kennedy had served as attorney general, made it impossible for presidents to appoint a relative to a position "over which he exercises jurisdiction."

To her grave disappointment, Hillary could not become an official member of the Clinton team.

She could, however, exercise informal power. The co-presidency would have to be understood, implied, "virtual," but not made official. Hillary would exercise the power, but could hold no title. The federal nepotism law would be honored, at least literally. But she *had* to have the authority. And everyone would have to know it.

That is why there was so much emphasis on cosmetics, why it was so important to give her portrait such a prominent place. That is why she went to a policy retreat at Camp David at which cabinet spouses had been pointedly excluded. That is why she allowed the staff to see her correct her husband in front of them.

"How could you be so damned stupid?" she barked at him in front of staff. "How could you do that?"[16]

"The President sits in the middle of the table, the Vice President right across from him, and Hillary wherever she wants," a Clinton aide said. "And the refrain we have all gotten used to is, 'What do you think, Hillary?'"[17] She quickly recognized that the speechwriting process was a central policy function in the White House. It was not long before she was calling to add last minute changes, or to get down on her hands and knees when need be to cut and paste drafts of major addresses herself.[18]

"What's it like to govern?" Bill Moyers asked Hillary at an Austin event that included Texas governor Ann Richards.

"It's been exhilarating, frustrating, eye-opening...."

Later in the conversation, Hillary caught the slip and said, "Just to set the record straight, I'm not really governing either."

"If you believe that," the sassy Texas governor retorted, "I've got a bridge I'd like to sell you."[19]

Hillary's ostentatious show of power generated little opposition and a great deal of media flattery.

In the first ten weeks of 1993, some fifty-seven minutes of network time were devoted to Hillary Rodham Clinton. Vice President Al Gore attracted four minutes.[20]

"If we could be one-hundredth as great as you and Hillary Rodham Clinton have been in the White House," Dan Rather gushingly told the Clintons by satellite at a meeting of CBS affiliates, "we'd take it right now and walk away winners…. Thank you very much, and tell Mrs. Clinton we're pulling for her."

This national anchorman who made his reputation by standing up at a White House press conference to talk back to Richard Nixon could not have made it plainer that he was pulling for Hillary, her husband, and for Hillary's health care plan, and that his news program would lead the Clinton cheering section.[21] Nor was Dan Rather the only journalist to be transformed into a quivering groupie by the Clintons. The reporting of *Newsweek*'s Eleanor Clift was embarassingly obsequious. Laura Blumenfeld of the *Washington Post* became a symbol of the lengths to which much of the national press fawned over the Clintons. She actually wrote that Roger Clinton's life was made more difficult by his brother's spectacular success. "If your brother is Christ, you have a choice: become a disciple, or become an anti-Christ, or find yourself caught somewhere between the two."[22]

A few journalists rebelled but found themselves under attack if they did, especially if they were male. "There was a kind of political correctness that applied to writing about her," complained Fred Barnes, then the White House correspondent for the *New Republic*. "The pieces were adoring: She was a wonderful mother, one of America's 100 best lawyers, politically shrewd. She had no flaws, except maybe her choice of husband."[23]

When Nancy Reagan borrowed a dress to wear to a public function, she was splashed with media vitriol and the Internal Revenue Service was sent to conduct an audit. Hillary was the toast of the town when she was photographed in the black bare-shouldered Donna Karan dress that Candice Bergen (a.k.a. Murphy Brown—how's that for politically correct?) had worn to the Emmys. Hillary's ever-mutating hairstyle became shorter, lighter, more layered under the talented fingers of Frederic Fekkai, known as "King Cut" among celebrity clients like Demi Moore, Emma Thompson, Jodie Foster, and Marla Maples.[24] A woman who ten years before had to be persuaded to shave her underarms and wear deodorant now accepted $2,000 in fees and airplane travel costs for a photo shoot that put her on the cover of the May 1993 *Family Circle*.[25]

Nor was her husband immune from fashion fever. It was in the first, error-prone spring of the Clinton presidency, an avalanche of gaffes that included the gays in the military fiasco, that Clinton sat in Air Force One on a Los Angeles runway, holding thousands of people hostage in the sky so he could receive his $200 haircut from Cristophe. (A White House spinmeister suggested, absurdly, that the commander-in-chief wanted to give the business to Cristophe to assuage the hairdresser after his wife took her business to Fekkai.)

As the Clintons remade themselves, they also remade the White House. They brought in Little Rock decorator Khaki Hockersmith to redo the Oval Office. Out went the Bushes' tasteful champagne-and-cream sofas and chairs, and the pale blue curtains. In came bold red stripes, red pillows, and a gold curtain with a blue laurel leaf motif, the slightly rakish suggestion of a Hot Springs bawdy house.

The White House changed in other ways. Gary Aldrich—an FBI agent assigned to do background checks on White House employees—described the new decorum in "the people's house." Aldrich often remarked to me how "shocking" it was to see the dress of the new Clinton White House when he was accustomed to the formality of the Bush staff. "It was Norman Rockwell on the one hand and Berkeley, California, with an Appalachian twist on the other."

And there were many other testimonials, to the change in attitude and respect for the White House with the change of administrations. "Reagan would not take off his jacket in the Oval Office out of respect for what he called 'the people's house,'" one Republican White House aide told me. "During the Bush years, we dressed every day as if we were attendees at a wedding." Young Clintonites flooded in with miniskirts, hair spikes, and T-shirts.

Before moving into the White House, Hillary's staff put out the spin that she read no fewer than forty-three White House biographies. (Slightly better than one every other day between the election and the inauguration for those gullible enough to believe the story.) She made a point of meeting with former first ladies, having tea with Jacqueline Kennedy Onassis at her Fifth Avenue apartment.[26]

For all her preparation, however, in the first half of the first term Hillary was too busy being co-president to worry much about the formal duties of actually being a first lady. Months went by before the first state dinners were held. Congressional leaders and powerful committee chairmen and their wives waited for White House invitations that never came. After bringing order to Clinton's life as governor, she allowed him to show up two-and-a-half hours late for the reception for the U.S. Holocaust Museum, standing up Polish President Lech Walesa and House Speaker Tom Foley. Some of the guests were Holocaust survivors, who were left to mill about in a tent as a hard rain turned the ground beneath them to mush.

Making people wait is standard procedure for the Clintons. A whole book could be written on stories of late arrivals and irritated guests. Years later, Bill and Hillary would leave the king and queen of Norway to stand at the landing of the White House on a frigid night, a scene that played over and over again on Norwegian television. This outraged the whole country, but was little noticed in America. In a sense, the Clintons allocated their time shrewdly. How many electoral votes does Norway have?

PARANOIA STRIKES DEEP

Hillary arrived at the White House after years of humiliation at the hands of state troopers who acted as procurers and protectors for her husband. This was undoubtedly painful for her, the constant presence of the troopers a visible reminder of Bill's other life. Yet she forced herself to live with the enablers of her husband's infidelity. What she could not live with was the presence of subordinates with political disloyalties, real or imagined.

In the governor's mansion Hillary had once tried to install a swimming pool, arguing it would be good for Chelsea. Dick Morris advised the Clintons that this would be a fatal mistake. Pools may be common features among the friends of Hillary in places like Scarsdale or Beverly Hills. In Arkansas, it would be taken as a sign that the Clintons had settled in as royalty. Hillary was dissuaded from installing the pool only by fierce and unrelenting opposition from two other Valkyries, Betsey Wright and press secretary Joan Roberts.

Now she was in the White House, the second most powerful person in the United States, perhaps the world. She would remake the White House and its staff in her own image, and this time no one would have the power to restrain or correct her mistakes.

She started with the official staff, a blunt exercise in power based on an astonishing ignorance of the folkways of the White House. Her paranoia would become a self-fulfilling prophecy, fed by her own mistakes and mistreatment of subordinates.

The Clintons themselves say it began one morning soon after the inauguration when a staffer walked into their bedroom to wake them up. To the Clintons' astonishment, staff members followed them around wherever they went, even in the residence. The Clintons found this disconcerting, which, to be fair, would be a typical reaction for most Americans.[27]

It wasn't long, however, before the Clintons became paranoid about the constant hovering staff, a fear that extended to a press corps that also seemed to appear in too many sensitive places. In short order, Hillary ended the practice of allowing reporters to stroll unescorted to press secretary Dee Dee Myers's office.

"She made it clear what she thought about reporters roaming around," a Clinton insider told the *Washington Post*. "She said the press were scum. That they would be standing around trying to read papers upside down on people's desks and doing gotcha interviews and just trying to make us look bad." A Democratic campaign official said, "She freaked. She could not abide the idea of having spies in her own home. She puts just an enormous store in having people around whose loyalty she trusts. Much more than he does. She really does have a feeling that if you are not with us, then you are against."[28]

"Hillary feels like she's walking into Washington with her arms wide open and smiling, but she's watching on both sides," said Linda Bloodworth-Thomason, putting her friend's behavior in a more charitable light. "She's not a fool. She knows that Washington is treacherous."[29] The Secret Service almost immediately became the focus of the Clintons' suspicions. Their silent, watchful, professional mien was incomprehensible to Bill, who was used to being surrounded by jovial fellow travelers and good ole boys like L.D. Brown and Larry Patterson. Their constant presence in the living quarters, a policy that began after the near assassination of Ronald Reagan, was deeply resented by the Clintons. They soon had them moved. Camera positions in the private residence were moved or eliminated as well. For their part, the agents felt mistreated by a first lady who openly regarded them as servants, asking agents to carry luggage, a humiliation for law enforcement officers and a distraction for agents who needed to keep their eyes on the surrounding crowds and hands free to act.

A widespread rumor had it that Hillary had once thrown a Bible at an agent for driving too slow. Another version had it that she had thrown a briefing book at her husband and hit an agent instead. There were also numerous reports of the Clintons openly bad-mouthing and violently chastising the

Secret Service. The fits of cursing from the Clintons not only betrayed a deeply ingrained disrespect for law enforcement but a complete contempt for the men and women ready to throw their bodies in harm's way to protect them.

The Secret Service was proud of its reputation for lifelong confidentiality. It took only a few months of exposure to the Clintons to wear away at that tradition. First, the Bible-throwing story made its way into print. Then, more disastrously for the Secret Service, the *Chicago Sun-Times* and *Newsweek* reported that Hillary and Bill had one of their knock-down, drag-out fights in the residence, with the first lady throwing a lamp at the president. Some assumed that the source must have been in the Secret Service. Hillary retaliated against *Newsweek* for reporting the story by canceling a scheduled interview.[30]

Things quickly grew worse. Unaware of the statutory role the Secret Service plays in protecting the president, the Clintons naively asked Harry Thomason to investigate the possibility of replacing them with private security guards or the FBI. Former bar bouncer and the Clintons's director of White House security Craig Livingstone told an FBI agent: "I wrote this memo, this four page memo, and I recommended that the Secret Service be dumped in favor of the FBI.... Someone got a hold of the memo, leaked it to the Secret Service, and they went ballistic." The project of "privatizing" the Secret Service function was mercifully short-lived.

"From the start, there was an atmosphere of chaos and paranoia, and it started with Hillary Clinton," a White House aide told the press.[31] After Hillary's old Watergate associate, Bernie Nussbaum, was brought in as White House counsel, he asked the cooks and gardeners to fill out a form with thirty-three questions, including questions about their political affiliations.

The paranoia extended to the White House telephone system. In his first days as president, Clinton was annoyed that operators came on every line. New lines were installed through a rush grant of a sole source contract that allowed him to place his own calls (this would later give him the false sense of security he needed to call Monica Lewinsky for phone sex and, undoubtedly, countless other equally willing associates). To ensure the president's privacy, it wasn't good enough to remove the outmoded telephone system at a cost to the taxpayers of more than $27 million. The Clintons removed the switchboard operators as well.

The paranoia extended to the official staff, the nonpartisan civil servants who kept the White House operating smoothly. Marsha Scott, self-described former "hippie girl-friend" of Bill's in the 1960s and now White House appointee as director of correspondence, summarily fired the ladies in the White House correspondence office. The official excuse was to live up to the promise to trim the White House staff by 25 percent.

"Of all the things the Clintons did, this was perhaps the most sickening," a Bush White House aide said. "Most of them had been there for many years, some were close to retiring. They were hard-working, dedicated, and good-humored. It was like beating up the town librarian." Soon mail was piling to the ceiling, and there were tales of mail being thrown out by the bushel. But room had been made for patronage employees, people who could be trusted.

HILLARY'S GUILLOTINE

The reign of terror proceeded into the White House kitchen. White House chef Pierre Chambrin was asked to leave, along with *sous-chef* John Moeller, assistant chef Sean Haddon, and dishwasher Adam Collick. Gone, too, was Milton Pitts, the barber who had trimmed the hair of numerous past presidents.

Chris Emery, one of four White House ushers, got the axe. His firing offense? He had spoken to former First Lady Barbara Bush on the phone about a computer he had programmed for her. There was nothing unusual in this; White House staff often took calls from former first family members. In this one act, Hillary revealed not only pettiness, but the inner workings of her own mind. She actually believed that it was possible that Barbara Bush was snooping and collecting dirt on her, using a valet as a spy.

In truth, it was a small act of courtesy, if not a part of Emery's job description. For answering that phone call, Emery lost the job by which he supported his wife, an eight-year-old daughter, and three older stepchildren.[32]

In all of these acts of vindictive housecleaning, Hillary and Bill showed one of their most striking traits. They are able to project great empathy to the stranger who has lost a house to a natural disaster, touching his shoulders and kneading his arms. They have immense compassion for humanity at an abstract level, and can tear up at the story of a Kosovar family's plight. But they are callous, even coldly cruel, to subordinates.

Worse yet, the Clintons's fear of the staff can't just be chalked up to a desire for privacy. Their overreactions to rumors betray the truth of those rumors.

That they fear being spied upon through absurd channels—cooks, gardeners, ushers—betrays their own experience with "opposition research" and private detectives. Previous presidents and first ladies had no problem with the White House staff, which prompts the question: What are the Clintons saying and doing that requires so much concealment? Monicagate provided one answer. But the reality goes deeper than that.

HELL TO PAY

The purge of the White House staff led to co-president Hillary's first big public relations disaster: the White House Travel Office.

After the election, campaign worker Catherine Cornelius, blonde and pretty, was brought into the White House to work at the White House Travel Office. It wasn't long before the White House started putting out the story that Cornelius was Clinton's cousin, as a peculiar and peculiarly Clintonesque way to explain her frequent appearances with the president on the road and trips to the Oval Office.

Once in the Travel Office, she began to conspire against her superior, Billy Dale, whose job she expected to take— because she was a Clinton loyalist and Dale and his crew were apolitical careerists of the sort the Clintons treated with contempt and as possible spies. Cornelius handed David Watkins—a former Little Rock ad man and now the White House director of administration—reports of bad record-keeping, poor money management, and sloppy handling of vouchers, all of which enabled her to help set Billy Dale and his fellow workers up for a claim that they had sticky fingers.

As Cornelius undermined Dale from the inside, Clinton

friend and campaign supporter Harry Thomason—who, in addition to being a Hollywood producer, had an interest in an air charter broker called TRM—made a direct assault from the outside. Anxious to obtain a White House contract for TRM, Thomason built on Cornelius's suspicions and brought them directly to the Clintons. The first lady was "pressuring" Chief of Staff Mack McLarty to act. Watkins describes "pressure for action" from Mrs. Clinton. White House counsel Vince Foster's notes disclose the continuing pressure over the Travel Office and that "the first lady was concerned and desired action." Foster wrote that he had to "defend HRC role whatever it is, was in fact, or might have been misperceived to be" in July 1993. Watkins and Foster were sent to investigate.

There was a nexus of motives that made the firing of the White House Travel Office seem like the proverbial killing of multiple birds with a single stone. One was to award business to friends. ("These guys are sharp," the president wrote in a memo after hearing of Thomason's plan to take over White House travel.) Another was to extend Hillary's purge, opening seven new jobs for loyal and trusted people. (David Watkins recounts his phone conversation with Hillary five days before the firings: "We need those people out—we need our people in—we need the slots.") Another was desire for good publicity at a time when the White House was under fire for the "gays in the military" controversy. Harry Thomasson is credited with stating that the firings would showcase the profligate ways if not outright stealing that had been tolerated under the Republicans and would favorably cast the White House as defenders of the taxpayer. He felt it would "be a great story," showing "Bill Clinton cleaning up the White House" after the Bush administration.

An accounting review by Peat Marwick was commissioned, and it did show careless record-keeping (including the commingling of personal and office accounts by Dale). But it revealed no graft. No matter. Dale was fired after thirty-two years on the job. He and his staff were given little more than an hour to clean their desks and were driven out in a windowless van under the watchful eyes of uniformed Secret Service.

In this act of gratuitous spite, Hillary had finally overreached. The White House worked hard, too hard, to make a felony case against Dale and his people. William Kennedy III —a Rose Law Firm partner, now in the White House counsel's office—called the FBI and set them loose on the Travel Office staff like dobermans to destroy Billy Dale's reputation and justify the firings. As Kennedy told the FBI: It came from "the highest level."

The error was compounded when press secretary Dee Dee Myers was sent out to tout what was meant to be a good news story about the Clintons' ferreting out corruption. But Myers did not know that a cardinal rule of the FBI was never to reveal the targets of an investigation until an indictment is about to be presented. In one clumsy move, the White House revealed that it, and not a disinterested FBI investigation, had initiated the firing of Dale.

Soon the White House was working furiously to contain the damage. New employees—from Worldwide Travel, which handled the Clintons' campaign flights—were in place in the White House and then released, so the White House could take back five fired Travel Office staffers who had had no role in money management.

After an internal investigation, Bill Kennedy and David Watkins were officially reprimanded. Dale, after offering to

plead to a misdemeanor to keep his legal bills down, was prosecuted for a felony, and after a brief deliberation was found
not guilty by a D.C. jury in a 1995 trial in which celebrity
supporters of the Travel Office staff, like ABC news reporter
Sam Donaldson, came to Billy Dale's defense.

One casualty from the Travel Office was David Watkins,
who was ostensibly fired for using a White House helicopter
for a trip to a golf course. But Watkins—a Clinton loyalist
who had been instrumental in keeping the Clintons' campaign
financially afloat in 1992—felt that he had been set-up to take
the fall for Hillary's Travel Office fiasco.

In January 1996 a memo Watkins had written to Chief of
Staff Mack McLarty surfaced. It had never been sent, for it
was the kind of letter one puts in a file to get a set of facts on
record in the event of an investigation or indictment.

"On Friday, while I was in Memphis," Watkins wrote,
"Foster told me that it was important that I speak directly with
the First Lady that day. I called her that evening and she conveyed to me in clear terms her desire for swift and clear action
to resolve the situation. She mentioned that Thomason had
explained how the Travel Office could be run after removing
the current staff—that plan included bringing in WorldWide
Travel to handle the basic travel functions, the actual actions
taken post dismissal, and in light of that she thought immediate action was in order.

"At that meeting you explained that this was on the First
Lady's radar screen. *The message you conveyed to me was clear:
immediate action must be taken.... We both knew that there would
be hell to pay if, after our failure in the Secret Service situation earlier, we failed to take swift and decisive action in conformity with the
First Lady's wishes.*"

Linda Tripp worked in the counsel's office at this time as an executive assistant. She was later deposed by Larry Klayman of Judicial Watch and asked about the Travel Office firings. Tripp testified that she saw a handwritten memo from Hillary demanding that the Travel Office staff be fired and replaced with "our people."

Long before Watkins's memo surfaced and Tripp was deposed, rumors about the first lady's involvement started to leak out. When the White House believed it could still contain the truth, Hillary put out a statement attesting that she "had no role in the decision to terminate the [Travel Office] employees."[33] Hillary repeated this statement under oath to questions by the General Accounting Office and to the twenty-six questions presented to her in my investigation. She denied having "first-hand knowledge" and did "not recall" most other information. These questions were signed by Hillary Rodham Clinton on March 21, 1996, under penalty of perjury.

That denial proved to be very much like Bill Clinton's finger-waving denial of having had sexual relations with Monica Lewinsky: categorically false. But if, as Clinton's defenders asserted, that it is only natural to lie about sex, perhaps Hillary's defense is that it's only natural to lie about the unpleasant business of firing people for no better reason than to replace them with "our people."

The Travel Office fiasco showed one more thing about Hillary Clinton and her husband. They had every right to replace the Travel Office empoyees. They did not have to smear them or lie about why they were being replaced. But it has become second nature to do both. The abuse of power, the destruction of people who are in the way, the lying, even when the truth might be entirely acceptable—these are the Clintons' *modi operandi*.

TROJAN WOMEN

"She has a huge cadre of friends and knows where she wants them in the administration," a White House aide told the press.[34] Hillary quickly fixed her imprint on the president's cabinet, subcabinet, and staff. The men she brought in were, conspicuously, the lawyers—Bernard Nussbaum, Webster Hubbell, William Kennedy III, and Vincent Foster. Elsewhere she exercised her veto authority to keep other white men out of jobs.

One of her early hires was a favorite of Marian Wright Edelman, Dr. Johnetta Cole. Dr. Cole was a former president of Spellman College, brought in to head the transition team's education cluster, making her a Secretary of Education-in-waiting.

Articles on Dr. Cole's past soon began to appear in *Forward*, a leading Jewish paper, and the *New York Post*. It turned out that Dr. Cole had maintained extensive ties with the Venceremos Brigade, an adjunct of the Communist Party of the United States (CPUSA), dedicated to the Havana government. She had founded a CPUSA front organization, the U.S. Peace Council.

Dr. Cole applauded Castro's military adventure in Angola, and was given to saying that American blacks need to "stand in solidarity with the Cuban Revolution." She was one of many notorious far-left activists (including Angela Davis) who denounced Joan Baez for signing an ad in the *New York Times* that criticized the Communist Vietnamese government for its human rights violations. "Some 400,000 servants of the former barbaric regime were sent to re-education camps," said the letter signed by Dr. Cole. "Should they not be re-educated?"[35]

The prospect was mind-boggling. A woman who took a public stand in favor of Communist reeducation camps was Hillary's first choice for America's Secretary of Education. It did not take long for the magnitude of Hillary's mistake to sink in. Before the nomination had been officially referred, the Clintons realized that sending Dr. Cole to a Senate confirmation hearing would be like tossing a T-bone into a den of starving rottweilers. They quietly dropped her.

Hillary would have to look elsewhere to make her mark. A natural place, of course, was the Department of Justice. The Justice Department transition team was firmly in her hands, led by an old friend, Peter Edelman, husband of Marian Wright and a law dean at Georgetown. One of their nominees was Lani Guinier, an old friend of the Clintons from Yale, to head the department's civil rights division.

Of all the embattled Clinton nominees, Guinier was one of the most embarrassing. The American Jewish Congress, which opposed Robert Bork and Clarence Thomas, found Guinier unacceptable, saying that her ideas would lead to "bad public policy." "Crowning a Quota Queen?" asked *Newsweek* in a headline. The term stuck, and was used to great effect by Clint Bolick, a conservative legal scholar, in the *Wall Street Journal*.

What made the Guinier nomination remarkable was that no one stood up for her. Columnist Mark Shields wrote that Clarence Thomas "had a staunch, unflinching champion in Senator Jack Danforth and a supportive White House." Guinier "had nobody on Capitol Hill for her, and the White

House was distracted, disorganized, and in disarray."[36] And, one might add, unwilling to commit to anything but polls.

With Guinier getting little visible White House support, even Carol Moseley-Braun, the liberal firebrand on the Senate Judiciary Committee, refused to meet with her.

Guinier was left, in the unforgettable phrase of an earlier administration, to twist slowly, slowly in the wind. What made the matter worse was that the very people who had put her in this embarrassing spot were thought of as friends. "We had known each other for a long time, after all," she wrote in her book *Lift Every Voice*. "When we were in law school, Bill Clinton and Hillary Rodham were directors of the Yale Barristers Union. They came to my rescue after another student supervisor neglected to recommend me for inclusion in the Prize Trial Competition."[37]

Now Bill claimed to have never read her work, implying that he was surprised by how radical she was after he had nominated her. Insult was added to injury when Hillary ran past her old friend with a dismissive, "Hi, kiddo" and walked on by.

If the Guinier nomination was an embarrassment, the long, problem-plagued attempt to secure a female attorney general was a farcical catastrophe.

It all began, of course, with the one person who most wanted the job—Hillary herself—being unable to have it as a matter of law. Hillary settled for deciding who would be second best. The person would have to be loyal and discreet, sufficiently liberal, and, of course, a woman.

The *New York Post* reported that Judge Patricia Wald, a U.S. Appeals Judge, had turned down the post because it was made clear that she would be expected to rubber-stamp the

Clintons choices for deputy attorney general, associate attorney general, and solicitor general.[38] Judge Wald proved to be very wise as the Justice Department was ultimately stocked with Clinton cronies and relatives of friends.

So the opening went to Zoe Baird, a wealthy corporate lawyer making $650,000 a year. Her nomination did not last long when it was discovered that she had not paid Social Security taxes for her nanny, an oversight that looked more than a little awkward for the nation's chief law enforcer. Then there was Judge Kimba Wood, the liberal scourge of Michael Milken. As with the other interviews, there was no mistaking who was going to make the call. Hillary interviewed Judge Wood for ninety minutes, twice as long as her husband did.[39] Judge Wood, too, had a nanny problem in that her Trinidadian babysitter was undocumented. As with Guinier, the Clintons lost their nerve and refused to risk any of their political capital on Judge Wood, even though it was shown that Judge Wood had violated no law.

The job finally went to Janet Reno, a Dade County, Florida, prosecutor who had made a name for herself by losing high-profile cases and for pressing dubious charges of child abuse.

Janet Reno had all the right qualifications—for Hillary Clinton, that is. She was loyal. She was liberal and warmly regarded by Marian Wright Edelman. And she was a woman, though Camille Paglia would say what everyone thought— that Reno was "the most masculine Clinton appointee."

Above all, Reno had a great desire to get and keep the job, which made her pliable. One condition of Reno's appointment was to accept a trusted Hillary ally—and soon-to-be-convicted felon—Webb Hubbell, who was made associate attorney general and the de facto attorney general. Another apparent condition, played out soon after Reno took office, was to fire all ninety-three U.S. attorneys. This was a break with the tradition of disinterested jurisprudence. Past presidents had replaced prosecutors gradually, preventing any disruption to their ongoing cases.

Reno's heavy axe cleared the way immediately for ninety-three Hillary appointees, including many friends from Wellesley. One appointee, Kris Olson, served as a deputy U.S. attorney in Oregon. There she intentionally wrecked the prosecution of a former Black Panther on a weapons charge. She had been fired for advocating the decriminalization of street prostitution. Now she was in the top spot as U.S attorney in Oregon. Olson celebrated her swearing in with a rendition of a Grateful Dead song by the Gay Men's Chorus.[40]

There was another reason for such haste, of course. Firing the U.S. attorneys stymied a potential fatal line of inquiry into all the assorted scandals that were clinking around in Arkansas.

HILLARY'S VULCAN MIND MELD

Ira Magaziner holds the distinction, along with Judge Robert Bork, of having his last name transformed into an active verb. To "bork" someone means to vilify a nominee with preemptive and baseless character attacks. In Washington today, to "magaziner" is to study an issue to death, then issue a report detailing a solution that can only be described by charts of inputs and outputs that resemble a Rube Goldberg contraption. Ira Magaziner, simply through the exertions of one remarkable career, ought to put to rest forever the excessive adulation accorded to Rhodes scholars in our society.

Magaziner got to know Bill Clinton at Oxford, but his real White House patron was Hillary. They did not merely hit it off. They locked onto each other with the intensity of a Vulcan mind meld, sharing the same corporatist, managerialist, quasi-socialist view of the world.

Hillary and Ira Magaziner served on the board of the non-profit project, the National Center on Education and the Economy, which in 1992 proposed that the Clinton administration enact a utopian scheme for national training. Government would guarantee three years of schooling beyond a basic "competence certificate" at age sixteen. It proposed a mandatory 2 percent levy on American business to pay for this training program. An NCEE experiment in the Rochester schools involved the fastest learners in the mentoring and the teaching of their slower-learning peers. Predictably, this resulted only in a dumbed-down curriculum. It also slowed down the progress of the fast learners. The Rochester experiment was an abject failure. Worse, it was described by biographer Joyce Milton as "corporate fascism—a partnership between government and big business to create a planned economy—with, of course, multiculturalism replacing the more traditional nationalism, racism and anti-Semitism as the unifying ideology."[41]

In 1990 and 1991, NCEE spent more than $100,000 in New York State grant money to pay Rose Law Firm for lobbying activity, with Hillary as the designated person to carry out its activities.

Several interesting questions come to light. One is the propriety of a first lady's being a paid lobbyist. To lobby the legislature? To lobby her husband across a pillow? The other is the fact that Hillary was paid not by the taxpayers of

Arkansas (which alone would have been a scandal), but, in part, by the taxpayers of New York State.

When the payments came to light, New York Governor George Pataki reacted with indignation, "To pay $100,000 to an Arkansas law firm out of scarce state education dollars where it seems no vital services were performed is an outrage."[42]

HEALTH CARE COLD FUSION

A particular meeting of minds occurred over the issue of health care. James Carville could attest to the power of the health care issue, having used it as a keystone of Pennsylvanian Harris Wofford's successful campaign for the U.S. Senate against former U.S. Attorney Richard Thornburgh.

Another health care advisor with a profound impact on Hillary's thinking was Vincente Navarro, professor of health policy at Johns Hopkins University. "Has Socialism Failed?" is the title of a Navarro article published in the *International Journal of Health Services* in 1992. You might guess the answer was obviously "yes!" But not to Dr. Navarro, who wrote "contrary to what is widely accepted today, the socialist experience (in both its Leninist and its social democratic traditions) has been, more frequently than not, more efficient in responding to human needs than the capitalist experience."

With advisors like Magaziner and Navarro, Hillary was determined to sweep aside the best medical delivery system in the world and to reshape 14 percent of America's economy by enacting a national health care plan.

She announced that the plan would be put together within one hundred days. The president pledged to pass it into law in 1993. That seemed like plenty of time. After all, the Lord had taken only seven days and had even rested on the seventh.

The effort began as soon as the Clinton White House opened for business. President Clinton immediately named his wife to head his Health Care Reform Task Force, and Ira Magaziner was brought in as director.

Hillary's task force grew to gargantuan size but operated in near total secrecy and without participation from private-sector health care companies, which were consciously excluded.

The task force experts were joined, however, by more than two hundred detailees from executive branch positions. The amalgamation of policy "wonks" eventually swelled to five hundred. Participants were not available to be interviewed; indeed, the White House refused to release their names lest they be compromised somehow by exposure to the American people. Not even a directory of members was published; someone would surely leak it to a conspiring world.

It was not long before the task force got bogged down. Snafus of every sort developed. They began with the simple logistics of holding meetings, and ended with management practices that explored the outreaches of asininity.

Task force members found themselves waiting in long lines to be cleared in by the Secret Service, day after day. There were meetings, which led to consensus conclusions, that were painstakingly reviewed at "tollgate" meetings that could last half a day, during which time Magaziner would review, evaluate, and correct recommendations before letting them proceed onward. One such tollgate lasted past 2:00 AM on a Sunday morning. One member of the task force revealed to *Time* that this was "Ira's own heuristic process. This is the way Ira decides things. He gets as many people in a room and talks as long as everyone can stand."[43]

When challenged to reduce the plan to a two-page memo, Magaziner refused. There was too great a danger, he said, that details would leak out. This plan had to spring fully grown from Hillary's forehead.

Meanwhile, Hillary lobbied Capitol Hill to the applause of Democratic representatives flattered by the first lady's attending on them. The tone of press coverage was no less spellbound.

"In the midst of redesigning America's health care system and replacing Madonna as our leading cult figure, the new first lady has already begun working on her next project, far more metaphysical and uplifting," gushed the *Washington Post* hagiographer Martha Sherrill. "She is both impersonal and poignant with much more depth, intellect, and spirituality than we are used to in a politician.... She has goals, but they appear to be so huge and far-off grand and noble things twinkling in the distance that it's hard to see what she sees."[44] The pages of the *Post* seemed not nearly large enough to write of Hillary's charisma, genious and prodigious output. Others had difficulty "seeing what she sees," but for entirely different reasons.

Right off the bat, she showed no deference to opposition leaders, or even potential allies, never a wise move in pushing a major agenda. Dick Armey, the powerful Republican congressman from Texas, had once referred to Hillary's health care plan as "a Dr. Kevorkian prescription" for American jobs. When they came face to face, Armey tried to make nice, without compromising his stance.

"While I don't share the chairman's joy at our holding hearings on a government health care system," Armey said, "I do share his intention to make the debate as exciting as possible."

"I am sure you will do that, you and Dr. Kevorkian," Hillary spat back.

Armey got in the last word. "The reports of your charm are overstated, and the reports of your wit are understated." The next Republican to speak started by saying, "After seeing how you impaled my colleague...."[45]

It soon became apparent on the Hill and to Clinton's cabinet that the only real function of the task force was to feed facts into Ira Magaziner's head like a stream of digits flowing into a supercomputer. Otherwise, it was utterly superfluous. As with the series of school reform meetings held by Hillary in Arkansas and as with much of the Watergate staffwork under John Doar, it was all so much window dressing.

"Ira Magaziner has mesmerized Hillary," complained Donna Shalala, Secretary of Health and Human Service.

"How can I advise the president on a plan Ira Magaziner won't let me see?" asked Robert Rubin, then chairman of the National Economic Council.[46]

Sara Singer, aide to health task force advisor Alain Enthoven, said that Hillary and Ira Magaziner would seem receptive to an idea, then "the next day Alain would hear from someone else with totally opposing ideas that they had seemed equally receptive to them. I think what they were doing was creating the illusion of participation."[47]

Whenever trouble erupted, Hillary diligently went to the Hill. Her talent for soothing egos and smoothing over disagreements was undermined by her absolute unwillingness to negotiate. She refused to come to terms with Democratic Congressman Jim Cooper and Democratic Senator John Breaux, who had plans of their own, and who were supported by moderate Democrats and some Republicans.

In truth, Congressman Cooper offered Hillary a great vehicle—congressional support that would have allowed her to negotiate from a position of strength and receive much of what she wanted. Saul Alinsky advocated asking for 100 percent, and settling for 30 percent in the knowledge that this is 30 percent more than you have. Hillary made it clear that 99 percent was unacceptable. "You can't fix part of this problem," she told Dick Morris. "If you do this over here, it causes this bad reaction over there. You've got to do it all or nothing."[48]

From start to finish, Hillary refused to acknowledge that compromise was possible. Rather than negotiate with Cooper, Hillary tried to marginalize him, just as she had marginalized Bill Clinton's cabinet. "We were met with a cold shoulder," Cooper said, in words not too different from the complaints of Shalala and Rubin, which they tactfully directed at Magaziner.[49]

When cabinet secretaries were finally allowed to see a rough first draft of the plan in mid-August, they had reason to be aghast. It filled more than 1,300 pages. It proposed to expand Medicare and absorb Medicaid in a new system of universal coverage. Employer mandates would open a rich new vein of wealth transfers, making American jobs as expensive to maintain as European jobs, without explicitly raising taxes (though the admitted costs would be tagged at $400 billion over a few years).

The centerpiece of the plan was a system of bureaucratic regional alliances from which consumers would have to choose their insurance plans. The alliances would, in the words of the Congressional Budget Office, serve as purchasing agents, contract negotiators, welfare agencies, financial intermediaries, collectors of premiums, developers and managers of information systems, and coordinators of the flow of information and money.

This level of control would necessarily involve public policy makers in the minutiae of medical care, with Ira Magaziner at the apex personally counting out the number of cotton swabs per jar. "I have never read an official document that seemed so suffused with coercion and political naïveté... with its drastic prescriptions for controlling the conduct of state governments, employees, drug manufacturers, doctors, hospitals, and you and me," concluded the University of Virginia's Martha Derthick.[50]

"What happens when you cross the worst management consultant blather with paleoliberal ambition?" asked the *New Republic*. "For starters, 268 boxes of paper and 1,300 pages of a health care bill."[51]

The "Jackson Hole Group" of congressional moderates, who had entered into the task force deliberations with great enthusiasm, now bitterly denounced the plan.

Daniel Patrick Moynihan, a liberal Democrat and a man who had, through the various twists and turns of a brilliant career, proved himself to be Congress's most prescient thinker, was clearly astonished by what Hillary and Ira Magaziner had thrown in front of the Congress.

In a lecture before the College of Physicians and Surgeons at Columbia University in 1997, Moynihan described his reaction in candid terms.

"By the time the first session of Congress was coming to a close, we still had not received a bill," Moynihan said. "On November 23, the day before we 'went out,' as our phrase has it, I finally was able as Chairman of the Senate Finance Committee to introduce, on request, a 1,362 page bill. I suspected it was not quite complete—it was not—but saved the honor of the task force to have got its work done in one year."[52]

Moynihan criticized the plan for proposing to limit the supply (hence the costs) of medicine by cutting the number of doctors by 25 percent and the number of specialists in half.

"If you have fewer doctors you have fewer doctor bills," Moynihan said. "But you don't associate it with improving medicine."[53]

Worse yet was the devastating effect the plan would have had on New York's teaching hospitals. "The university presidents were right to have been incredulous at this proposal," the senator said, calling it the "deliberate dumbing down of medicine."[54]

"Working in secret," Moynihan said, with regard to Hillary's methods, "[is] an abomination where science is concerned and [is] no less an offense to democratic governance." Soon, the long knives were out. Elizabeth McCaughey, an analyst with the Manhattan Institute, wrote a devastating critique of the plan in the liberal *New Republic*. Republicans gleefully began to call the proposal "Hillarycare."

Former Quayle Chief of Staff William Kristol acted as a kind of high-tech Paul Revere, blast-faxing a memo that warned Republicans that the future of their party—and the free economy—would rest on the utter defeat of any version of Hillary's plan.

In truth, it was not much of a contest. The obsessive secrecy of the plan was its worst political shortcoming, one that drew a rebuke early on. In March 1993, U.S. District Judge Royce C. Lambeth ruled on a lawsuit filed by the Association of American Physicians and Surgeons, finding

that Hillary and the top-tier, twelve-person task force had blatantly violated "open-meeting" laws. The White House was
in a bind. Hillary could avoid the law if she were deemed a
federal employee, but that would constitute nepotism. If she
were not such an employee, she and her cohorts were acting
illegally. The White House counsel's office chose instead to
argue that Hillary was neither fish nor fowl, just the "func-
tional equivalent" of a federal employee.

Judge Lambeth scolded President Clinton for deliberately
ignoring the open meeting laws. "While the court takes no
pleasure in determining that one of the first actions taken by
a new president is in direct violation of a statute enacted by
Congress, the court's duty is to apply the laws to all individuals," he said.[55] Even after receiving an order to post advance
notice of meetings, the White House chose to disobey. In
time, Magaziner (who confided to friends that the secrecy
rules were forced on him) became the scapegoat, and lived for
some time under investigation and fear of an indictment. The
first federal judge to experience the contempt with which the
Clintons treat subpoenas and testimony under oath, accused
the White House of being "dishonest with the court." He
added, "Some government officials never learn that the
cover-up can be worse than the underlying conduct."[56]

Hillary went into high spin. She played some defense, ridiculing the notion that her plan was "socialist," telling readers of
Parade magazine how scared she had been by the visions of
Aldous Huxley in *Brave New World* and George Orwell in *1984*.
"I find it so amusing when people think that I'm in favor of big
government or big anything, because I'm not."[57] She sprang
into "war room" mode. Hillary instigated a mean-spirited campaign of call-in critics to blast Congressman Cooper when he

unveiled his own alternative plan on radio talk shows. Hillary allies Senator Harris Wofford and Tom Daschle of South Dakota ridiculed Cooper's plan as "rock-bottom Wal-Mart."[58]

The Democratic National Committee ginned up a campaign to save Hillary's plan, with Hillary working overtime as an editor of political copy and videotape. Hillary's aides lobbied the House Ways and Means staff so ferociously that Democratic chairman Dan Rostenkowski called them "paranoids."[59] Rostenkowski had little patience with Hillary's "with us or against us" style of negotiating. Ultimately, Hillary tried to revive her plan with an outright campaign of vilifying insurance and pharmaceutical companies. Industry, predictably, did not take this lying down.

They produced and aired the "Harry and Louise" ad campaign that undercut and subtly ridiculed Hillarycare. The ads fomented public opposition far beyond the health care plan itself. It crystallized disgust with liberal Democrats, a building anger that would eventually end their forty-plus years of rule in the House of Representatives, making Hillarycare one of the most self-destructive political maneuvers committed by liberal Democrats in this century.

Hillary handled the growing public reaction against her plan by trying to create a new set of villains. She branded the insurance industry as liars: "It is time for… every American to stand up and say to the insurance industry, 'Enough is enough. We want our health care system back.'" She lashed out at Representative Cooper. She flew around the country and was astonished to find hecklers in the audience. At a rally in Seattle, demonstrators carried "Heil Hillary" signs. She had to turn up the microphone and shout to be heard over the protestors.

Hillary saw enemies everywhere, and saw any dissent as a

Republican put-up job. "She's a glib speaker," noted a retired family practitioner who had seen her up close. "She can really rattle off the answers. But she doesn't like you to argue with her."[60] When a health insurance agent asked the perfectly reasonable question of what would happen to his job under her plan, Hillary answered, "I'm assuming anyone as obviously brilliant as you could find something else to market." Then she added, just for fun, "I can't go out and save every undercapitalized entrepreneur in America."[61]

It did not seem to occur to Hillary that hecklers were prompted by her own tendency to attack, and counterattack, that her biggest problem was her own thin skin. Hillary's moral standing to take on corporate medicine was also compromised when it was revealed, in the spring of 1994, that she was profiting from her attacks as her hedge fund shorted her health stocks.

It soon became apparent that the health care campaign was a frantic race into oblivion.

Her desperation showing, Hillary now saw opposition to her plan as nothing less than an assault on American democracy. "This personal, vicious hatred that for the time being is being aimed at the president, and, to a lesser extent, myself, is very dangerous for our political process," she said.[62]

Without directly repudiating Hillary, Bill Clinton tried to signal that he was ready to compromise. "Clinton seems to be waffling," a prominent Oregon Democrat said. "He puts out this 95 percent, and Hillary says, 'No, universal coverage,' and all of a sudden Bill's saying, 'Yeah, universal coverage.' It's like she hit him over the head with a frying pan."[63] Bill would praise a Senate bill, and then Hillary would denounce it as an "untested approach."

It was George Mitchell who performed the act of mercy, sitting down with the Clintons in August 1994 to tell them that no version of their plan could pass the Senate. A few months later, the American people went to the polls and took out their frustrations on Democratic members of Congress, most of whom were actually opposed to her plan. Democrats not only lost control of the House, but major Democrats like House Speaker Tom Foley, New York Governor Mario Cuomo, and Texas Governor Ann Richards were tossed out of office.

Hillary's poll numbers confirmed that she was at the center of voter dissatisfaction. Five months before the election, an NBC–*Wall Street Journal* poll found that 51 percent of respondents felt that the first lady had too much influence.

Depressed, Hillary absented herself from political and strategy meetings in the White House. Her co-presidency had slammed into a retaining wall.

"Remind me," she asked an aide, dripping with self-pity. "Have I ever done anything right in my life?"[64]

NINE
WHITE HOUSE PLUMBER

"He knows that all values are relative,
in a world of political relativity."

— SAUL ALINSKY, *RULES FOR RADICALS*

DEATH ON THE POTOMAC

Hillary's first two years in the White House were a litany of disasters. Her health care initiative was not only a bipartisan disaster, it was exposed as a colossal piece of political knavery. Hillary's exalted ethical opinion of herself, which she repeatedly invoked to friendly reporters, was not shared by the Washington press corps that exposed her early refusal to put her investments in a blind trust.

Numerous White House staff still had temporary passes after nine or more months on the job. Many could not receive necessary clearances due to reports of recent drug use and tax problems. Ultimately, the White House had to operate a random drug testing program in order to obtain FBI clearances.

The relentless investigations of Jeff Gerth at the *New York Times* began to peel off one layer of lies after another on Whitewater, exposing such a tangle of political and business dealings that the appointment of an independent counsel became inevitable. Her role in the Travel Office firings was widely suspected from the beginning. Her nominees for attorney general had been failures. Her early interest in Lani Guinier ended in a withdrawn nomination and a lost friendship. The new surgeon general, Dr. Joycelyn Elders, was a walking embarrassment who felt it necessary to publicly promote teen masturbation. Her old Watergate mentor Bernie Nussbaum was fired by her husband. Her Rose Law Firm partner Webb Hubbell was indicted on mail fraud and tax evasion charges. Janet Reno was receiving withering criticism over her handling of the Waco–Branch Davidian disaster that left eighty-four people dead and almost ended Reno's Washington career before it had begun. The congressional Democrats had marched like lemmings off a cliff to the beat of Hillary's drum. And there had been much more.

But worst of all for Hillary was the death of Vince Foster in July 1993.

The case is curious, poignant, and, like many suicides, mysterious. Foster's wife, Lisa, had never wanted to move to Washington. She stayed in Little Rock until June, leaving Foster to live alone in an unfamiliar and very tough city.

Foster himself seemed to waver between attraction and repulsion for his new job, with repulsion often winning out. "No one back in Little Rock could know how hard this is," Foster told Skip Rutherford, an aide to Mack McLarty. He told an Arkansas lawyer, "You try to be at work by 7 in the morning, and sometimes it's 10 at night when you walk out just dog-tired. About the time you're thinking, 'What a load,' you turn around and see the White House lit up, and the awe of where you are and what you're doing hits you. It makes you realize it's worth it."[1]

Over time, his characterizations would dwell less and less on how much it was "worth it," and more on how he could get out of his job alive. And there was another thing. Webb Hubbell, among others, noticed that Foster appeared depressed by Hillary's lack of attention to him. Foster's relationship with Hillary, always complex, was now strained and fraught with tension.

Foster saw himself as the protector of and counselor to Hillary, sometimes a big brother, sometimes a pseudo-husband, sometimes a calm port in a stormy sea. But no lawyer could have protected her from her mistakes, from the daily pummeling she was getting over health care and the Travel Office. Someone else might have been glad that only Bill Kennedy and David Watkins had been officially reprimanded. But according to his friends, Foster felt guilty. He was depressed over the lawsuit against the health care task force, worried about problems with the Clintons' tax returns and, some have suggested, depressed at the blood spilled at Waco.

But more than that, there was almost a sense of betrayal. Foster's experience at the White House had turned his self-image upside down. Foster was not used to having his integrity criticized or compromised, or as being regarded as anything but a top-flight litigator. One of his Rose Law Firm partners was quoted saying that Foster had never suffered a defeat.

Now he felt overwhelmed, even incompetent, to deal with

an avalanche of trouble and with Hillary's violent fits of temper about how everything was going wrong. Foster not only dealt with the Clintons' personal legal affairs, dating back to the tangled webs of Arkansas, but also with the fallout from the seemingly innumerable and unending political scandals.

During the investigation of Travelgate, Foster joined Watkins in denying that the first lady had a significant interest in the Travel Office firings. Foster knew that this statement would soon be tested, in congressional hearings and perhaps even by a prosecutor. Days before his death, he had called his good friend Jim Lyons about the need for outside counsel for the Clintons. His loyalty to Hillary kept putting him in positions that forced him to choose between compromising his principles or failing to be a stalwart protector of Hillary. Foster knew he had to "defend" Hillary regardless of what her role might have been.

Then came a *Wall Street Journal* editorial that asked "Who Is Vincent Foster?" The White House had made the inexplicable and utterly stupid decision to refuse to supply the *Journal* with a picture of Foster, so the inset art in the column had a cutout of Foster's face, a silhouette with a question mark in the middle. By this time, Foster had begun to lose weight, subsist on junk food, and take antidepressants.

In another place, his distress might have been more noticeable. He was obviously stressed, but then who wasn't in the battlefield environment of the White House's first year? All seemed well on his last weekend, when he seemed to have enjoyed himself with his wife and the Hubbells. Their host was Nathan Landow, a wealthy donor whose eagerness to please would later allegedly lead him to attempt to buy Kathleen Willey's silence about being groped by the president.

The Tuesday after Landow's retreat, July 20, 1993, Foster left the White House to drive up a beautiful green expanse of the George Washington Parkway. He pulled into Fort Marcy Park. He parked his car and stood at a rise where one can see across the Potomac River valley, put a gun to the roof of his mouth, and squeezed the trigger.

TRENCH WARFARE

Artful and heavy-handed White House damage control began immediately. Foster possessed many of Hillary's personal records. Hillary was at her mother's home in Little Rock when Mack McLarty called at 9:45 PM and notified her of Foster's death. The President was appearing on *Larry King Live* that night. Following the call that evening and into the early morning there was a flurry of telephone exchanges between Hillary and Maggie Williams, Harry Thomason, and Susan Thomases. Thomases paged Bernie Nussbaum at about 8:00 AM the next morning—then more calls between Hillary, Nussbaum, McLarty, Williams, and Thomases. No mention is ever made of a call to Lisa Foster.

By the next morning, Nussbaum was imposing strict restrictions on how Foster's office would be searched by official investigators. It would not be until 5:00 PM day that an agreement was reached—and not until 10:00 AM the following morning, July 22, that it actually took effect—to allow investigators into Foster's office.

It was soon revealed that the night of the suicide, Maggie Williams and Patsy Thomasson went into Vince Foster's White House office. Williams and Thomasson have both denied under oath that they were doing anything other than wanting to "feel the presence of Vince" or looking for a suicide note.

Shortly after lunch, the day after the suicide, Nussbaum gave a verbal description of the files in Foster's office, but refused to allow investigators to see any of them. For the remainder of the day, Nussbaum and Williams separated Hillary's and Bill's personal files from White House business and Foster's personal files. Secret Service agent Bruce Abbott would later testify that he saw Craig Livingstone, Hillary's director of White House security under the command of Nussbaum, carry a briefcase and several loose-leaf binders out of the White House. Maggie Williams was also seen by Secret Service agent Henry O'Neill leaving the office with a stack of file folders. All this was denied by Williams and Livingstone.

Six days after the suicide, according to the White House, a suicide note was found torn into pieces at the bottom of Foster's briefcase. The first thing the counsel's office did was to patch the note back together and inform Hillary and then Susan Thomases. Hillary directed that Mack McLarty, President Clinton's chief of staff, not tell the president about the note until a decision was made about turning it over the the Justice Department. It then took the White House thirty hours to decide to turn it over to the FBI and Park Police who were investigating the incident.

Throughout the crisis, Hillary kept a firm hand on the investigation. She had seen Richard Nixon destroy himself by erecting a stone wall, then giving ground with investigators, then trying to build another stone wall. Hillary did not give ground. She did not want the Justice Department to have "unfettered access" to Foster's files, according to testimony from associate counsel Stephen Neuwirth. The stone wall remained secure, even after her chief of staff and other White

House aides watched as their reputations were sacrificed during investigations of the special prosecutor.

Hillary's people seemed more than willing to suffer embarrassment to protect *her* from embarrassment. Some time later, White House lawyer Jack Quinn even tried to rewrite the factual record, deleting words in the titles of memos, changing "HRC's Travel Office Chronology" to "Chronological Analysis of Travel Office Events." "HRC Role" became "Draft chart analysis and comparison of various Travel Office investigations." The removal of the first lady's initials from White House memos, said Chairman William Clinger, brought "a scent of obstruction of justice... [to the] changing of documents in an attempt to rub out... the role of the First Lady." Throughout my investigation, facts surrounding Hillary seemed to be erased from memory or "deleted."

FILEGATE

The next big challenge was the revelation that the White House had been illegally collecting secret, sensitive, and personal FBI files of nine hundred–plus Reagan and Bush officials, including the files of the fired Travel Office staff.

Past administrations kept such files under lock and key, and carefully limited access to them. Even the president could not have access to them, except, perhaps, on a strict "need to know" basis. In a counsel's office run by Hillary's lieutenants, these files were shipped over wholesale from FBI secure rooms to the White House and were kept in an open vault, where any secretary, any intern, could leaf through them. That is if Craig Livingstone approved.

"The prior system of providing files to the White House relied on good faith and honor," FBI Director Louis Freeh publicly complained. "Unfortunately, the FBI and I were victimized." It was quite clear that the FBI director had been stunned to learn that the White House had so misused the FBI's records, damaging his credibility and the FBI in the process, and making it appear that the FBI would be used for political purposes by White House opposition researchers.

"When I worked in the White House," said a former Bush aide, "the people who handled personnel security were very button-down, very discreet. When one goes into government service, a contract is made. You allow the FBI to review your most intimate secrets—your personal, financial, and employment history—in exchange for an understanding that this stuff is used only to gauge your fitness to work near the president and to be granted the security clearance needed to review highly classified documents."

Under Hillary, this very sensitive job went to Craig Livingstone, a former bar bouncer and a professional dirty trickster who had distinguished himself by following the Bush campaign dressed up in a chicken suit. He was also well known in Democratic circles for "opposition research"—that is to say, dirt digging. Dennis Casey, a former aide in Senator Gary Hart's campaign in Pennsylvania, recounted to me how Livingstone came to him to offer up dirt on former Vice President Walter Mondale in the 1984 primary.

In his deposition of Linda Tripp, Larry Klayman asked who had hired Craig Livingstone:

> **TRIPP:** I can only tell you who Craig Livingstone told me hired Craig Livingstone.
>
> **Q:** What did he tell you?
>
> **TRIPP:** He told me Mrs. Clinton hired him.
>
> **Q:** When did he tell you that?

TRIPP: Relatively shortly after my arrival in the counsel's office, when he asked me how I managed to get a job like that. So I asked him, how did he manage to get a job like that?

Q: Where was he when he made that statement?

TRIPP: In the counsel's office....

Q: Give me an example of how he led you to believe that he was acting at the direction of Mrs. Clinton?

TRIPP: Well, there were times when he was very frustrated with me personally, because I wouldn't let him in to see Mr. Nussbaum, who had an extremely busy schedule and who clearly had made it rather plain to me that he didn't have any wish to deal with Mr. Livingstone, and that [Livingstone] should deal with Bill Kennedy....

Q: To continue, what was it that Mr. Livingstone told you, by way of example, that created your belief that he was trying to convey that he was acting on behalf of Mrs. Clinton?

TRIPP: He would talk into his watch and act as though he were a covert agent. He didn't have an ear piece.... It was a regular watch.

Q: Was he talking to Mrs. Clinton at the time?

TRIPP: He would like you to believe so.... Overall, the impression I had was that he, as I said, was well connected, and that he had a direct pipeline into Mrs. Clinton. Whether or not that was true, I never formed an opinion one way or another. I didn't see them having lunch. It seemed a form of self aggrandizement. It didn't seem necessarily true. However, that said, this is a man whose very existence in that position in the White House was beyond comprehension for someone like me....

Q: Did Mr. Livingstone ever tell you that he had access to the White House residence?

TRIPP: Oh, on more than one occasion, yes.

Q: On how many occasions?

TRIPP: Several times. Remember when I say this, please put it
in context. He—and you couldn't know this—but he, for
instance, was in the process of trying to date one of my volunteers; so we received often very unsolicited, bizarre information
that none of us cared to know, about access and his access, his
proximity to the first family. None of this fazed any of us, but
clearly impressed him.

Early on, Hillary used Livingstone to track down the
leaker responsible for stories about her throwing things (such
as lamps) during arguments at the White House residence.
Harry Thomason, according to his notes, even suspected that
"two agents" had been "talking [to] Bob Woodward." She also
invested more trust in Livingstone after Foster's death. This
"cop without a gun" was the one sent to confirm that the body
found in the park was Foster. He was the one trusted to help
clean up the mess in Foster's office. After Foster's suicide,
Tripp testified that Livingstone "seemed to have more access.
He seemed to be over more. He had a different air, completely
different demeanor. He was more confident...."

The White House spin on how it came to be that
Livingstone had been illegally collecting FBI background files
was that it was a matter of miscommunication between
Livingstone, the FBI, and the Secret Service. But it was difficult for anyone in Washington to believe that the same White
House that allowed hundreds of their own staffers' security
clearances to languish, including that of press secretary Dee
Dee Myers, had a dispassionate interest in examining and
maintaining the personnel files of the previous administration.

The question of "Who Hired Livingstone" set off a

remarkable public show of "hot potato." White House Counsel Bernard Nussbaum and William Kennedy shrugged their shoulders. Hillary even denied knowing who he was.

Former FBI agent Gary Aldrich recounts the beginning of Livingstone's tenure: "There was an investigation to find more than $150,000 worth of equipment lost or stolen from the inauguration. This equipment had been in the charge of Craig Livingstone." When Aldrich suggested that the security post should be held by someone "squeaky clean," Aldrich said, White House Counsel William Kennedy cut him off, saying, "I guess I see your point, but it doesn't matter. It's a done deal. Hillary wants him."

A White House intern undermined Hillary's denials of knowing Craig Livingstone by testifying before House investigators that he overheard the first lady warmly greet Livingstone in a White House hallway.

Some writers have speculated that the FBI files were gathered to defend the White House staff against the slow security clearance of its personnel. Other observers surmised that the White House sought ammunition to point to Bush or Reagan appointees whose foibles were overlooked.

The Clinton administration was eager to have the public accept these rather benign explanations. On the Clinger committee, I was always struck by one anomaly in this explanation, one fact I can never put out of my mind: Why were these files in the hands of an opposition research specialist?

Cracks later began to appear in the more innocent explanations. One big crack appeared in the syndicated column of Bob Novak. Leslie Gail Kennedy, the ex-wife of William Kennedy, the associate counsel who became Hillary's ally at the Rose Law Firm, told Judicial Watch lawyers that Kennedy "brought FBI files from his White House office to their home in Alexandria." Several times, she said, she observed him "making entries from the files into a database he maintained on his lap top computer." The reason? Leslie Gail Kennedy testified that her then-husband told her the files were "intended to make FBI file information accessible and useful to the Clinton administration."[2] Whether Mrs. Kennedy actually saw FBI files is being investigated by the Starr team.

Hillary elsewhere expressed a similar appetite for maintaining intelligence files on individuals. WhoDB, a White House database, was developed by FOB Marsha Scott at a cost to the taxpayers of more than $1.6 million. Known among the staff as "big brother," it tracks the vital statistics, Social Security numbers, ethnicity, diet, political associations, and sexual preferences of more than 350,000 members of Congress, state and local officials, journalists, and supporters and donors from the lists of the Democratic National Committee.

President Nixon's "enemies list" ignited a political firestorm when it became public. But first lady Hillary's creation of a taxpayer-funded political database created scarcely a ripple from watchdogs of civil liberties. When the existence of WhoDB came to light, the White House was ready with a typically benign spin—it was used, we were told, to keep track of correspondence. It was portrayed as a mid-level staff project that was overzealously pursued.

In truth, WhoDB is a cybernetic version of the handwritten index cards started by Betsey Wright for the Clinton's comeback bid in the early 1980s. Its purpose is to keep track of supporters and major donors, a software that correlates perks with donations, in an effort to wring the maximum from supporters. It could also be used as a virtual "enemies list."

Such an idea—no less than the raid on Vince Foster's office or the accumulation of FBI files for a White House blackmail database—could only come from the mind of someone who thinks like Nixon. And it apparently did—from Hillary Rodham Clinton, Nixon's disciple of hardball politics.

"I wanted you to be aware of the fact that the First Lady has set up an appointment to see the software tomorrow at 11:45," Marsha Scott wrote in a memo to Bruce Lindsey on January 16, 1995, meant to "keep you and the First Lady informed with progress reports." She referred to it as Hillary's "no. 1 project."[3]

In her bid to rise from the ashes of her disastrous first few years, Hillary has resorted to schemes that make the Watergate conspirators look weak for lack of ambition. She masterminded a bold and unashamed obstruction of justice in the office of Vincent Foster. She politicized the FBI and trampled on the law, giving the most private personal background files to opposition research specialists while simultaneously dismantling the normal White House security clearance system for new employees.

Hillary has indulged a despotic hunger for information on enemies and friends better suited to an Eastern bloc tyrant—like Elena Ceausescu—than to a first lady of the United States. And she did most of these things with a shocking lack of protest from Congress, civil libertarians, and much of the press, despite the controversy stemming from her political activities—from Whitewater to Travelgate and beyond. In her own Nixonian way, Hillary has proved to be as slick as her husband.

TAKE TWO

Foster's death had a big emotional impact on Hillary. Hillary sent her chief of staff, Maggie Williams, to most high-profile policy meetings. Bill's childhood friend, Mack McLarty, was replaced as chief of staff by OMB Director Leon Panetta, a skillful and cunning former congressman from California. Panetta's power grew, in part, because Hillary had withdrawn, allowing him to discipline and shape the White House staff. He prioritized policies and brought coherence to a chaotic White House that had tried to remake American politics, culture, and economics in the first months of its first year.

Hillary, for a time, was content to let Panetta run the show. But she only withdrew to lick her wounds, to analyze her failure, to regroup. She had dug herself into a hole. Now she had to dig out. And the hole was deep.

In January 1996 a *USA Today*/CNN/Gallup Poll remarked that 51 percent of the American people disapproved of her. She was the most unpopular first lady in history. Even worse, 52 percent of the American people believed Hillary was a liar, and 68 percent believed she had probably done something wrong or illegal.[4]

Hillary worked hard to soften her public image. She even allowed Annie Leibowitz to photograph her in a slinky, almost sultry, pose, wearing a black $975 Donna Karan. The *piéce de résistance* of this kinder, gentler Hillary was the rollout of the rumor that the first couple was thinking of adopting a baby.

While the charm offensive went forward, Hillary kept her distance from the working press and any potential critics. She ordered lists compiled of enemies to be excluded from White House movie screenings.[5] She restricted the movement of the press corps in the White House, and she kept them off the plane as she traveled on a below-radar sweep of grassroots gatherings from coast to coast.

And then she began to find the ways to redefine her public

persona. She tried out a pink sweater, over a demure black knit skirt and matching high heels. The flavor and image of Eleanor Roosevelt's "My Day" reflections were recycled and used to humanize her own nationally syndicated newspaper column. And then there was *It Takes a Village*, the success of which took Hillary from being the nation's power-mad scold to being the nation's thoughtful den mother.

It Takes a Village was used to define Hillary Clinton. It weaves personal anecdotes from her own upbringing, about her daughter Chelsea's birth by caesarian section, and defends the Clinton marriage by coming out strongly against divorce.

Village even plays to conservative sympathies, quoting Bill Bennett on rap music, and advancing the idea of school uniforms (a cause Bill Clinton later picked up). To borrow another of Saul Alinsky's memorable phrases, she had learned not to eat a ham sandwich while trying to organize a community of orthodox Jews.

The sound rejection of her health care plan was enough to convince Hillary that her liberal agenda was far ahead of the American people. So she dressed up traditional "family values" arguments once again to put forward universal health care. She praised the comprehensive welfare states of Western Europe, from the French day-care system to the generous leave policies of Germany, without ever noting that these economies suffered double-digit unemployment for more than a decade while the U.S. economy burgeoned.

A minor controversy erupted over the writing of her book. Hillary had claimed to have written the book herself, only to have it revealed that Simon & Schuster had paid a $120,000 advance to Georgetown journalism professor Barbara Feinman, a woman who had worked seven days a week to complete the book. The book contained no word of appreciation to the long-suffering Feinman, who had traveled with Hillary on a Western vacation, undoubtedly with tape recorder in hand. "All she expected was 'Many thanks to Barbara Feinman, whose tireless efforts were greatly appreciated,'" said Sally Quinn. "She [Feinman] would have died and gone to heaven."[6]

Hillary actually tried to withhold a fourth of the payment to Feinman as a punishment for talking to reporters. It was a very *It Takes a Village* crisis, because Feinman was counting on the income to help finance the adoption of a baby girl from China. In the end, Feinman was paid. But Hillary's pique had underlined the most vindictive aspects of her character. She became so defensive about her authorship that she called *Time* correspondent James Carney to her private study to examine legal pads filled with her handwriting.

One has to wonder why Hillary went to such great lengths to deny that she had help with the book. That is no crime, especially in Washington. No one would have denied a busy first lady the right to have research and writing help on a project such as this. In the end the book expressed *her* ideas. But Hillary can never seem to give anyone else credit, and she can never seem to admit that she is anything less than "super-woman." In the end she undermines the very image she works so hard to construct.

When all was said and done, however, the authorship squabbles didn't matter, because they didn't carry much beyond the jaded Eastern corridor of the *Washington Post* Style section and the *New Yorker*. In America-at-large, *It Takes a Village* hit the best-seller list and stayed there for twenty weeks. It raised not a few eyebrows when it won Hillary a Grammy for the audiotape version. More important, it gave her the image of a PTA mom and displaced the image of the secretive, power-obsessed woman pushing behind the president.

HOLDING THE LINE

No sooner did Hillary begin to bask in the adulation of her book tour than the long-awaited, and dreaded, Rose Law Firm records materialized in the White House residence to contradict virtually everything she had been saying about the matter.

When former Rose aide Carolyn Huber, then in the White House, found the printouts of Hillary's billing records in her private residence, it revealed that Hillary had, in fact, lied under oath when she said she had not worked on the Castle Grande land scam. When Hillary offered the lamest of excuses, claiming she had known the Castle Grande project by another name, *New York Times* columnist William Safire publicly labeled her a "congenital liar."

Safire traced the movement of the records, from their removal from Foster's office on the night of his suicide, to Webb Hubbell's basement, to the president's secretary's personal files, and then Hillary's closet.[7]

The president responded to Safire with an indirect second-hand threat to punch him in the nose. This display of manly protectiveness struck the public as very incongruous. When Harry Truman had lashed out at a music critic who had savaged his daughter, he did so by angrily jotting his vituperation in his own hand. Clinton offered his "en garde" in the form of a studiously clever riposte through an intermediary, White House press secretary Mike McCurry. A patented Clinton ploy to have it both ways, to appear offended and manly, but not really concerned.

Hillary's response was even more to type.

William Safire has earned an enviable reputation for his hard-nosed stance on ethics, taking on old friends like the late CIA director William Casey, and showing no deference to Ronald Reagan and George Bush on Irangate. Hillary ignored this and centered her attack on Safire's service several presidents earlier as a White House speechwriter for Richard M. Nixon.

Hillary chose a friendly format, an interview on National Public Radio, and said she did not take seriously a man who had once worked for Nixon, and "best I can tell, is still working for him." She professed complete ignorance of how the papers had come to be so close to her, but did offer journalists an interesting double reverse.

When she was working on the Watergate committee, Hillary said, if missing records under subpoena for two years had come to light, "we would have been delighted. The problem back then, you'll remember, is that documents were destroyed, tapes were missing 18 and a half minutes. The White House was not cooperating.... I think the contrast is so dramatic."[8] The implication was not concealed: Think about Nixon and all those really bad people. The Clintons on the other hand discovered and produced the documents. And please overlook the fact that they were "found" and produced by a secretary, not by the person who had been holding them during their time in the wilderness.

Also left unsaid, of course, was that any Nixon official who had been caught with documents that Leon Jaworksy had demanded by subpoena for two years would have likely been indicted and gone to prison.

CHELSEA: CONVENIENT COVER

The billing records weren't the only new evidence of deceit surfacing from the Clintons. When the *American Spectator* magazine and the *Los Angeles Times* published the revelations of state troopers Larry Patterson and Roger Perry who had guarded Bill as governor, the White House realized it could no longer talk about the Clintons having had a "pain-in-our-marriage" *phase*. The reality testified to by the state troopers was of a governor-turned-president who was an out-of-control sex addict and who used law enforcement officials with uniforms and weapons to procure women and to cover his tracks.

These disclosures were a direct threat to Hillary's image as well. "Lately, I find people who know Hillary better than I do who tell me that the only reason she has put up with Bill's philandering is that she loves the trappings of high office," John Robert Starr mused in one of his *Arkansas Democrat-Gazette* pieces. "She likes having taxpayer-financed servants, of whom she has more than 100 in the White House."[9]

Family was the antidote to this unpleasantly frank talk, and for all practical purposes, Chelsea was her family. Hillary writes that she wanted a child in their marriage from the start. Perhaps she saw it as the only way to secure a marriage with a husband who pursued other women with relentless abandon. Perhaps there were ideological reasons. "You can't be a woman if you don't have children," she told a friend.[10]

Named after the Joni Mitchell song "Chelsea Morning," the president's daughter had spent almost her entire life living in the governor's mansion or the White House. She seemed to have been raised as much by Bill and nannies as by her mother. "Mommy go make peech," she would say at age two.[11] Former Arkansas State Trooper L. D. Brown—who married one of the Clintons' nannies—paints a picture of Saturday night Bill as a loving father, and Hillary as a harsh, neglectful shrew.

As the illusion of a strong and stable marriage began to unravel, the Clintons broke their own rule and resorted to using their daughter, with Hillary appearing more and more with her in innumerable photo ops on foreign trips. Cloying stories began to appear in the press of how the Clintons spent their family time playing word games and doing homework. Later, when the Monica Lewinksy scandal broke, Bill and Hillary invited the world to watch them depart as a family on Air Force One, to take their daughter across the country to attend Stanford. For years, the privacy of their daughter had been the Clintons' genuine concern. In extremism, they used her in a cynical way to stave off impeachment.

TRIANGULATION

"You know, you have to stop having to be rescued like this," Morris recalls Hillary telling her husband. "Last time, I swear," he replied.[12]

The multiple catastrophes of the first term had brought the Clinton presidency to its knees. Clinton had, on a more sophisticated level, reproduced his first term as governor, showcasing a mixture of arrogance, indifference to his legislative allies, and contempt for business interests. As before, he had tried to achieve everything: opening military barracks to gays, enacting universal health coverage, and putting economic and environmental regulation on an aggressive footing.

At home, the agenda was a patchwork quilt. Abroad,

Americans watched as U.S. troops were dragged through the streets of Mogadishu and the Navy had to deal with a gang of rock-throwing Haitian thugs.

Forty years of Democratic rule of the House was broken, and the former governor accustomed to the one-party rule of Arkansas had to work with a Republican Congress equipped with the power of subpoenas.

As the president's reelection began to seem in jeopardy, a curious role reversal took place for Hillary. It was Hillary who now pushed a more centrist agenda. It was Leon Panetta, the former Republican and Washington insider who led the "liberal" wing of the White House staff, aided by George Stephanopoulous and Harold Ickes, while the president himself grew solemn and withdrawn.

Hillary recognized that Bill would have to mount a comeback bid no less dramatic than the one he had launched to retake the governor's mansion in 1982. While this left Clinton on the verge of despair, Hillary quickly grasped that a massive course correction was needed, that to retain power he had to run to the center.

And she knew that the right man to lead her husband in that direction was not Leon Panetta or James Carville. It was a sometime-Republican then working for Senate Majority Leader Trent Lott, Dick Morris.

Night show comedians would later joke about the twin sex scandals of the president and his top political advisor. In truth, it is difficult to imagine two people more unalike than Dick Morris and Bill Clinton. Morris's understanding of the unsentimental uses of power is Machiavellian—deeply grounded in history and in a penetrating observation of people and current events. He is also Machiavellian in another sense, for

Machiavelli was a great analyst of power, but a poor practitioner. He ended up in penury and alienated from his patrons.
Morris is unlikely to end up poor. But for all his touted cynicism, he has served himself poorly. He often shows a disarm-
ingly naive streak and a deep and genuine fascination with
power politics that leads him into divulging trade secrets.
Morris seems oblivious to the cynical uses of interviewers who
would manipulate his almost scientific interest in his craft.

Morris joined Hillary and her top aides Maggie Williams
and Melanie Vereer at secret "girls club meetings" in the
White House solarium to plan the comeback bid.[13] The secret
alliance soon led to Morris's writing focus-group–tested
speeches for Clinton, which the president, needing to conceal
Morris's involvement from his own staff, rewrote by hand to
make them look authentically his. When Morris telephoned
the president, Clinton was told that "Charlie" was on the line.[14]

Morris offered Clinton the perfect foil for the popularity of
the Republican Congress's brilliant "Contract with America"—
which had set out a detailed reform agenda. In *Behind the Oval
Office* Morris reveals how he saw a parallel between Clinton and
Republican House Speaker Newt Gingrich and the powershar-
ing in France between socialist President Francois Mitterrand
and conservative Prime Minister Jacques Chirac. Rather than
paralyzing the government by fighting Chirac, Mitterrand "fast-
forwarded" the agenda of the right and therefore removed any
incentive for the electorate to support right-wing candidates,
because they had no issues to run on.[15]

Morris's "triangulation" allowed Clinton to do much the
same thing to Newt Gingrich. The president embraced the
Republican tenets of welfare reform and a balanced budget,
leaching these issues of their salience to the Republicans.

To protect himself against the Republicans, Bill Clinton had to jettison many of his closest friends in the social welfare lobby, angering Marian Wright Edelman and prompting her husband, Peter, to resign from his senior post at the Department of Health and Human Services.

"I know the politics, I know the numbers, but it still bothers me deeply," Hillary told Morris.[16] Morris doesn't say so in his book, but surely he saw the crocodile's tears.

Clinton staked out a place of his own with a "values" agenda designed to appeal to women voters and showcase Bill Clinton as a compassionate alternative to the congressional Republicans who allowed themselves to be portrayed as Snidely Whiplashes.

In time, the identity of "Charlie" became known and deeply resented by the White House staff, especially by Harold Ickes and George Stephanopoulos. Morris not only began single-handedly to supersede the White House staff, he also began to outshine them, showing a political acumen and degree of cynicism absent among Bill Clinton's true believers.

As Morris's strategic vision guided the 1996 campaign, the White House staff began its assault on its own strategic genius. Morris relates that a story was first put out among the press that he was billing the campaign for pornographic movies in his hotel room. The story wasn't true, but a little detective work likely ordered by White House enemies exposed a personal foible that was far more embarrassing.

Dick Morris was spending his own money for room service in the Jefferson Hotel from a $300-an-hour prostitute who was happy to take the money to have her toes sucked. The prostitute was persuaded to take Morris onto the balcony where the two of them could be photographed. (Fortunately for Morris she had her shoes on.)

When the tabloids ran the story, Morris was finished. As so often happens with the Clintons, the people who give them the most, suffer the most.

But as also so often happens, the Clintons gain everything they need from their victim before discharging him. Morris's strategy was masterly. He revived his tactic of advertising early and often—which had worked so well in Clinton's comeback bid against Frank White in 1982.

Now, as Gingrich and Clinton locked horns over the budget in the fall of 1995, shutting down much of the government, the early ad strategy was dusted off.

The Democrats aired a battery of radio and television ads to defend the president and his party. The ads aired in swing districts, in swing states. Morris and Clinton refrained from airing their ads in Los Angeles, New York, or Washington, D.C., hoping that the Republican political apparatus would be too lethargic to notice.

In truth, Republicans noticed what was happening. They knew all too well that the Clinton ad strategy was winning the election before it even began. They simply had no way to match the Democratic onslaught, one that we now know was paid for by Bill Clinton's unprecedented prostitution of his administration, his office, even the White House itself.

HUANG, CHUNG, AND TRIE

Dick Morris and Harold Ickes had clashed since their days as West Side, New York student activists. But the fights over how much to spend on political advertising a year before the 1996 election were the most monumental yet. Eventually, the

Democratic National Committee (DNC) agreed to borrow money, with Ickes masterminding a scheme to make every stick of furniture in the White House, every presidential M&M, and every cocktail napkin on Air Force One pay for itself. The White House and the presidency were put up for sale on a scale theretofore unimaginable.

Under Clinton, anything and everything had a price: the Lincoln Bedroom, rides on Air Force One, state dinners, personal tours of the White House by the president, the presidential suite at the Kennedy Center, the weekly presidential radio adresses to the nation, jogging or golf with the president, first-run movies at the White House, trips abroad with the Secretary of Commerce, even burial at Arlington Cemetary. All could be had for the right price.

Ten thousand dollars would get you into a coffee, or even a dinner with the president. For $100,000 you could join the president at his table. For $1.5 million, a New Jersey donor of Polish descent got to fly with Clinton to meet Pope John Paul II at Newark Airport.[17]

In the midst of the Waco tragedy on April 19, 1993, when at least twenty-four children and more than fifty Branch Davidians burned to death, Bill Clinton escorted privileged donor James Riady, an Indonesian businessman with links to Communist China, to the White House situation room to view the action.[18]

Vice President Gore was similarly busy, making fundraising calls from the White House and visiting sham donors at a Buddhist temple in California—actions that would lead Gore into political trouble of his own.

The administration's unprecedented practice of blatantly selling seats on the Department of Commerce's foreign trade missions for $50,000 apiece raised hackles even from the slick cabinet officer charged with doing it. "I'm a motherfucking tour guide for Hillary," Commerce Secretary Ron Brown told his business partner and lover, Nolanda Hill, shortly before his death.

Nolanda Hill later told journalists that Secretary Brown was ordered by Hillary herself to bring into the Commerce Department none other than John Huang, a LippoBank executive who had squired Governor Clinton and his wife around Hong Kong in 1985. Since then, Huang had made a number of interesting career decisions, including moving to Arkansas to work at the Riady-controlled Worthen Bank.

It was Riady money that had rescued Clinton's first presidential campaign when it was at its most vulnerable. Riady cash made a big difference in Georgia, where Clinton beat Bush by a razor-thin 13,000 votes out of 2.4 million cast. James Riady and John Huang each gave $100,000 to the Clinton inaugural.[19]

Joe Giroir, a former Rose partner who had been pushed out of the firm by Hillary, Vince Foster, and Webb Hubbell, now became a certified FOB, giving hundreds of thousands of dollars to the DNC as a representative of the Lippo Group.

During the mid-1980s, the Riadys had shifted much of their wealth from Indonesia into the People's Republic of China (PRC). They relied on Chen Xitong, Politburo member and mayor of Beijing, to break the lease of the most profitable McDonald's in the world to clear the way for them to build the immense and profitable Wangfujing project.[20]

The CIA reported to Senate investigations that "Lippo has substantial interests in China—about US $2 billion in the Riady's ancestral province of Fujian alone. These include real estate, banking, electronics, currency exchange, retail, electricity and tourism... Lippo has provided concessionary-rate loans to finance many of these projects in key [Communist] Party members' home areas.[21] The close ties between the Riadys and the Communist government in Beijing became even closer when the Indonesian economy plummeted, prompting the PRC-controlled China Resources to buy up Lippo shares. The latter, of course, is controlled (as are so many entities in the PRC) by Chinese intelligence.

The Riadys soon learned to wire their deals with Washington as neatly as they did in Beijing. On the very day a Riady-controlled company steered $100,000 in business to Hillary's friend Webb Hubbell, who had left the Justice Department under investigation, was out of funds, and who needed to be kept happy and quiet, John Huang, a Riady "fixer" and Democratic fund-raiser, was hired at a very sensitive position at the Commerce Department.

There, Huang could dip into the flow of U.S. cable traffic at will. He had access to hundreds of CIA documents, including sensitive files on technology transfers. He had access to information that, if revealed to a foreign power, would have exposed informants to torture or execution. Curiously, when Huang wanted to make an overseas phone call or send a fax, he did so on his lunch hour from the Stephens, Inc., branch office in Washington.

Huang was given liberal access to the White House because of his fund-raising prowess, and would escort high-level Communist Chinese officials to watch President Clinton deliver his radio address. Huang's amazing access was duplicated by Johnny Chung, a southern California businessman who later admitted to making campaign donations on behalf of the daughter of one of the most senior generals in the Chinese Communist army. When Chung delivered a $50,000 check to Hillary Clinton's chief of staff—who inappropriately accepted it on behalf of the DNC—Hillary was on hand to greet Chung and a Communist Chinese delegation in the White House map room. Chung came to the White House more than fifty times. Twenty-one of those times, he was "cleared in" by Hillary Clinton's office.[22]

Then there was Charlie Trie, a veritable Horatio Alger of foreign influence peddlers. From his humble position as a Little Rock restaurateur, Trie had morphed into a major donor and even foreign policy advisor.

In the spring of 1996, Trie brough bags of phoney money orders and cash totaling a half-million dollars to the president's legal defense fund. But with the money came a letter protesting the deployment of U.S. aircraft carriers and cruisers in the Straits of Taiwan.

"Why U.S. has to sent the aircraft carriers and cruisers to give China a possible excuse of foreign intervention and hence launch a real war?" the letter asked in broken English. "It is highly possible for China to launch real war, based on its past behavior in sino-vietnam war and then Bao-Tao war with Russia."[23] This is the first time an American president has ever received a threat of war from a fund-raising bag man who ran a Chinese restaurant in Little Rock.

MARRIED TO THE MOB

For a first lady willing to secure money from a Communist government, there was little reason not to embrace the mob.

Arthur A. Coia, general president of the Laborers International Union of North America, was charged by the Justice Department for being "associated with and controlled and influenced by organized crime." For years, prosecutors alleged, Coia had helped the mob loot pension funds of some of the hardest working people in America. Such a background did not deter Hillary Clinton from flying to Miami to appear with Coia on stage at a Laborers International Union of North America convention at the Fontainebleau Hotel. He had already made his investment, beginning with a $100,000 donation to the inaugural committee. Hillary invited him to the White House to have breakfast with her. Several times, she earnestly solicited his advice on health care reform. Coia attended a reception for the Japanese emperor, and flew on Air Force One to Haiti.

In years past, the Justice Department has moved with alacrity to prosecute and remove from office union bosses with ties to organized crime. Not this Justice Department. A week after Hillary's appearance with Coia in Miami, the Justice Department agreed to an unusual deal that allowed Coia to keep his presidency (a direct election was permitted, but no one of any rank dared to take him on). The Laborers International Union of North America held out against the Justice Department on the direct election of officials below the rank of president and secretary-treasurer.[24] The same Justice Department that had once been tough enough to launch a takeover of the Teamsters behaved with remarkable timidity when it came to Coia.

But perhaps even more remarkable is that the Clintons thought they needed financial support from the mob and the Communist Chinese in order to beat the hapless campaign of Bob Dole and Jack Kemp that started on empty and never bothered to stop for gas.

TEN
HILLARY AND THE DEVIL IN THE BLUE DRESS

"One's concern with the ethics of means and ends varies inversely with one's profound interest in the issue."

— SAUL ALINSKY, *RULES FOR RADICALS*

Having bought, spun, and triangulated her husband's reelection—making Bill Clinton the first Democrat since Franklin Roosevelt to be elected to two terms—Hillary found that her popularity had also been solidly restored.

On the other hand, she was constantly absorbed with damage control. The Clintons and their administration careened like a drunken sailor from one scandal to another sometimes producing two or more at a time.

Already, in Clinton's first term she had had to provide sworn testimony to special prosecutor Robert Fiske. Then she had to deal with Fiske's replacement, Ken Starr. And Starr's investigation not only wouldn't end quietly, it kept getting bigger.

Starr won his first big scalps in May and June 1996, with the twin Whitewater-related convictions of Governor Jim Guy Tucker and Susan McDougal. White House aide Bruce Lindsey was named but not convicted as unindicted co-conspirator.

The Starr investigation intensified the pressure on Hillary in 1996. She went through a grueling four hours of testimony before a federal grand jury on the disappearance and embarassing reappearance of her billing records. She was questioned again in 1998 by Starr and his lieutenants about the FBI files. In April 1998 she underwent almost five hours of questioning in the White House as a Whitewater witness.[1]

As the Clintons saw their legal exposure widen (and legal bills stack up into the millions) over Whitewater, Travelgate, and Filegate, another aspect of Bill's past opened up. As Arkansas state troopers began to talk freely of their exploits to David Brock and the *American Spectator*, Clinton tried to move swiftly to plug the leaking dike. He saw to it that the head of his security detail, Raymond "Buddy" Young, received a $92,000-a-year federal post as a regional manager for FEMA (Federal Emergency Management Agency). He even found time in his busy schedule to make two calls to trooper Danny Ferguson to dangle the promise of federal jobs in front of him.

THE ANIMAL HOUSE PRESIDENT

"This is fun," Clinton had once confided to Susan McDougal. "Women are throwing themselves at me. All the while I was growing up, I was the fat boy in the Big Boy jeans."[2] Arkansas

State Trooper L.D. Brown would later charge that he had solicited more than one hundred women for Governor Clinton during their years of hounddogging in the dance clubs and honky-tonks of Arkansas. Now Bill's prolific past finally began to catch up to him. When the *American Spectator* printed its story about Clinton's women procured by the state troopers, Paula Corbin Jones filed a lawsuit to clear her name.

It is a measure of the discipline, tenacity, and viciousness of Hillary's War Room that at first the story of the Jones lawsuit and its repercussions did as little damage as it did.

Nevertheless, Jones's story would soon become world famous. Jones, a low-level state employee during Clinton's governorship, was working at a hotel for a trade show when she caught Clinton's eye. Given all that is now known about Clinton's behavior—the combined weight of partially corroborated testimony from women like Gennifer Flowers, Kathleen Willey, Juanita Broaddrick, and others, and what Clinton and his defenders no longer bother to deny—we know that a state trooper did ask her to see the governor in his hotel room. Clinton, with his usual directness, allegedly dropped his pants in front of Jones, asked her to fellate him, and warned her, when she refused, not to talk.

The War Room response was immediate and effective. Hillary's people took a handful of rhetorical razors and went to work on Jones. James Carville, a man who apparently has no princples or scruples and will say anything no matter how outrageous or stupid, to advance his own interests, told a national television audience, "Drag a $100 bill through a trailer park, you never know what you'll find."

To disparage Jones, the Clinton people resorted to crude stereotypes, and unashamed class warfare—pitting middle-class sensibilities that found it hard to imagine such an accusation could be true, against the underlying prejudice against the white poor, the sort of people who punch, betray, and lie about each other on "trash TV" shows like those hosted by Jerry Springer. Ironically, the same stereotypes that Clinton's upbringing calls to mind.

Hillary's War Room skillfully portrayed Jones as a greed-stricken creation of the radical right. But Jones struggled on with a lonely campaign. When her lawyers urged her to settle for cash, she refused and took new legal counsel. She wanted justice. She got, at a minimum, headlines. The Jones scandal was a shot across the bow of complacent Democrats—if not, ultimately, one that altered the behavior of the president himself.

"He can't play JFK," a major Democrat said. "If he does, it would be a killer. All bets would be off."[3]

Hillary had assiduously cultivated a picture of family normalcy in the White House. *It Takes a Village* spoke warmly of what it was like "to live above the store." Journalists were fed images of a president who, in a memorable 1993 portrait in *U.S. News and World Report*, "often pads down to the Oval Office wearing jeans, sneakers, and an open-collared work shirt and sits at the big desk that John F. Kennedy used, doing paperwork and making phone calls. Clinton loves the fact that next door, in the small study where George Bush ran the Persian Gulf War, Chelsea will sometimes do her homework, sometimes shouting a question about an algebra problem to Dad."[4]

Time portrayed a family that spent hours gathered around the piano, or on the rug playing Pictionary, Scrabble, and Hungarian Rummy.[5] And they painted a homey portrait of the use of the room adjacent to the Oval Office wildly at variance to what the American public was soon to discover.

Hillary went to great lengths to let no one see the truth, that for her living above the store could sometimes be like living above a brothel. How did she reconcile it? She resorted to another favorite Clinton gambit. Bringing history's greats down to the Clintons's level.

"I remember when I read *The Autobiography of Benjamin Franklin*," Hillary recounted in *American Heritage* in 1994, "I discovered things about Franklin's personal life that at the age of fourteen I was shocked by. I remember going to my English teacher and saying, 'I just can't believe it.' I felt I had been disillusioned about Benjamin Franklin. And I'll never forget my teacher saying, 'But why should you be disillusioned? He was a great man; he wasn't a statue somewhere. Men have faults as well as virtues; the real challenge is to see people in their humanity and then admire them even more because of what they were able to accomplish.'"[6] Bill Clinton could thus be portrayed as another great man like Benjamin Franklin, who also had faults—because Bill Clinton and Ben Franklin were after all just human.

MONICA

The story the world would know simply as "Monica" broke at the worst possible time for Hillary. Safe in the White House for another four years, the president talked of delegating major responsibilities to his wife. Hillary herself went further, speaking of a "formal" role in welfare policy.[7]

But Hillary's bid once again to act as co-president of the United States was overtaken by a new scandal.

When Bill Clinton submitted to questioning from Paula

Jones's lawyers in January 1998, he was asked about "Jane Doe Number Six," a zaftig twenty-four-year-old intern from Beverly Hills. He must have known the game was up when the questions turned specific. Did you give her a T-shirt? *Leaves of Grass*? Call her at home?

Jane Doe Number Six, of course, was Monica Lewinsky, a by-product of the Clinton White House's solicitous attitude for donors—in this case, Lewinsky's family friend, Walter Kaye. With Monica, the commanders of spin were forced to move into the fog of battle without a good compass or a map. One line, sold around town by Sidney Blumenthal, portrayed the president as a victim, the "I-was-stalked" defense.

Why the White House would allow the commander-in-chief and leader of the free world to be victimized by a libidinous sexual predator was never fully explained. The story was simply not credible. The really incredible thing about it, however, was the number of Clinton sycophants and journalistic supporters who not only bought but willingly peddled the story.

The other line could be called the Gladstone defense, after the nineteenth century prime minister who was famous for approaching street prostitutes, and converting them from a life of sin by taking them upstairs and "ministering" to them. In much the same way, the staff (and Hillary herself) trotted out this excuse, speaking of the president's interest in ministering to and counseling a troubled young woman.

"You poor son of a bitch," Morris said to the president of the United States over the telephone in a conversation he recounted for *Vanity Fair*. "I've just read what's going on."

"Clinton's whole tone between the lines," Morris remembered, "was 'Oh God, have I fucked up this time.'"[8]

When all else failed, the Clintons went to straight denial and attacking their enemies. It had, after all, worked before. The line, "I did not have sexual relations with that woman," the rehearsed finger wag, likely even Hillary's sun-yellow made-for-television dress, had all been stage-managed by Harry Thomason.

Hillary's signal moment came early, when she appeared on the *Today* show to denounce her husband's detractors as agents of "a vast right-wing conspiracy." The word "vast" was overdone, the kind of adjective that, in a previous era, had been used to describe Communist purveyors of fluoride in our drinking water. Otherwise, her *Today* show appearance was dead-on. She was the essence of a moderate and thoughtful woman, a middle-class mom with a Midwestern twang and a gentle manner. For those anxious to see no futher than what Hillary had to tell them, it was the most effective damage control appearance since Nixon's "Checkers" speech.

But as the months of 1998 marched on, and the facts began to emerge on the front pages of the *New York Times* and the *Washington Post*, it became harder and harder to hide the truth. Worse, what had begun as a sexual indiscretion was now a matter of possible perjury and the beginnings of an impeachment process.

The president's legal defense had to resort to absurd interpretations of conventional words like "sex" or "is."

By many accounts, Hillary was most dismayed by Monica's version as her supporters leaked it to the press that Bill had encouraged her fantasies of dumping Hillary and spending the rest of his life with Lewinsky. "And then I said something about... us sort of being together," she told Starr's investigators. "I think I kind of said, 'Oh, I think we'd be a good team'.... And he... jokingly said, 'Well, what are we going to do when I'm seventy-five and I have to pee twenty-five times a day?'"

If Hillary was angry, hurt, and humiliated by her husband, she was positively seething with hatred at Starr for exploding the myth of the happy family that lived above the store. It was Starr, not Bill, she blamed for splashing the revelation that her husband had admitted to Lewinsky that he had had "hundreds of affairs" earlier in his marriage.

Proven a liar by the presence of his own DNA on Monica's dress, Bill Clinton finally went on national television on August 17 to lance the boil and cut his losses. His brief appearance was a devastating failure, an angry self-pitying whine; an effort at one time to paint himself as a contrite victim, but also to attack his enemies. I was in the green room waiting to appear on *Larry King Live* while watching the speech. It was painful to watch. Even James Carville looked unusually reserved. It was, as America saw it, a thin-skinned attack on Starr disguised as a national apology.

According to White House spin, it wasn't until just before that speech that a reluctant president, his head bowed, went to his wife and told her the truth. The same woman who had not missed a beat to launch a counterattack on the "vast right-wing conspiracy" was now portrayed as a national victim.

The Clintons then left for a vacation at Martha's Vineyard, one in which Hillary allowed the press corps to see her batting away Bill's hand. Another well-rehearsed gesture, probably as carefully orchestrated as the "I-did-not-have-sex" finger wag. The new spin from press secretary Mike McCurry was a kind of amused, boy-he's-in-for-the-spanking-of-his-life story, letting Hillary stand as a surrogate for America's anger. Otherwise, she was to be admired for standing by her man.

"Rather than jump ship or turn on her husband, she turned to him with her daughter and offered love and support when he needed it the most and perhaps deserved it the least," the Reverend Jesse Jackson said after counseling (rehearsing with) the first family. "Many women would have been nursing their wounds or in private solitude. She was in the room helping to chart the plan for his testimony."[9]

She also spearheaded strategy sessions on the November congressional elections, and shrewdly allowed aides to see her bark instructions at a meek Bill Clinton.[10]

The staff Hillary had assembled to defend a president who had obviously lied to the American people were unshakable. Only George Stephanopoulos, who was trying to recreate himself as an ABC journalist, denounced the president's abuse of trust. Otherwise, no Clintonites resigned or seriously criticized the president. Only Health and Human Services Secretary Donna Shalala dared to express her disappointment in a meeting in which the president called ostensibly to apologize to his cabinet. She was rudely slapped down by an aggrieved Clinton, who challenged her to answer whether she preferred a president like Richard Nixon with his abuses of power, or a John F. Kennedy, who slept around? Of course, with Bill Clinton she got both. But like a good Clinton cabinet member, she shut up.

By all the political rules of the past, the War Room–style counteroffensive should have been a disaster. But Hillary and Bill have a way of making the world play by their rules. Many of the advisors to the president argued against the attack on Starr in the national apologia speech.

But the president's astute advisors were ultimately proven to be wrong. A direct frontal attack was, perhaps, Clinton's only hope of staving off a forced resignation or removal from office. Here a good offense was not only a good defense, it was essentially the only defense. As she had done before to try to rescue her health care agenda, Hillary went to the Hill. She addressed House Democrats, whipping up a fury against Starr and the House impeachment managers. She assured them she was a "wife who loves and supports her husband," and was standing firm to keep the vast right-wing conspiracy from "hounding him out of office." She told them that the real fight was not over the impeachment issue, but over whether the Republicans would be allowed to break the back of the Democratic Party.

Hillary even attributed the attacks on her husband to "prejudice against our state." "They wouldn't do this if we were from some other state," she said, ignoring the fact that Kenneth Starr had lived near the Arkansas border and attended two years of college at Harding University at Searcy, Arkansas.[11] And ignoring also the fact that no one had thought to link perjury, obstruction of justice, witness tampering, and intimidation to the state of Arkansas. But Hillary knew that her only salvation was attack, attack, attack. It mattered less that there was any substance to the attack.

There were the predictable confessions, the prayer breakfast, all the tearful Jimmy Swaggart moments. Hillary actually went public with praise for her husband for his *courage and for his willingness to do the right thing*. Clinton himself characteristically slipped into self-pity. At one gathering in late August, he recounted a conversation with Nelson Mandela: "You can't make me believe you didn't hate those people," Clinton told the South African leader. "And then [Mandela] said, 'They could take everything away from me—everything—but my mind and my heart." The implication, of course, was that both men had been unfairly persecuted, as though being imprisoned for decades on Robben Island was the moral equivalent of committing perjury under oath and masturbating in the Oval Office in front of a young intern.[12]

If Bill was helpless, Hillary's War Room was gaining ground. The congressional Republicans were effectively portrayed as the ideological descendants of Thaddeus Stevens and the Radical Republicans who had railroaded the impeachment of President Andrew Johnson. Senator Joseph Lieberman, a respected centrist Democrat, appeared to turn the tide for impeachment when he lashed out against the president. The appearance was deceiving, however, for Lieberman's attack was based only on sex. It was intended and had the same effect as Hillary's public vacation reprimand to her husband—to inflict some public pain on Bill Clinton and to relieve some of the mounting pressure for him to resign. This was an enormous favor to the president in the wrappings of a rebuke. The Democrats succeeded in defining the issue as wholly about sex, as though perjury under oath were of no consequence.

Meanwhile, the Republicans not only misread the tea leaves, they ignored them all together. House Speaker Newt Gingrich had been warned in late summer by GOP pollsters that the public attitude was turning against impeachment. The American people were disgusted with President Clinton's behavior. Their anger toward Clinton, however, was modified by a horror that the most powerful man in the country (and therefore anyone) could be dragged into a courtroom and subjected to such extensive questioning over the most embarrassing aspects of one's life. They rebelled against the explicitness of the Starr report, and blamed Republicans for dragging the whole country through the mud.

What could the Republicans have done?

They needed to reinforce the fact that Bill Clinton was a victim not just of his own actions but also of his and his wife's Orwellian approach to the law. It was Clinton, after hard lobbying by Hillary, who had signed the Violence Against Women Act and supported other legislation that had allowed sexual harassment suits to open up a man's whole life to microscopic examination in civil suits. They could have reminded the American people that the independent counsel's office, which the public increasingly agreed with James Carville was out of control, was advanced by the very Watergate lawyers who protected Clinton and was reauthorized by the president himself, with one hundred Republican House members voting against it. They could have forcefully reminded the public that the whole process had been started by Attorney General Janet Reno.

In short, the Republicans could have portrayed the president as a man pursued by Frankenstein monsters of his own creation. Instead, they proceeded methodically, overriding the Democrats in bitter, contentious proceedings that played right into the "Radical Republicans" stereotype.

Even after all of this, the presidency hung by a thread. There was a brief period in which the senior leaders of the Democratic Party seemed to weigh whether it would be better to jettison Clinton and go with an incumbent Gore. All it would take for that to happen was for the right Senate Democrat to stand up and call on him to resign. John Glenn could have done it. Joseph Lieberman could have done it. Patrick Moynihan could have done it. Dianne Feinstein seemed at times to come the closest, unafraid to express her outrage that the president had lied to her, point blank. The Senate Democrats could have played the honorable role that Republicans Howard Baker and Watergate counsel Fred Thompson played during Watergate, going where the facts led them.

But party discipline—and Clinton's brazen defense—reigned over conscience. The Clintons maneuvered senators of stature and conscience into defending him as a matter of constitutional propriety. The national feminist organizations, so certain that Clarence Thomas had been a sexual harasser, were by now transformed into a kind of Clinton pep squad. At worst, they would issue Delphic pronouncements about the slight but ultimately unimportant degree of Clinton's culpability.

Below the surface, Hillary unleashed the secret police. The director of White House records later admitted in a deposition that he ordered a search for "anything and everything we might have in our files on Linda Tripp," the former White House and Pentagon employee whose taped conversations with Monica Lewinsky helped prove that Clinton was lying. Pentagon spokesman Kenneth Bacon likely broke the law by divulging an embarrassing juvenile arrest from Linda Tripp's personal security file.

Meanwhile, the president refused to distance himself from the very public efforts of pornographer Larry Flynt, who offered a small fortune for sex dirt on members of Congress, managing to smear House Judiciary Chairman Henry Hyde for a decades-old affair. The president's attorney, even hired Terry Lezner and his private detective firm, IGI, with the implied threat that if the president was going to go down because of sexual improprieties, he was going to take others with him. As it turned out, of course, others would go down, like the new House Speaker Bob Livingston, who sought to do the noble thing by resigning. But President Clinton would never have followed that course. If the worst thing that could happen to Clinton was also the worst thing that could happen to America, it simply was not going to happen. By slinging dirt and wrapping himself in a "zone of privacy" against Starr and the apparent Puritans of the radical right, Clinton no doubt felt he could beat the rap.

The Clintons had a long history of using private detectives to sniff out vulnerabilities of enemies and keep track of each other's private lives. In 1992 Betsey Wright hired Jack Palladino, San Francisco detective and student of Hal Lipset, who had served as a private investigator in many Black Panther cases. Palladino's job was to ransack the lives of women who could have turned on Clinton during the campaign.

This time round, the focus seemed to be on getting the bimbos to shut up. Kathleen Willey, who would later claim Bill Clinton had groped her, had her tires slashed. In another incident, a stranger jogged next to her in a park and inquired about the health of her cat, calling it by name.

Other inducements were used. Elizabeth Ward Gracen, a former Miss America, got the carrot—offers of acting roles dangled in front of her by FOB Mickey Kantor—and the stick, when someone ransacked her room.

While the Clinton machine worked—allowing the Clintons to claim victory in the congressional elections and to survive the Congress's impeachment proceedings—it had forced the Clinton machine to run to the last dregs of support. And the sweet savor of victory was short-lived. The next Jane

Doe would rock the administration, permanently mar the president's image and throw the liberal establishment into crisis.

'EVERYTHING YOU DO FOR BILL'

The Juanita Broaddrick interview with NBC's Lisa Meyer was a story to push every feminist button. As a "police rape," it fit the feminist need to seek out the ideological underpinnings of a crime. It was the perfect example of how women at that time were reluctant to charge rape, fearing that cross-examination would reveal their most intimate and embarrassing secrets. We have long been assured by feminists that women do not lie about such things.

But the very same feminists who had so savagely denounced Clarence Thomas for allegedly making off-color remarks to and asking for a date with an employee—an employee who nevertheless followed him to his next job—were willing to give Clinton the benefit of the doubt. Susan Estrich, herself a rape victim, pointed out on *Crossfire* with me that the statute of limitations had long passed, and that absent any evidence, we were just back to the he said/she said, in which case Clinton had to be considered innocent.

The Broaddrick rape story was met with glacial silence and indifference by Barbara Boxer, Gloria Steinem, and the country's leading feminist icon, Hillary Rodham Clinton.

It is highly doubtful that Hillary believes that her husband is innocent, not with a history like his.

After all that has come to light about Clinton's telling Paula Jones to "kiss it," the groping of Kathleen Willey in the presidential study, and the exploitation of an immature and unsteady White House intern, can Hillary be free of doubts that her husband is a rapist?

Only Andrea Dworkin, a radical feminist, seemed willing to demand that Hillary throw away the shield she had erected for Clinton. "What Hillary is doing is appalling," she said. "Being a feminist has to mean you don't use your intellect and your creativity to protect a man's exploitation of women."[13]

But Hillary's betrayal was of more than a mere abstraction like feminism. It was a betrayal of humanity for power. In an interview with Matt Drudge in August 1999, Juanita Broaddrick claimed that she met Hillary Rodham Clinton at a political rally in the spring of 1978, just weeks after Mrs. Broaddrick was allegedly raped by the then–Attorney General Bill Clinton.

According to Mrs. Broaddrick, Hillary "caught me and took my hand and said, 'I am so happy to meet you. I want you to know that we appreciate everything you do for Bill.'… I started to turn away and she held onto my hand and reiterated her phrase—looking less friendly and repeated her statement—'Everything you do for Bill.'"

ELEVEN
THE PHILOSOPHER QUEEN

"Power is the very essence, the dynamo of life. It is the power of the heart pumping blood and sustaining life in the body."

— SAUL ALINSKY, *RULES FOR RADICALS*

GETTING SPIRITUAL

"You know, I'm beginning to think there must be more to life than this greasy pole, this rat race," Hillary once said to friends in the late 1970s on a vacation to England with Bill to meet his old Oxford friends.[1]

Whatever their private compromises with themselves and their consciences, the Clintons continue to project a robust religious life. They worship together in Foundry United Methodist Church, where J. Philip Wogaman, a social-ethics professor and liberal pastor, can be counted on to address topics in such a way as to cause the Clintons no embarrassment.

Hillary's turn to the spiritual intensified in her first year as first lady, when Hugh Rodham suffered a massive stroke and slipped into a three-week coma.

The day before his death, Hillary gave the commencement address at the University of Texas, where she made a famous speech on America's "crisis of meaning and spiritual vacuum," and our national "sleeping sickness of the soul."

"We are at a stage in history in which remolding society is one of the great challenges facing all of us in the West. If one looks around the Western world, one can see the rumblings of discontent, almost regardless of the political systems, as we come face to face with problems that the modern age has dealt us."

These problems, she suggested, were the result of a "lack of meaning" in individual lives and society. She positioned herself between a market economy, "which knows the price of everything, but the value of nothing" (an unintended description of the Clinton White House approach to the use of the presidency to raise reelection funds), and the "state or government, which attempts to use its means of acquiring tax money, of making decisions to assist us in becoming a better, more equitable society…. Neither is adequate to address the challenge confronting us." Then she cut to the chase.

"We need a new politics of meaning. We need a new ethos of individual responsibility and caring." This could be attained, she suggested, as millions of individuals "reject cynicism, as they are willing to be hopeful once again, as they are willing to take risks to meet the challenges they see around them, as they truly begin to try to see others as they wish to be seen and to treat them as they wish to be treated, to overcome all of the obstacles we have erected around ourselves that keep us apart from one another, fearful and afraid, not willing to build the bridges necessary to fill our spiritual vacuum."

It was a stylistic and conceptual return to her Wellesley

commencement address of 1969. As Michael Kelly pointed out in his astute "Saint Hillary" piece in the *New York Times Magazine*, the speeches share "all the same traits: vaulting ambition, didactic moralizing, intellectual incoherence and the adolescent assumption that the past does not exist and the present needs only your guiding hand to create the glorious future."

Many were appalled by Hillary's reference to Lee Atwater's deathbed regrets—printed in *Life* magazine—that he had spent his short life as a campaign attack dog for the right. It was a perfect Hillary trope, to weave an attack on an opponent and his ideology into a speech that seemed to have a self-confessional tone.

"Never mind that the limits of materialism are not best learned on somebody else's dime," objected the *New Republic*'s Leon Wieseltier, certainly no apologist for Atwater, Reagan, or the right. "The politics of meaning turns out to be, negatively, just an ornate rejection of Reaganism. But it is historically incorrect, and politically foolish, to mistake Reaganism for meaninglessness."[2]

Perhaps more worrying was Hillary's belief that something was so wrong in Western society that it required not reform, but a thorough "remolding." Re-creation, of course, from the top—by planners, reformers, experts, and the intelligentsia. Reconstruction of society by those smart enough and altruistic enough to make our decisions for us. People like Bill and Hillary Clinton. Hillary, throughout her intellectual life, has been taken by this idea, which is the totalitarian temptation that throughout history has led to the guillotine, the gulag, and the terror and reeducation camps of the Red Guard.

The phrase "politics of meaning" was coined by Michael Lerner, who launched the magazine *Tikkun* as a Jewish, liberal, intellectual counterweight to Norman Podhoretz's Jewish, neo-conservative *Commentary*, one of the most respected and influential intellectual magazines in the country. But it doesn't stack up. To read a copy of *Tikkun* is to wade through a pool of self-indulgent New Age twaddle and psychobabble indistinguishable from Hillary's worst speeches or *It Takes a Village*.

Lerner's book, *The Politics of Meaning*, can readily be sized up by the subtitles of its chapters, "Give Men a Chance: Understanding Homophobia and the Desperate Struggle to Prove One's Manliness," or "Overcoming Patriarchy as Family Support," or "The Tyranny of Couples." At his wedding to his first wife, Lerner cut into a cake with the inscription "Smash Monogamy." The couple exchanged rings hammered out of metal from downed U.S. military aircraft.[3]

Lerner, who liked to invoke the phrase "Hillary and I believe," turned out to have an ideological bottom line in his dealings with the Clintons. As an activist whose left-wing pedigree is unassailable, Lerner soon lost interest in the Clintons when he saw that polling and focus groups were leading into "triangulation," welfare reform, and spending cuts.

After Kelly's lacerating "Saint Hillary" piece appeared in the *New York Times Magazine* —and after another devastating review of Hillary's "politics of meaning" came from columnist Charles Krauthammer—Hillary withdrew from Lerner, and referred to his visits to the White House as mere "courtesy calls." Lerner, unlike most people who are used as Clinton fodder, turned on her.[4]

Lerner criticized the Clintons' apologetic triangulation. "So here was one of the most powerful men in the world telling the rest of us that he did not have enough power to pursue his principles, and that instead he must watch out for himself. And this, sad to say, was the same man to whom the rest of the world had listened when he told us in 1992 that we as a community could move beyond self-interest to fight for a common vision of mutual caring."[5]

THE SEEKERS

One would expect a president and first lady to arrive at the White House psychologically and spiritually mature. But Hillary and Bill dealt with national criticism of their first term by turning to, among others, fringe spiritualists. One of them was Marianne Williamson, a Jewish charismatic spiritualist from Texas who sports Armanis and presided over one of Liz Taylor's weddings. Another is Tony Robbins, known to millions of cable TV viewers as the smarmy hawker of expensive self-help videos that can help you "awaken the giant within." And, of course, there was Jean Houston, co-director of the Foundation for Mind Research in Pomona, New York, who believes that her personal archetypal predecessor was Athena. Dr. Houston—who misrepresented her doctorate, awarded by Union Institute in Cincinnati, as coming from Columbia University—used hypnosis to guide Hillary into a seance/conversation with Eleanor Roosevelt.

The revelation of the Eleanor exercise in Bob Woodward's book *The Choice* was a major embarrassment to a woman who prided herself on projecting intellectual and moral strength. It was widely compared with published stories a decade earlier concerning Nancy Reagan and her interest in astrology.

Hillary, however, has not fled from the comparison with
Eleanor Roosevelt. At a speech at Georgetown University in
December 1998, Hillary noted:

> Wherever I go as first lady, I am always reminded of one thing:
> that usually Eleanor Roosevelt has been there before. I have been
> to farms in Iowa, factories in Michigan, and welfare offices in New
> York where Mrs. Roosevelt paid a visit more than a half-century
> ago. When I went to Pakistan and India I discovered that Eleanor
> Roosevelt had been there in 1952, and had written a book about
> her experiences.

In the Clintons' communion with Dr. Jean Houston, the
president was advised to "deepen the elder in himself."[6]

Dr. Houston had a deeper message for the first lady.

The human race, she said, was at a five-thousand-year
turning point, a moment when women were at the brink of
finally achieving equal partnership with men. Joan of Arc had
been a vital actor, the one who moved the progress of women
more forcefully than anyone else. But Hillary had a special
place reserved for her. It was up to her to finish the job, to be
a stand-in for all of womankind at the moment of equality.

Dr. Houston told Hillary that if she could do this, Hillary
would become the most consequential woman in human history.[7]

Finally, a properly ambitious undertaking, but certainly
not beyond the reach of someone who had done so much
already.

THE CANDIDATE

At one of her lunches with John Robert Starr at Little Rock's
Cafe Saint Moritz in 1989, there was a lapse in the conversa-

tion about Bill's ambitions for national office. Starr took the opportunity to ask Hillary what she wanted to do. "She leaned toward me," he recounted, "eyes ablaze, and said in as an intense voice as I have ever heard, 'I want to run something!'"[8]

As a young law professor, Bill Clinton had confided in friends that he recognized that Hillary was putting her own political future into escrow by coming to Arkansas. Now the long years of waiting are over. The Monica Lewinsky scandal has, ironically, made Hillary one of the most popular women in the world. She has become a celebrated and sympathetic popular figure in another ironic turn of fate: The most powerful woman in the world cast as a victim. As her popularity rose, as the crowds became larger and more enthusiastic, Hillary could think about fulfilling her ambition for power.

Long before Hillary announced she was considering a run for the U.S. Senate from New York, knowledgeable Democrats connected to the White House and on the Hill were talking about Hillary's real ambition to run something big. Very big. One possibility I thought of was the World Bank. Her college roommate and close friend Jan Piercy was already there.

Though a multinational panel governs the bank, the president generally comes from its largest shareholder, the United States.

As president of the World Bank, Hillary would have tens of billions of dollars at her fingertips to effect social experimentation on a global scale. And she could be appointed without having to go through either the nastiness of a Senate confirmation process or the untidiness of a popular election. Of course she could still be appointed after the 2000 presidential election. There still would be time before the next president is sworn in.

But the real question is: Would that be enough?

Hillary in office—any office—will finally be free from the troubled trajectory of her husband's career. She will be free to take back her old name. She will be free to create her own legacy. Divorce or at least some degree of separation will allow her to establish herself as a world stateswoman, as the death of FDR at Warm Springs freed Eleanor Roosevelt to become an international figure in her own right. Then she will "run something."

If not politics, President Clinton could make a recess appointment to the Supreme Court. Her mother's dream would be fulfilled. It has been done before. Justice Brennan was a recess appointment. That would suit Justice Rodham Clinton just fine.

If she has her way, it could be the United States itself that will have the opportunity for rebirth in the hands of Hillary. Indeed there are rumors in Washington, surely untrue, that she is not at all disturbed by the troubles Al Gore is experiencing, because if a Republican is elected in 2000 she can be the Democratic presidential heir apparent in 2004. That is if Al Gore is unsuccessful in 2000.

We already know that in her relentless quest for power Hillary has been as financially acquisitive and ethically agile as any politician. But she also has pursued a politics of vendetta, deceit, and extremist ideology to a remarkable degree.

Hillary's embryonic Senate campaign has shown that she is determined to let nothing stand in the way of the next step in her ambitious career. She has also proven that for those who are in her way or who fail to help her, there will indeed be "hell to pay." Never have the stakes been so high—both for her and for her opportunity to change this nation.

The Clinton years might seem like a long national nightmare of scandal, sleaze, and ruthless acquisition of power. Hillary herself is the link from the excesses of the Watergate staff, to the Whitewater fiasco, to abuses of executive power, to the defense of her husband's perjury and obstruction of justice. But now it is Hillary's turn. The Clinton era is far from over and Hillary's ambitions far from satisfied.

AFTERWORD
SHE'S BACK

I t was bound to happen. The reemergence of Hillary Rodham Clinton from self-imposed obscurity to incandescent super-celebrityhood was only a matter of time. Not that Hillary was going to overdo the demureness routine. She had duly bided her time for weeks as a quiet "backbencher" after her election to the United States Senate from her adopted state of New York, downplaying the idea that she would be taking a leadership role soon after her swearing-in, mildly insisting, "I'm only here to learn." But her modest and self-effacing demeanor was a necessarily prudent course given the spectacular finale she and her husband had orchestrated for their last few weeks in the White House. Once the headlines about the pilfered furniture, the ostentatious and unseemly giftfest, and the last-minute deluge of indefensible pardons receded from view (and, she hoped, from memory), Hillary was anxious for the moment when she could reassert her position on the national stage, a position she seems to regard as hers by divine right.

That moment came in late May 2001 when Republican senator Jim Jeffords of Vermont announced that he was bolting his party to become an independent, throwing the balance of power in the Senate to the Democrats (a moment that had been otherwise breathlessly anticipated by Senate Democrats as they kept a barely concealed round-the-clock death watch on ninety-eight-year-old GOP senator Strom Thurmond).

Little noted in all the voluminous commentary about what the Jeffords move meant for President Bush's agenda, and for the Democrats' efforts to oppose it, was what it meant for Hillary Rodham Clinton—a little detail of the historic shift in power that may well prove the most significant part of the Jeffords transformation. In that one moment, Hillary suddenly found herself with a position of real authority as the point woman and leading Democratic authority on the very wedge issue she has always wished to ride to victory, her ticket to another Clinton administration: health care reform. As Peggy Noonan, the *Wall Street Journal*'s Hillary watcher, so colorfully wrote, "You lock the door and she comes in the window, you lock the window and she comes through the floor boards. This is like 'Alien'—she lives in Tom Daschle's stomach. Just as the music gets soft and the scene winds down you hear the wild 'Eek! Eek!' and she bursts out of Tom and darts through the room."

For those who have observed Hillary closely over the course of her long and determined climb to the pinnacle of national power and influence, this latest resurrection comes as no surprise. She shares with her husband a preternatural capacity to spring back from the most appalling and embarrassing—even seemingly fatal—revelations with newfound strength and with no apparent sense of shame, remorse, or even memory of her past missteps. She has performed more escapes from impossible situations than Houdini.

Before she even took office in January, Senator-elect Clinton was at the epicenter of an immense controversy. This one concerned the granting of eleventh-hour pardons to individuals represented by her lawyer-brother Hugh Rodham, who just happened to be residing at the White House as a sort of "live-in guest" during the last weeks of the Bill and Hillary administration. That story is told in detail in my newest book, *The Final Days*. Suffice it to say here that Hillary's reaction was Rodham-Clintonian in its most classic form—a categorical denial she had any clue as to what her brother was doing right under her nose, in her own house, in concert with her own husband; a public hand-wringing over his lamentable behavior; a self-pitying performance of how tragically she had been victimized yet again; and a self-righteous insistence that her brother return all the fees he had earned from his pardon-seeking clients.

Such strict ethical standards did not, of course, apply to the $190,000 worth of "gifts"—including china, rugs, televisions, sofas, and expensive furniture—Hillary solicited from friends and political supporters for their new homes in Washington and Chappaqua. Only when confronted with a media firestorm did the former first couple offer to return about half of the ostentatious gifts, an offer that has yet to be fulfilled. As Brit Hume of Fox News pointedly asked, "[I]f it was wrong to accept the gifts, how is that wrong corrected by giving back half their value?"

Another ethical lapse that was not allowed to crack Hillary's icy veneer was her $8 million book deal with Simon & Schuster, which was inked in the short interval between her election and her swearing-in so as to escape Senate rules on gifts. In the wake of the controversy swirling around her book deal, her husband's last-minute pardon orgy, and the first

couple's gift haul, Hillary spent her first weeks in office giving
new meaning to the phrase "keeping a low profile." Reporters
were reduced to shouting questions to her on the run, questions that she studiedly ignored as her Secret Service detail
helped her scurry to her Senate office sanctuary. Ironically,
after repeatedly criticizing her Republican opponent in the
New York senatorial campaign, Rick Lazio, for missing votes in
Congress, Hillary kicked off her legislative career by missing
her very first vote in January. Temerity is not a quality missing
from Hillary's bag of tricks.

Then came the revelation that Hillary had attended the
meeting between the leader of a Hasidic community in New
York and President Clinton where pardons were discussed for
four Hasidic felons who had stolen $40 million of federal
money intended for the poor. Hillary predictably claimed that
she had never discussed the issue with her husband. The sen-
tences of all four were commuted shortly after their Hasidic
communities voted overwhelming (1,400 to 12) for her in the
November election as neighboring Hasidic communities went
overwhelmingly for her opponent, Mr. Lazio. Just another
one of those funny coincidences that follow Hillary around
like so many obedient cocker spaniels.

Lest anyone think that Hillary's humble, "just here to
learn" performance was a sign that she had set aside any
higher political aspirations, there were ample clues as to her
actual ambitions. In her first formal interview after taking
office, Hillary announced the formation of her own national
political action committee, HILLPAC (strangely missing her
patented exclamation point), which would raise money from
the "many friends I've made over thirty years" across the
country in order to help "the Democrats regain the majority

in the House and Senate." As *Human Events* understatedly noted at the time, "When a politician forms a PAC, especially one that will accept $150,000 increments of 'soft money,' it usually means that official has higher aspirations."

A hint of those "higher aspirations" came shortly after President Bush gave his first State of the Union address. *The American Spectator* reported that Senator Clinton had made known her desire to give the televised Democratic response to the next major prime-time address by the president. "She understood she couldn't do the response to the State of the Union address," an aide to the Democratic Senate leadership was quoted as saying, "but she requested dibs on the one after that." Perhaps when she had been given the perfunctory task of presiding over the Senate on January 24—and had been addressed as "Madam President" according to Senate protocol—the experience had served to remind her of her true calling. Remaining a "quiet back-bencher" was not the path for someone with Hillary's much more lofty ambitions.

But her early Senate learning tour, like her early Senate campaign listening tour, was merely prelude to the real campaign to follow. Neither her radical ideological proclivities nor her brazen hypocrisy on ethical issues was ever far from the surface. One of the first bills that Mrs. Clinton cosponsored in February was a measure that would force private insurance companies to provide birth-control coverage. If enacted, it would cover approximately 20 million women, cost the insurance companies billions, and, as always with mandated care, drive premiums sky high. Something of a sneak preview, perhaps, of her priorities in future "health care reform" legislation.

Another "reform" measure cosponsored by Senator Clinton was the McCain-Feingold campaign finance reform bill.

Did Hillary see any contradiction at all between her vocal
support for campaign finance reform and her behavior when
she used "joint-fundraising committees" to solicit and raise
her own soft money? Not likely. Hillary was, in fact, the overwhelming leader in using this deceptive technique in 2000,
raising over $9.6 million in soft money, $9 million of which
was "transferred" to the New York State Democratic party.
One campaign finance expert described this practice as "violating the spirit and letter of the federal law limiting contributions to Senate candidates." But as one who has a history of
violating the spirit and letter of federal law with impunity, and
as the spouse of the all-time leader in that category, Mrs.
Clinton was not likely to be discouraged by such trifles. And
it was classic Clintonese to call for laws to prohibit the type of
conduct for which they are being criticized. That enables the
wrongdoer to simultaneously deny the wrongdoing and
assume the mantle of reformer.

One ethics rule the Senate might want to consider tight-
ening in light of its new member is the one that applies to
speech fees—for Senate spouses. While Bill's $100,000
speeches before business and trade associations may not be
unusual for ex-presidents, what is unprecedented is for a
former inhabitant of the White House to receive so much
money from groups that have an interest in bills on which his
wife will vote. Existing Senate rules put a $50 limit on the value
of gifts to senators but no limit on the amount that one can
give to a Senate spouse. Professor Randy Barnett of the Boston
University Law School, for one, thought that there wasn't
much ambiguity about the propriety of such fees: "You don't
need to be an ethics expert" to question the appropriateness of
such fees, he told *The Hill*. "This is obviously a legal way of

funneling hundreds of thousands of dollars into the joint bank account of a senator." (Professor Barnett presumes, undoubtedly correctly, that Mrs. Clinton and her husband are not going to put the money anywhere other than a joint account!)

Talking about President Bush's tax bill in an interview with the *Poughkeepsie Journal*, Senator Clinton complained that facts seem to have little impact on Washington's entrenched interests. The federal city, she said, is "like an evidence-free zone." With regard to incriminating evidence concerning her own relationship to scandals past and present, Hillary can only hope that this continues to be the case. In the same interview, she was asked about the relationship of the pardons granted by her husband in the administration's final days and assistance given to her campaign by some of the pardonees. Her response was classic—a prototype for its genre: "We'll just let it run its course. There was no quid pro quo. There wasn't any connection whatsoever. That's what is going to be determined and it will all fade away, as these things usually do. And we are just going to wait for that to happen." Remarkable. A categorical denial along with a suggestion that a proper investigation should be allowed to run its course, tied together with a detached suggestion that we're all in this together and we'll just have to see what happens.

Since letting scandals "run their course" has been the successful modus operandi of the Clintons for decades, there is no reason to believe that the junior senator from New York will alter her carefully perfected techniques after they have worked so well for so many years. We have to assume that the voting public will tolerate the same type of ruthless and vindictive political behavior that has worked so well for her entire public life. I have explained in this book where she learned it, as well as how she has put it in practice. No one has denied that these depictions are true.

No, hours after the Jeffords announcement, which vaulted the Democrats into power in the Senate and opened up new avenues of advancement for Hillary, she indicated a heightened aggressiveness. As the Senate overwhelmingly confirmed Bush appointees Viet Dinh and Michael Chertoff as assistant attorneys general, Mrs. Clinton cast the sole vote against both men. It was only a coincidence, of course, that both men had served as lawyers with the Senate Whitewater committee. All of the other senators expressed with their votes their respect for the integrity of these men and their respective talents. The junior senator from New York, however, had personal reasons for voting against them. They had dared to help investigate her and her husband. There would be no forgetting that.

NOTES

CHAPTER ONE: HILLARY'S BABY

1. *New Yorker*, June 10, 1996.

CHAPTER TWO: DREAMS OF POWER

1. *Washington Post*, January 11, 1993.

2. *Washington Post*, January 25, 1999.

3. *Washington Post*, June 23, 1996.

4. Dick Morris, *Behind the Oval Office*, p. xxx.

5. Webb Hubbell, *Friends in High Places*, p. 153.

6. *New York Daily News*, May 27, 1999.

7. *Crains Insider*, May 20, 1999.

8. *Wall Street Journal*, April 28, 1999.

9. *New York Times*, March 4, 1999.

10. *Washington Post*, March 28, 1999.

11. *New York Post*, May 12, 1992.

12. *Tikkun*

13. *Washington Post*, March 28, 1999.

14. MSNBC, May 24, 1999.

15. CNN, May 26, 1999.

16. *New York Post*, August 12, 1992.

17. *New Yorker*, May 30, 1994.

CHAPTER THREE: "SEE HOW LIBERAL I'M BECOMING!"

1. Hillary Rodham Clinton, *It Takes a Village*, p. 20.

2. Ibid., p. 33.

3. *People*, February 17, 1992.

4. Hillary Rodham Clinton, *It Takes a Village*, p. 24.

5. *Newsweek*, February 28, 1994.

6. Hillary Rodham Clinton, *It Takes a Village*, p. 171.

7. *Newsweek*, January 15, 1996.

8. Hillary Rodham Clinton, *It Takes a Village*, p. 178.

9. Judith Warner, *Hillary Clinton: The Inside Story*, p 19.

10. *American Heritage*, December 1994.

11. *Washington Post*, January 11, 1993.

12. Meredith Oakley, *On the Make*, p. 97.

13. Warner, *Hillary Clinton: The Inside Story*, p 29.

14. *American Spectator*, August 1992.

15. David Maraniss, *First in His Class*, p. 225; *Boston Globe*, January 12, 1993.

16. *Boston Globe*, January 12, 1993.

17. *Washingtonian*, January 1993.

18. *Boston Globe*, January 12, 1993.

19. Ibid.

20. *New Yorker*, May 30, 1993.

21. *American Spectator*, August 1992.

22. *Newsweek*, February 3, 1992.

23. *New Republic*, March 4, 1992.

24. *Washington Post*, January 12, 1993.

25. Ibid.

26. Saul Alinsky, *Rules for Radicals*, p. 100.

27. Ibid., p. 185.

28. Ibid., pp. xxi, xxii.

29. Ibid., p. 139.

30. Ibid., p. 140.

31. *Yale Review of Law and Social Action*, Winter 1970, p. 93.

32. Robert H. Bork, *The Tempting of America*, p. 208.

33. David Brock, *The Seduction of Hillary Rodham*; p. 30. Joyce Milton, *The First Partner*, p. 37.

34. Joyce Milton, *The First Partner*, pg 39.

35. David Brock, *The Seduction of Hillary Rodham*, p. 33.

36. Joyce Milton, *The First Partner*, p. 53.

37. Ibid.

38. *New York Times Magazine*, May 23, 1993.

39. *Newsweek*, October 31, 1994.

40. David Brock, *The Seduction of Hillary Rodham*, p. 18.

41. *American Spectator*, August 1992.

42. Ibid.

43. David Brock, *The Seduction of Hillary Rodham*, p. 35.

CHAPTER FOUR: OF ONE MIND

1. *Time*, October 26, 1996.

2. *Newsweek*, March 9, 1992.

3. David Maraniss, *First in His Class*, p. 247.

4. Ibid.

5. *Vanity Fair*, February 1999.

6. *Washington Post*, January 11, 1994.

7. *Oxford Mail*, October 13, 1992.

8. *New Yorker*, May 30, 1999.

9. David Maraniss *First in His Class*, p. 39.

10. *Vanity Fair*, February 1999.

11. Dick Morris, *Behind the Oval Office*, p. xxvii.

12. Ibid., p. 25.

13. Ernest Dumas, ed., *The Clintons of Arkansas*, p. 57.

14. *Time*, April 4, 1993; Ernest Dumas, ed., *The Clintons of Arkansas*, p. 113.

15. Ernest Dumas, ed., *The Clintons of Arkansas*, p. 54.

16. David Maraniss, *First in His Class*, p. 264.

17. *Washington Post*, December 1993.

18. *Newsweek*, March 30, 1992.

19. *Time*, January 4, 1994.

20. *American Heritage*, December 1994.

21. *Newsweek*, February 3, 1992.

22. *Newsweek*, March 30, 1992.

23. David Maraniss, *First in His Class*, p. 326.

24. *Time*, January 4, 1993.

25. Webb Hubbell, *Friends in High Places*, p. 33.

26. Ernest Dumas, ed., *The Clintons of Arkansas*, p. 62.

27. Ibid., p. 63.

28. Ibid.

29. *Time*, January 4, 1993.

30. David Brock, *The Seduction of Hillary Rodham*, pp. 57-60.

31. Dick Morris, *Behind the Oval Office*, p. 45.

32. *Newsweek*, March 30, 1992.

33. Dick Morris, *Behind the Oval Office*, p. xviii.

34. *People*, April 15, 1996.

35. *U.S. News and World Report*, April 20, 1998.

36. David Brock, *The Seduction of Hillary Rodham*, p. 64.

37. Ibid., p. 65.

38. Dick Morris, *Behind the Oval Office*, p. xviii.

39. *Washington Post*, June 23, 1996.

CHAPTER FIVE: VILLAGE SOCIALISM

1. *Newsweek*, January 15, 1996.

2. *Washington Post*, December 5, 1992.

3. *National Review*, February 15, 1993.

4. *Boston Globe*, February 7, 1993.

5. *Washington Post*, January 12, 1993.

6. Meredith Oakley, *On the Make*, p. 105.

7. Joyce Milton, *The First Partner*, pp. 55-59.

8. *Newsweek*, September 21, 1992.

9. Ibid.

10. *U.S. News and World Report*, September 7, 1992.

11. *Criticism*, October 1992.

12. Meredith Oakley, *On the Make*, p. 497.

13. Associated Press, August 12, 1997.

14. *Washington Times*, August 21, 1992.

15. "Product Liability Coordinating Committee Report."

16. *Free Market*, December 1992.

17. *Newsweek*, January 18, 1993.

18. *Arkansas Democrat-Gazette*, May 12, 1992.

CHAPTER SIX: WATERGATE TO WHITEWATER

1. *New Republic*, April 1994.

2. Webb Hubbell, *Friends in High Places*, p. 60.

3. *Newsweek*, March 11, 1996.

4. *Investor's Business Daily*, December 6, 1990.

5. Jerry Zeifman, *Without Honor: The Impeachment of President Nixon and the Crimes of Camelot*, pp. 151-152.

6. Judith Warner, *Hillary Clinton: The Inside Story*, p. 71.

7. David Maraniss, *First in His Class*, p. 311.

8. Michael Ledeen, *Machiavelli on Modern Leadership*, p. 139.

9. *American Spectator*, August 1992.

10. Joyce Milton, *The First Partner*, p. 130.

11. *American Spectator*, August 1992.

12. David Brock, *The Seduction of Hillary Rodham*, p. 100.

13. David Brock, *The Seduction of Hillary Rodham*, p. 101.

14. Ibid.

15. Ibid., p. 100.

16. Daniel Wattenberg, *American Spectator*, August 1992

17. *New York Times*, January 20, 1993.

18. Ibid.

19. Meredith Oakley, *On the Make*, p. 496.

20. *American Spectator*, August 1992; David Brock, *The Seduction of Hillary Rodham*, p. 112.

21. *New Yorker*, May 30, 1994.

22. *Business Week*, April 18, 1992.

23. Saul Alinsky, *Rules for Radicals*, p. 150.

24. *Newsweek*, March 14, 1994.

25. *National Review*, April 4, 1994.

26. *Newsweek*, March 14, 1994.

27. *National Review*, April 4, 1994; *Vanity Fair*, May 1993.

28. *New Republic*, January 4, 1994.

29. *Business Week*, April 18, 1994.

30. *American Spectator*, December 1993.

31. *Washington Times*, March 31, 1994.

32. *Newsweek*, March 14, 1994; *Money Magazine*, July 1993.

33. *American Spectator*, August 1992.

34. *Business Week*, April 18, 1994.

35. *New York Times*, February 18, 1994.

36. *Washington Post*, April 12, 1994.

37. *Newsweek*, April 25, 1994.

38. *Newsweek*, April 11, 1994.

39. *New York Times*, March 18, 1994.

40. *Washington Times*, April 3, 1994.

41. Ibid.

42. *USA Today*, April 7, 1994.

43. *Time*, April 1, 1994; *New York Times*, April 11, 1994.

44. *National Review*, February 20, 1994.

45. *New York Post*, April 1, 1994.

46. *Washington Times*, April 3, 1994.

47. *New York Times*, March 18, 1994.

48. Webb Hubbell, *Friends in High Places*, pp. 46-47.

49. Ibid.

50. Ibid., p. 50.

51. Ibid., p. 67.

52. *Tallahassee Democrat*, August 19, 1993.

53. *New Yorker*, May 30, 1994.

54. *Tallahassee Democrat*, August 19, 1993.

55. Webb Hubbell, *Friends in High Places*, p. 34.

56. Ibid.

57. Ibid., p. 35.

58. *National Review*, April 4, 1994.

59. Ibid.

60. Webb Hubbell, *Friends in High Places*, p. 14.

61. Ibid.

62. Ibid., p. 66.

63. Ibid., pp. 55-56.

64. Ibid., p. 41.

65. *Washington Times*, January 12, 1996.

66. L. D. Brown, *Crossfire*, p. 63.

67. Saul Alinsky, *Rules for Radicals*, p. 12.

68. *Time*, March 30, 1992.
69. Ibid.
70. *New Yorker*, January 17, 1994.
71. *Washington Post*, January 24, 1994.
72. Ibid.
73. Joyce Milton, *The First Partner*, p. 174.
74. *New Yorker*, January 17, 1994; *Washington Post*, November 3, 1993.
75. *New York Times Review of Books*, March 24, 1996.
76. *Time*, March 18, 1996.
77. *Time*, March 21, 1996.
78. *Wall Street Journal*, January 19, 1996.
79. *Newsweek*, January 26, 1996.
80. *New York Post*, January 20, 1996.
81. *Newsweek*, January 15, 1996; *Newsweek*, January 22, 1996.
82. *Vanity Fair*, February, 1997.
83. Joyce Milton, *The First Partner*, p. 195.
84. Ibid., p. 165.
85. David Brock, *The Seduction of Hillary Rodham*, p. 213.
86. *New Republic*, April 4, 1995.
87. Ibid.
88. Edward Timperlake & William C. Triplett II, *Year of the Rat*.

CHAPTER SEVEN: THE CAMPAIGN MANAGER

1. David Maraniss, *First in His Class*, p. 345.
2. Meredith Oakley, *On the Make*, p. 517.
3. Dick Morris, *Behind the Oval Office*, p. 13.

4. Webb Hubbell, *Friends in High Places*, p. 76.
5. *People*, February 17, 1992.
6. Dick Morris, *Behind the Oval Office*, p. 51.
7. *People*, February 17, 1992.
8. Webb Hubbell, *Friends in High Places*, p. 85.
9. *New Yorker*, May 30, 1994.
10. *Time*, August 17, 1992.
11. David Maraniss, *First in His Class*, p. 399.
12. *New Yorker*, May 30, 1994.
13. Webb Hubbell, Friends in High Places, p. 103.
14. David Maraniss, *First in His Class*, p. 400.
15. *New Yorker*, May 30, 1994.
16. *Vanity Fair*, May 1992.
17. Dick Morris, *Behind the Oval Office*, p. 35.
18. *New Yorker*, May 30, 1994.
19. David Maraniss, *First in His Class*, p. 408.
20. *New Yorker*, May 30, 1994.
21. Ibid.
22. David Maraniss, *First in His Class*, p. 439.
23. Webb Hubbell, *Friends in High Places*, p. 144.
24. *New Yorker*, May 30, 1994.
25. *Vanity Fair*, May 1992.
26. Dick Morris, *Behind the Oval Office*, pp. 64-64.
27. Meredith Oakley, *On the Make*, p. 459.
28. *New Yorker*, May 3, 1994.
29. *American Spectator*, August, 1992.

30. *National Review*, March 4, 1996.

31. *Washington Post*, March 2, 1993.

32. Ibid.

33. *Vanity Fair*, February 1994.

34. *Time*, March 21, 1994.

35. *National Enquirer*, January 26, 1999.

36. Joyce Milton, *The First Partner*, p.142.

37. *National Enquirer*, January 26, 1999.

38. *Vanity Fair*, May 1992.

39. Judith Warner, *Hillary Clinton: The Inside Story*, p. 170.

40. *Newsweek*, February 3, 1992.

41. *Vanity Fair*, May 1992.

42. Saul Alinsky, *Rules for Radicals*, p. 136.

CHAPTER EIGHT: THE BLUE LIGHT SPECIAL

1. *Washington Post*, August 24, 1992.

2. *Washington Post*, March 31, 1992.

3. *Time*, January 4, 1993.

4. *Boston Globe*, January 19, 1993.

5. *Richmond Times-Dispatch*, January 31, 1994.

6. *Philadelphia Inquirer*, February 14, 1993.

7. *Time*, May 10, 1993.

8. Joyce Milton, *The First Partner*, p. 268.

9. *Ladies Home Journal*, August 1993.

10. *Wall Street Journal*, March 19, 1993.

11. David Maraniss, *First in His Class*, p. 413.

12. *New Yorker*, May 30, 1994.

13. Ibid.

14. *Wall Street Journal*, March 19, 1993.

15. David Brock, *The Seduction of Hillary Rodham*, p. 175.

16. *U.S. News and World Report*, February 5, 1996.

17. *Time*, May 10, 1993.

18. Ibid.; Dick Morris, *Behind the Oval Office*, p. 169.

19. *People*, May 10, 1993.

20. *Harper's*, May 1993.

21. *American Journalism Review*, February 1994.

22. Ibid.

23. *Washington Post*, March 7, 1994.

24. *People*, May 31, 1993.

25. *New York Times*, May 28, 1993.

26. *Time*, May 10, 1993.

27. *U.S. News and World Report*, February 15, 1993.

28. *Washington Post*, February 9, 1996.

29. *New York Times Magazine*, January 17, 1993.

30. Joyce Milton, *The First Partner*, p. 271.

31. *U.S. News and World Report*, July 8, 1996.

32. *Washington Post*, March 5, 1994.

33. *Newsweek*, December 2, 1996.

34. *U.S. News and World Report*, January 31, 1994.

35. *New York Post*, December 17, 1992.

36. Lani Guinier, *The Tyranny of the Majority*, p. xi.

37. Lani Guinier, *Lift Every Voice*, p. 53.

38. *New York Post*, February 8, 1993.

39. Ibid.

40. Joyce Milton, *The First Partner*, p. 40.

41. Ibid., p. 246.

42. *New York Post*, January 11, 1996.

43. *Time*, September 20, 1993.

44. *Washington Post*, May 6, 1993.

45. *Washington Post*, September 30, 1993.

46. *Newsweek*, November 1, 1993.

47. *New Yorker*, May 30, 1994.

48. Dick Morris, *Behind the Oval Office*, p. 111.

49. *Washington Post*, February 9, 1996.

50. George F. Will, *Washington Post*, March 24, 1999.

51. *New Republic*, October 3, 1994.

52. Senator Moynihan, speech, December 10, 1997.

53. *Washington Post*, March 28, 1999.

54. Senator Moynihan, speech, December 10, 1997.

55. *Washington Times*, March 11, 1993.

56. *Washington Post*, March 28, 1999.

57. *Parade*, April 11, 1993.

58. *Newsweek*, November 1, 1993.

59. *U.S. News and World Report*, January 31, 1994.

60. Ibid.

61. *Newsweek*, February 21, 1994.

62. *Washington Post*, August 19, 1994.

63. *New York Times*, July 25, 1994.

64. *Newsweek*, January 15, 1996.

CHAPTER NINE: WHITE HOUSE PLUMBER

1. *Time*, August 2, 1994.

2. *Washington Post*, July 8, 1999.

3. *National Review*, March 24, 1997; Joyce Milton, *The First Partner*, p. 333.

4. *USA Today*, January 17, 1996.

5. *U.S. News and World Report*, January 31, 1994.

6. *New Yorker*, March 24, 1996.

7. *New York Times*, January 8, 1996.

8. *Washington Post*, January 11, 1996.

9. *Arkansas Democrat-Gazette*, November 27, 1997.

10. *Time*, March 18, 1996.

11. *Vanity Fair*, May 1992.

12. Dick Morris, *Behind the Oval Office*, p. 24.

13. Ibid., p. 136.

14. Ibid., p. 90.

15. Ibid., p. 37.

16. Ibid., p. 300.

17. *Washington Post*, December 15, 1996.

18. Edward Timperlake and William C. Triplett II, *Year of the Rat*, p. 14.

19. Ibid., p. 13.

20. Ibid., p. 16.

21. Ibid.

22. *Newsweek*, March 17, 1997.

23. Edward Timperlake and William C. Triplett II, *Year of the Rat*, p. 113.

24. Eugene H. Methvin, *Reader's Digest*, April 1996.

CHAPTER TEN: HILLARY AND THE DEVIL IN THE BLUE DRESS

1. *Time*, August 23, 1998.
2. *Time*, March 18, 1996.
3. *New York Times Magazine*, January 17, 1999.
4. *U.S. News and World Report*, May 10, 1993.
5. *Time*, September 24, 1992.
6. *American Heritage*, December 1994.
7. *Time*, December 2, 1996.
8. *Vanity Fair*, February 1999.
9. *Washington Post*, August 19, 1998.
10. *U.S. News and World Report*, September 28, 1998.
11. *New York Times*, August 16, 1998.
12. *Washington Post*, August 29, 1998.
13. *U.S. News and World Report*, September 28, 1998.

CHAPTER ELEVEN: THE PHILOSOPHER QUEEN

1. David Maraniss, *First in His Class*, p. 375.
2. *National Review*, July 18 and *New Republic*, 26, 1993.
3. Joyce Milton, *The First Partner*, p. 282.
4. *New Yorker*, February 26, 1996 and March 4, 1996.
5. Michael Lerner, *The Politics of Meaning*, p. 317.
6. *Maclean's*, July 8, 1996.
7. *Washington Post*, July 23, 1996.
8. *Arkansas Democrat-Gazette*, November 27, 1997.

ACKNOWLEDGMENTS

This book is the product of work performed on a series of teams on which I have been fortunate to have played a role. When I first arrived on Capitol Hill in 1995 as Deputy General Counsel and Solicitor to the House of Representatives, one of the first issues I confronted was the Clinton administration's resistance to the House Banking Committee's efforts to review President Clinton's activities concerning the Madison Guaranty Bank investigation. This was my first encounter with the full frontal assault mounted by the White House whenever evidence pointed towards Hillary Rodham Clinton. That customary reaction was repeated for the next three years—whether in response to queries about Ron Brown, Whitewater, Vince Foster, Travelgate, FBI files, or the Senate China investigation. Any door which seemed to lead in the direction of Hillary was immediately slammed, barricaded, and wired with explosives.

My interest in Hillary's political background and her potential as a candidate for future office evolved out of the House and Senate investigations in which I participated over the next several years. From the moment I read former White House administration chief David Watkins's "soul searching" memo about the consequences of not performing up to the first lady's expectations, I felt that Hillary Rodham Clinton's influence on the Clinton administration was much greater than the public was being led to believe—much greater than the president himself. David Watkins said it best: "I was convinced that failure to take immediate action in this case would have been directly contrary to the wishes of the first lady, something that would not have been tolerated in light of the Secret Service incident earlier in the year."

Haley Barbour opened the door for the new majority in the House in 1994, which gave me the opportunity to work for the House of Representatives. I am now practicing law with Haley in Washington, D.C. Thank you for continuing to open new doors.

Without the perseverance and dedication to the good government of House Government Reform Committee Chairman William F. Clinger, much that we know about this administration would never have been made public. He more than anyone was responsible for investigating the White House's firing and character assassination of seven career government employees in the White House Travel Office. Had he not been willing to pursue the Travel Office investigation, the fact that hundreds of secret FBI files on former Republican government employees were sent over to the Clinton White House's opposition research operatives might have never surfaced.

The dedication of our small team of House investigators is unparalleled. Phil Larsen and Lisa Kaufman handed over critical evidence on the Commerce Department and Ron Brown investigations which required Attorney General Reno (even under her own impossible standards) to appoint an Independent Counsel to investigate potential criminal wrongdoing there; an investigation that ended with Brown's death.

Working with Barbara Jean Comstock is like having the entire IBM mainframe working with you. Besides being an incredibly gifted congressional investigator and lawyer, she worked literally around the clock to expose the well-concealed wrongdoing in the White House. Her dedication has set a standard for all future House Committee counsel.

Kristi Remington went from a young bright staff lawyer to a seasoned congressional veteran by the end of our investigation. She provided careful analysis of issues and a much-needed perspective whenever tensions ran too high. The other two members of our House investigative team, Lauri Taylor and Joe Loughran were an equally important part of the team that kept the investigation moving forward. Committee Chief of Staff Jim Clarke was always willing to go to the end of many limbs for our investigation and always supported our work. Ed Amarosi stayed with us and tried to translate our work for public consumption.

Although our House Government Reform and Oversight investigative team numbered only four lawyers and one investigator, we uncovered a level of wrongdoing and potential criminality that resulted in numerous criminal referrals to the Justice Department.

After Chairman Clinger's retirement, I continued to investigate wrongdoing in the Clinton administration for a man I admire greatly, Senate Assistant Majority Leader Don Nickles. Senator Nickles devoted long hours to the Government Affairs committee campaign finance investigation, determined that no foreign country, corporation, or individual should be able to buy his way into the White House or dictate the policy initiatives for the presidency. His leadership and integrity restores the sense of pride and honor we all used to have in government service.

I want to thank Mark Davis whose help brought so much to this book. He immediately understood why it was important to trace the politics of Hillary Rodham Clinton from her days as a Goldwater girl to Senate candidate and to commit her past to paper for the future.

The numerous friends and Capitol Hill staffers who so generously provided background information and insight into the politics of Mrs. Clinton are too numerous to name and I am sure will be relieved not to be identified. Thank you. Thanks to my good friend Carol Janeway for her encouragement and wise words. Her love of books and writers gave me the courage to believe that I could do this. The Independent Women's Forum, especially Ricki Silberman who has been my mentor since I met her, Barbara Ledeen whose drive and determination gives us all hope for our future, and all my other talented friends there provided encouragement and advice when I needed it most. I also want to express my gratitude to my secretary Diana Davis, who helped me steal the time away from my practice to finish this book and still remain gainfully employed.

Finally, my husband's wisdom, insights, and sharp pencil have guided me since I first met him. All accomplishments are the result of team effort. But none has been so profound and total in my life as the team of Olson and Olson. We became engaged during the Vince Foster phase of the investigation, got married in between depositions and hearings, and heard about the first FBI file while on our honeymoon. Ted's encouragement, patience, and editing made this book possible. This book signifies the closing of an important part of my life and the beginning of a new one.

INDEX

Emerson, Thomas, 54, 56
Emery, Chris, 240
Enterprise, 10
Enthoven, Alain, 255
Episcopalians, 29
Equal Rights Amendment, 146
Estrich, Susan, 307
Evening Shade, 200
Eyrie, 23

family socialism, 112
family unit, 107
Father Knows Best, 25
FBI. *See* Federal Bureau of Investigations
FDIC. *See* Federal Deposit Insurance
   Corporation
Federal Bureau of Investigations (FBI), 238;
   Alinsky and, 46; Foster's suicide and,
   268; illegal collection of files of, 269–70,
   272–74; scandal in, 2–3; White House
   Travel Office scandal and, 243
Federal Deposit Insurance Corporation
   (FDIC), 162
Federal Emergency Management Agency
   (FEMA), 294
federal school lunch program, 113
Feinman, Barbara, 277–78
Feinstein, Dianne, 304–5
Fekkai, Frederic, 233
FEMA. *See* Federal Emergency Manage-
   ment Agency
Ferguson, Danny, 294
The First Partner (Milton), 39–40
Firtzgerald, Peter, 14–15
Fiske, Robert, 293
Florida, 111, 186
Flowers, Gennifer, 92; Bill Clinton's affair
   with, 151, 154, 169; Hillary and, 94,
   211–14; Paula Jones lawsuit and, 295
Flynt, Larry, 169, 305
Foley, Tom, 235, 262
Ford administration, 9, 126
Fortas, Abe, 78
Forward, 246
Foster, Jodie, 233
Foster, Lisa, 153, 264, 267
Foster, Vince, 199; character of, 152–53;
   depression of, 265–66; FDIC and, 162;
   Hillary's litigation skills and, 118;
   Hillary's records and suicide of, 267–69;
   Hillary's relationship with, 144–47,
   151–56, 211; ransacking of office of, 10;
   relationship with Clintons of, 144; Rose

Law Firm and, 149–50; suicide of, 264,
   267; Travelgate and, 242, 244, 265–66;
   as White House counsel, 246;
   Whitewater scandal and, 164
Foundation for Mind Research, 313
Foundry United Methodist Church, 309
France, 284
Fray, Mary, 82, 87, 89, 92–94
Fray, Paul, 89, 92–94, 180
"freedom flotillas," 186
Freeh, Louis, 269–70
Fulbright, J. William, 157, 158, 161

GAO. *See* General Accounting Office
Garry, Charles, 54, 56, 59
Gates, Bill, 138
Gault decision, 112
Gekko, Gordon, 134
General Accounting Office (GAO), 130–31
Georgia, 128
Gerth, Jeff, 264
Gigante, Robert, 12
Gingrich, Newt, 15, 194, 284, 303
Giroir, Joe, 148–50, 288
Giuliani, Rudolph, 15–16, 19–21
Glenn, John, 304
The Godfather, 153
Goldeberg, Rube, 250
Goldman, Marshall I., 38
Goldwater, Barry, 33, 40, 63
Gooden, Benny, 229
Goodwin, Tommy, 172
Gore, Al: Bill Clinton's doubts about, 13;
   Clintons' cattle futures profit and, 138;
   Hillary's co-presidency and, 232;
   Hillary's White House makeover and,
   222–23; *New Republic* and, 16; presiden-
   tial hopes of, 14, 316; 1996 campaign
   fundraising and, 287
Gore: A Political Life (Zelnick), 223
Gracen, Elizabeth Ward, 306
Grassroots International, 17, 132
The Gray Ghost, 81
Great Depression, 71
Greenberg, Stanley, 209
Greening, 59
The Greening of America (Reich), 53
Greenwood, Stanley, 141
Grenada, 56
Grunwald, Mandy, 12
Guernica (Picasso), 32
Guinier, Lani, 51, 247–48, 264

Navarro, Vincente, 252
NCEEP. *See* National Center on Education and the Economy
Nelson, Sheffield, 204
nepotism, 222, 231
Netanyahu, Benjamin, 20
Neuwirth, Stephen, 268
New Jersey, 33
New Republic, 232, 311; Hillary's board positions and, 136; Hillary's health care initiative and, 257, 258; Hillary's Senate campaign and, 16
Newsweek, 104, 232; Bill and Hillary's early relationship and, 68; Bill and Hillary's fighting and, 238; Guinier nomination and, 247; Hillary's arrival in Arkansas and, 82; Hillary's interest in radical publications and, 58; Hillary's interview with, 41
New World Foundation, 17, 132
New York: Bill's appearances in, 11; Giuliani as mayor of, 15; Hillary as junior senator from, 5; Lindsay as mayor of, 35
New York City Transit Authority, 129
New Yorker, 228; Hillary's campaign management and, 189; Hillary's name issue and, 190; Hillary's temper and, 147; *It Takes a Village* crisis and, 278; profile of Hillary by, 38
New York Post, 142, 246, 248
New York Times, 138, 246, 264, 279, 299
New York Times Magazine, 58, 311
New York Yankees, 18–19
Nicaragua, 56
Nicaragua Contra movement, 150
Nichols, Larry, 150–51, 167–69
Nigeria, 14
Nightline, 211
1974 congressional campaign, 87–94
1984 (Orwell), 259
1988 presidential campaign, 196–99
1992 presidential campaign: Bill Clinton's decision to run in, 204–5; Bill Clinton's team for, 205–9; "bimbo eruption" in, 13, 79, 151; children's rights and, 115–16; Clinton criticism in, 156: criticism of Hillary in, 104–5; disclosure of Bill Clinton's personal life in, 210–15; Hillary's management of, 204–10
1996 presidential campaign: fundraising in, 287–91; Hillary's management of, 283–86
Nitze, Paul, 45

Nixon, Richard, 44, 268, 301; Brooke and, 42; Cambodia bombing and, 121, 124; "enemies list" of, 274; Hillary and, 4, 80, 119, 123–24; House Judiciary investigation of, 120–21; investigation committee's goal of removal of, 122; nomination of, 36; Rather and, 232; Safire as speechwriter for, 280; Vietnam War and, 39; Watergate investigation and, 121–25
Novak, Bob, 273
Nussbaum, Bernie: deposition of, 3; firing of, 264; Foster's suicide and, 267–68; Livingstone and, 271, 273; Watergate investigation and, 122; as White House counsel, 121, 238–39, 246

O'Neill, Henry, 268
Oakley, Meredith, 32, 213
Oglesby, Carl, 58
Olson, Kris, 250
Onassis, Jacqueline Kennedy, 234
"open-meeting" laws, 259
Ortega, Daniel, 56
Orwell, George, 259
Oslo Peace accords, 132
Oxford University, 69

Paglia, Camille, 41–42, 43, 207, 249
Palestine Liberation Organization (PLO), 17, 19, 20, 132
Palladino, Jack, 306
Panetta, Leon, 276, 283
Parade, 259
Park-O-Meter, 174
Park Place Baptist Church, 76
Park Police, 268
Park Ridge, 24, 27, 71
Pataki, George, 21, 252
Patterson, Larry, 237, 281
Peace Corps, 42
Penn, Mark, 13
Penn State, 60
Pennsylvania, 26
People, 186
People's Republic of China (PRC), 287, 288–90
People for the American Way, 131
Percy, Chuck, 24
Perils of Pauline, 178
Perry, Roger, 281
Persian Gulf War, 204–5
Phelan, James, 61
Picasso, Pablo, 32